# Personality and Depression

# MENTAL HEALTH AND PSYCHOPATHOLOGY
## A MacArthur Foundation Research Network Series

## DAVID J. KUPFER, Series Editor

PERSONALITY AND DEPRESSION:
A CURRENT VIEW
Marjorie H. Klein, David J. Kupfer, and M. Tracie Shea, *Editors*

# PERSONALITY AND DEPRESSION
## A Current View

*Edited by*

**MARJORIE H. KLEIN**
*University of Wisconsin–Madison*

**DAVID J. KUPFER**
*University of Pittsburgh School of Medicine*

**M. TRACIE SHEA**
*Brown University*
*Butler Hospital*

THE GUILFORD PRESS
*New York   London*

© 1993 The Guilford Press
A Division of Guilford Publications, Inc.
72 Spring Street, New York, NY 10012

Printed in the United States of America

This book is printed on acid-free paper.

Last digit is print number: 9 8 7 6 5 4 3 2 1

Library of Congress Cataloging-in-Publication Data

Personality and depression: a current view / edited by Marjorie H.
  Klein, David J. Kupfer, M. Tracie Shea.
     p.    cm.—(Mental health and psychopathology)
  Includes bibliographical references and index.
  ISBN 0-89862-118-6
    1. Depression, Mental. 2. Depression, Mental—Research—
Statistical methods. 3. Personality and emotions. 4. Personality
assessment. 5. Personality assessment—Statistical methods.
I. Klein, Marjorie H. II. Kupfer, David J., 1941–    . III. Shea,
M. Tracie. IV. Series.
    [DNLM: 1. Depression—psychology. 2. Models, Psychological.
3. Personality. WM 171 P467]
RC537.P43 1993
616.85'27—dc20
DNLM/DLC                               92-48737
for Library of Congress                        CIP

# Contributors

**Peter A. Barnett, Ph.D.,** Department of Psychology, Victoria Hospital, London, Ontario, Canada

**Lorna Smith Benjamin, Ph.D.,** Department of Psychology, University of Utah, Salt Lake City, Utah

**C. Robert Cloninger, M.D.,** Department of Psychiatry, Washington University School of Medicine, St. Louis, Missouri

**Allen Frances, M.D.,** Department of Psychiatry, Duke University Medical Center, Durham, North Carolina

**Robert D. Gibbons, Ph.D.,** Departments of Psychiatry and Biometry, University of Illinois at Chicago, Chicago, Illinois

**Robert M. A. Hirschfeld, M.D.,** Department of Psychiatry and Behavioral Sciences, University of Texas Medical Branch, Galveston, Texas

**Brian W. Junker, Ph.D.,** Department of Statistics, Carnegie Mellon University, Pittsburgh, Pennsylvania

**Marjorie H. Klein, Ph.D.,** Department of Psychiatry, University of Wisconsin–Madison, Madison, Wisconsin

**Helena Chmura Kraemer, Ph.D.,** Department of Psychiatry and Behavioral Sciences, Stanford University School of Medicine, Stanford, California

**David J. Kupfer, M.D.,** Department of Psychiatry, University of Pittsburgh School of Medicine, Western Psychiatric Institute and Clinic, Pittsburgh, Pennsylvania

**Paul A. Pilkonis, Ph.D.,** Department of Psychiatry, University of Pittsburgh School of Medicine, Western Psychiatric Institute and Clinic, Pittsburgh, Pennsylvania

**M. Tracie Shea, Ph.D.,** Department of Psychiatry and Human Behavior, Brown University, Butler Hospital, Providence, Rhode Island

**Larry J. Siever, M.D.,** Department of Psychiatry, Mount Sinai School of Medicine, New York, New York; Outpatient Psychiatric Division, Department of Veterans Affairs Medical Center, Bronx, New York

**Thomas A. Widiger, Ph.D.,** Department of Psychology, University of Kentucky, Lexington, Kentucky

**Stephen Wonderlich, Ph.D.,** Division of Psychiatry–Behavioral Science, University of North Dakota School of Medicine, Fargo, North Dakota

# Preface

The area of personality and depression represents a key domain in our attempt to understand the affective disorders. Personality factors may play a major role in the pathophysiology, course, and treatment of depression. However, relatively slow progress has been made toward elucidating the contributions of personality traits to the development and maintenance of depressive symptomatology, or the potential interaction between personality and affective disorders.

Not surprisingly, this area has become a focus of attention for the Research Network on the Psychobiology of Depression and Other Affective Disorders, an association of research scientists supported by the John D. and Catherine T. MacArthur Foundation. Discussions during the initial planning phase of this research network in 1988 suggested that we examine the conceptual and methodological issues that impede more rapid progress toward understanding the role of personality in depression.

A conference was held in September 1988 to review in depth and with leading experts the current knowledge base on personality and depression. The conclusion from this meeting was that a lack of conceptual clarity concerning underlying models of the relationships between personality and depression was hampering comparison of results across studies and study domains, as well as unambiguous communication among investigative groups from these domains. Issues of instrumentation were viewed as tightly linked to these conceptual issues, since the inability to differentiate clearly between assessments of mood and personality could be seen as rooted in the lack of conceptual clarity on underlying models.

These conclusions led to the formation of a Network Task Force on Personality and Depression. Several key researchers in the area of personality and depression were invited to participate, and the task force was charged with the development of an initiative that would serve to drive this important area of research toward more rapid progress. In an iterative process of task force discussions, it was concluded that the network should focus attention on basic impediments of a conceptual and methodological nature that appeared to hamper progress in this area. A three-pronged initiative was developed and implemented; it included conceptual development, methods development, and supporting pilot research activities.

In November 1989 two working groups were formed by the task force to focus specifically on issues that appeared to be central impediments to progress. A Working Group on Models was organized to examine in depth existing models of the relationship between personality and depression, with the intent to make explicit the diverse conceptual constructs that underlie different strands of research in this area and to develop integrated models. A Working Group on Instrumentation was constituted to review assessment issues—specifically, existing difficulties in differentiating between the assessment of mood and that of personality traits. To facilitate the activities of these working groups, the network commissioned extensive review papers on these two core issues.

After reviewing existing models on the relationship between personality and depression, the Working Group on Models sought to develop an integrated model that would incorporate biological and psychological variables and their potential mode of interaction in forming pathways toward the expression of depression. The working group concluded that such a model should differentiate between pathways toward initial and subsequent episodes of the illness. In further exploring this notion, the group members felt that issues of basic biogenetic "endowment" may play a greater role in the initial expression of the disorder than in subsequent episodes, in which the outcome of the first episode of illness (such as residual symptoms and resulting changes in the interpersonal and cognitive domain) may determine to a great extent the susceptibility to developing future episodes.

In a parallel fashion, the Working Group on Instrumentation reviewed existing measurement approaches from a range of conceptual domains (biological, interpersonal, cognitive, and dynamic) and summarized key pathological processes thought to be involved in the relationship between personality and depression. The difficulty and possible artificiality of separating conceptions of mood from personality traits were noted.

With the active assistance of the participating scientists, the review papers commissioned to support the activities of the two working groups were revised and expanded in an iterative process. Once these materials were in their final form, the working group members felt that they would prove helpful and thus should be made available to an audience broader than that of the immediate task force and its working groups. The two core chapters were augmented by a third chapter on statistical issues, and critical commentaries were solicited for all three chapters. This monograph is the product of these efforts, published with the intent to share with the scientific public the perspectives of more than a dozen leading researchers in this area.

The first chapter, by Klein, Wonderlich, and Shea, reviews existing models on the relationship between personality and depression, and suggests the existence of a variety of causal and/or temporal relationships between the two domains. It examines the extent to which these models are overlapping to mutually exclusive, and elucidates how research in this area has been rooted in these various models (at times without being made explicit as underlying constructs). This chapter also seeks to integrate existing models. Furthermore, it proposes differential models of the development of first/single episodes and multiple episodes/recurrent depression. The accompanying commentaries by Siever, Cloninger, and Barnett incorporate perspectives of both the biological and psychosocial research domains.

The existing difficulties in distinguishing between mood states and personality traits are documented by Widiger in the second chapter, which reviews existing assessment methods and discusses various approaches for addressing their differentiation. The chapter concludes with a set of explicit recommendations for further research. The commentators for this chapter, Benjamin and Hirschfeld, are individuals whose research has focused on the development of assessment instruments in the area of personality, incorporating psychosocial and psychodynamic perspectives.

In the third chapter, Junker and Pilkonis review statistical issues involved in research on personality and depression. This chapter proposes approaches to test the models described earlier. Special attention is given to statistical approaches of particular interest to this area of research. The commentaries by Kraemer and Gibbons represent critical reviews of the material presented in this chapter by leading methodologists/biostatisticians familiar with this area of research.

In his epilogue, Frances reviews the importance of expanding research efforts in the area of personality disorders and notes some future lines of research that are likely to be informed by the methodological clarifications offered in the book.

With this monograph, we submit to the broader field the final product of efforts conducted under the auspices of the Task Force on Personality and Depression. We view the conceptual and methodological work conducted by this task force as a significant contribution toward progress in this area. We hope that this volume will clarify the relationship between personality and depression and related measurement issues, facilitate a more meaningful consideration of personality factors in research on the pathophysiology, course, and treatment of the affective disorders, and thus ultimately enhance our understanding of depression and its treatment.

We would like to thank all the researchers—too many to list individually—who have contributed to this monograph, either through direct authorship, by participating in the many discussions that preceded and stimulated the preparation of these materials, or by providing extensive input into various draft versions of the monograph's core chapters. We would also like to express our gratitude to the John D. and Catherine T. MacArthur Foundation for its continued support of this and other initiatives conducted by the Research Network on the Psychobiology of Depression and Other Affective Disorders.

DAVID J. KUPFER

# Contents

# CHAPTER ONE

# Models of Relationships between Personality and Depression: Toward a Framework for Theory and Research

MARJORIE H. KLEIN
*University of Wisconsin–Madison*
STEPHEN WONDERLICH
*University of North Dakota School of Medicine*
M. TRACIE SHEA
*Brown University*
*Butler Hospital*

## INTRODUCTION

The purpose of this chapter is to review and analyze the various models that have been proposed to explain relationships between personality and depressive disorders and to consider how these models apply to specific clinical syndromes. We also review ways in which models of personality–depression relationships are currently being defined within different theoretical perspectives and propose a model that integrates biological, cognitive, and interpersonal–developmental perspectives. A distinction is also made between models for the development of initial and repeated episodes of depression.

The close associations between depression and a number of personality traits and disorders have been the subject of much attention in the psychiatric and psychological literature. The placement in the *Di-*

*agnostic and Statistical Manual of Mental Disorders,* third edition (DSM-III) of the affective and personality disorders on separate axes has also led to observations of their high level of comorbidity (e.g., Farmer & Nelson-Gray, 1990; Mellsop, Varghese, Joshua, & Hicks, 1982; Pfohl, Stangl, & Zimmerman, 1984; Shea, Glass, Pilkonis, Watkins, & Docherty, 1987) and to discussions about the nature of the relationships (Frances, 1980; Widiger, 1989; Widiger & Hyler, 1987). Even in the absence of full-blown personality disorders, dysfunctional personality traits such as neuroticism, introversion, dependency, and/or perfectionism, as well as other cognitive and social styles that are closely akin to personality traits, have been found to be associated with a variety of depressive conditions (e.g., Barnett & Gotlib, 1988; Block, Gjerde, & Block, 1991; Hirschfeld & Klerman, 1979; Hirschfeld et al., 1983, 1989a; von Zerssen, 1982). Moreover, there is a growing body of evidence that personality comorbidity is associated with earlier onset, more severe symptoms, poorer outcomes, and more frequent recurrences of affective disorders (e.g., Charney, Nelson, & Quinlan, 1981; Farmer & Nelson-Gray, 1990; Klein, Taylor, Dickstein, & Harding, 1988; Pfohl, Stangl, & Zimmerman, 1984; Pilkonis & Frank, 1988; Weissman, Leaf, Bruce, & Florio, 1988).

Discussions of the meaning of these relationships, however, have been complicated by a number of unresolved issues about the disorders on the two axes and their underlying constructs, as well as by questions about the relationships between affective states and personality traits. What, if any, are the conceptual differences between the disorders on Axis I and Axis II, or between depression and the personality features that are associated with depression? Are different biological and psychological processes involved, and does the balance of these factors differ in various conditions? Are different temporal courses involved? Do these differences represent different levels of severity or kinds of impairment?

Other conceptual and methodological concerns plague this area of theory and research. For example, the definition of the personality disorders as categorical has complicated the picture by making it necessary to conceptualize the role of personality traits in relation to both axes (Frances, 1982; Widiger, 1989; Widiger & Frances, 1985a, 1985b; Widiger & Kelso, 1983). Furthermore, the conceptual separation of personality and depression seems artificial to some; as Widiger (1989) and others have pointed out, it is artificial to remove considerations of mood from conceptions of personality in general (Tellegen, 1985). Variations in affect are part of the definitions of certain of the personality disorders; personality constructs are central to many clinical formulations of depressive disorders. Also, the assignment of some disorders with chronic and characterological features, such as dysthymia and cyclothymia, to Axis I rather than Axis II has raised questions about their degree of distinctness from the disorders assigned to Axis II (Frances, 1980; Kernberg, 1984; Kocsis & Frances, 1987). Implicit in each of these concerns are open questions about the differences between the theoretical constructs of "mood" and "personality trait": Are distinctions between mood and trait theoretically meaningful? Can mood and trait be validly distinguished empirically? To what extent do commonly used measures tap the same or closely overlapping constructs? At what point in a chronic course do moods become trait-like? Or, if mood and trait are indeed distinct, how precisely do they interact over time to create, shape, or complicate disorders?

A number of models have been suggested to account for different temporal and/or causal relationships between personality and depression (Akiskal, Hirschfeld, & Yerevanian, 1983; Akiskal & McKinney, 1975; Farmer & Nelson-Gray, 1990; Shea, Hirschfeld, & Lavori, 1989; Widiger, 1989). In some models these relationships are inherent in the nature of the constructs involved, but are not spelled out in much detail. Akiskal's subaffective model, for example, assigns considerable explanatory power to certain biological variables (e.g., genetic history, biological markers such as rapid-eye-movement [REM] latency, response to pharmacological challenge), with minimal specification of hypotheses about the underlying mechanisms or processes involved in these relationships (e.g., Akiskal et al., 1983, 1985a; Akiskal, Djenderedjain, Rosenthal, & Khani 1977). Other models go further, spelling out the specific processes or mechanisms involved in these relationships and suggesting varying balances between biological and psychosocial factors in the development of clinical phenomena (e.g., Cloninger, 1987; Siever & Davis, 1991). Some models attempt to reduce the conceptual distinction between personality and depression constructs by attributing a common cause to both (e.g., Akiskal, 1988; Benjamin, in press), while other models maintain and even highlight the distinction by focusing on the interactions between personality and depression (e.g., Beck, Freeman, & Associates, 1990; Pilkonis, 1988). Concepts from dynamic, interpersonal, social learning, cognitive, and biological perspectives are generally introduced as the means by which the two states or clinical entities are linked.

## MODELS OF DEPRESSION AND PERSONALITY AS ABSTRACTIONS

The function of models in scientific investigation is to state hypotheses in abstract form in order to communicate and highlight key assumptions and guide the development of inquiry. If one accepts, at least for the purposes of discussion, the basic assumption that "personality" and "depression" are distinct and distinguishable concepts, and solves the associated measurement problems (i.e., untangling measurement of state and trait; eliminating overlap from general factors such as response bias, symptom reporting, and negative or positive affectivity), a number of models and hypotheses can be (and have been) developed on logical grounds. In this section, these models are described and discussed as general hypotheses about the nature of the relationships between personality and depression in the development and course of clinical phenomena; a description of their application and development in relation to specific clinical syndromes follows.

As outlined in Table 1.1 and diagrammed in Figure 1.1, the hypothetical models range from complete independence to complete interdependence of personality and depression at different stages in the development of pathology. In Table 1.1 and Figure 1.1, and in the discussion that follows (unless otherwise noted), the word "depression" is used to denote either dysphoric mood states or full-fledged affective disorders, and the word "personality" will be used to denote either personality traits or full-fledged personality disorders.

## Common-Cause Models

"Common-cause" models assume that personality and depression are distinct psychological phenomena that are each determined by the same underlying process (core liability). Although biological processes (e.g., noradrenergic dysregulation) are most often suggested as causal, psychological mechanisms (e.g., attributional style) or environmental circumstances (e.g., poor parenting) are also sometimes indicated, as are more hybrid concepts (e.g., temperament) that bridge or blend the two domains. Thus, in these models, each of the two independent pathological conditions or disorders is caused by a single process. In addition to requiring that personality and depression be thought of as distinct, the logic also requires that they be functionally independent, so that their association exists only through their linkage to the common cause; otherwise, "pathoplasty" would be the more appropriate descriptor.

Although these models are logically compelling, parsimonious, and consistent with theoretical integration, they are extremely difficult to test. Although retrospective assessment of a hypothesized causal factor might serve for exploratory purposes, for any definitive test the hypothesized causal factor would have to be clearly defined and measured well before the onset of either condition. In addition, depression

**TABLE 1.1.** Temporal/Causal Models of the Relationships between Depression and Personality

---

*Independence:* Depression and personality are distinct conditions with completely independent causes. Any specific mixture results either from chance or from operation of general risk or help-seeking factors. (This model is not reviewed in this chapter.)

*Common cause:* Personality and depression have a shared etiology, arising from a "common core liability."

*Spectrum or subclinical:* The two conditions can be located on the same continuum or "spectrum" of related disorders, in which one form is a prodromal, subclinical, or attenuated manifestation of a common pathological process.

*Predisposition or vulnerability:* When one condition occurs, it is a risk factor for the development of the other.

*Pathoplasty or exacerbation:* Although the conditions are not causally related, the presence of one condition influences the presentation, course, or outcome of the other.

*Complication or scar:* Residual effects associated with one condition, which has remitted, influence the course or presentation of the other.

---

and personality would have to be clearly defined and measured as distinct constructs, and independent linkages from the common cause to each of the hypothesized effects specified and established, either from experimental or from correlational designs. Even in a well-designed longitudinal study, questions about the relative timing and the possible interaction of the two processes, once established, can be extremely difficult to resolve, and the picture would be complicated still further if more than one common causal factor were proposed (e.g., faulty parenting *and* negative cognitive styles).

Appropriate control or contrast groups for tests of such models must include groups without the marker associated with the common causal factor; it would be hypothesized that these groups would show neither the personality nor the mood disorder. Additional groups with the depressive and/or personality disorders but *without* the core liability would also be useful. If, for example, the model were to stipulate that the common cause is a necessary condition for each outcome, then these groups should not be found; if the model were to state that the common factor is not a necessary, but simply a sufficient, condition, then these additional groups might provide information about the mode of action of the causal factor or about the importance of other causes. Another important control for the specificity issue would be a group composed of subjects with other disorders or core defects.

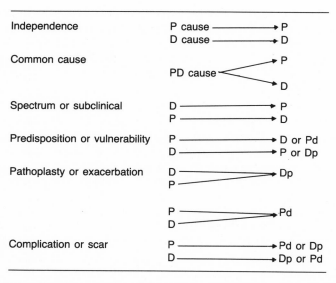

FIGURE 1.1. Diagram of models of personality–depression relationships. P, personality; Pd, personality with depressive features; D, depression; Dp, depression with personality features.

## Subclinical or Spectrum Models

"Subclinical" or "spectrum" models, which are the logical cousins of the common-cause models, assume that personality and depression are related but different manifestations or phases of the *same* underlying disease process, with a shared etiology and risk factors. Generally, the two forms of the underlying disorder are related in time (i.e., one is an early-stage or less fully developed form of the other), or they share some clinical features but differ in severity or type of impairment; thus these models hypothesize that one disorder is really a manifestation or variant of the other, rather than a distinct disorder. Two kinds of spectrum or subclinical models have been discussed in the literature.

1. *Affective spectrum models.* "Affective spectrum" models assume that a personality style or disorder is an early-stage or attenuated manifestation of a primary affective disease process (e.g., subaffective disorders). In other elaborations, the personality or character disorder is an alternative expression of common risk factors, and other factors such as stressors are hypothesized to account for whether (or when) personality or affective features may predominate. In either case, the spectrum involved is generally a continuum of severity or impairment, on which

characterological problems may be considered to be less severe and/or more chronic forms of a primary affective disease process; in that sense they can be considered a "phenocopy" of a "true" personality disorder. Although affective spectrum models share premises with common-cause models, the focus in the former is on a common pathological process, rather than on two distinct, but related, forms of a common etiology.

2. *Character spectrum models.* The assumption of "character spectrum" models is that the personality traits are primary and depression is secondary. Either biological or psychosocial causal factors may be implicated in the development of the character pathology. However, when a biological basis for the personality or character traits is hypothesized, the biological causes are not the same factors that were involved in the development or transmission of the affective disorder. In this sense, the affective disorder is not a "true" affective disorder, but, as Shea et al. (1989) suggest, is a "phenocopy." Because the depression is viewed in these models as secondary to the personality traits or disturbance, they may be more accurately classified, from the perspective of depression, as "vulnerability" models; from the perspective of personality, they are "complication" models. And to the extent that the depression is shaped and colored by the same personality traits, pathoplasty or interaction may also be involved.

Although correlations and between-group contrasts are typically offered in support of subclinical and spectrum models, longitudinal data carry greater weight. Development of these models in practice is also complicated by their complexity: Multiple risk factors and/or clinical features may be grouped together; causal mechanisms are assumed but not always spelled out. Since conceptually related variables and/or continua are assumed, it is very difficult to rule out alternative models (e.g., vulnerability, pathoplasty, or complication), particularly as explanations for why a particular case or group of conditions is located at a given point on the spectrum or course. These alternative models are especially salient when the depression associated with the characterological disturbance has distinct or atypical characteristics.

Appropriate contrast groups for tests of these spectrum models depend on the focus of the investigation. At a minimum, the "spectrum" group must be contrasted with "true" forms of each disorder (depression, personality), as well as with groups selected to control for psychiatric disorder in general. Here the hypothesis would be that the spectrum group will resemble the "true" group to which it is supposed to be related more than the other "true" group that it is thought to be "copying." In the case of spectrum models, however, it would also be important to develop and test hypotheses about the reasons why the full-blown forms of the disorders fail to develop, or to understand the circumstances in which spectrum disorders "convert" to their "true" forms.

## Predisposition or Vulnerability Models

The basic assumption of "predisposition" or "vulnerability" models is that one condition precedes *and* increases the risk of the other condition. In this respect, these models overlap somewhat with the spectrum models, and in practice the distinction may sometimes seem quite arbitrary. The difference, however, is that in the predisposition models no other, more fundamental cause of either condition is assumed (as in the spectrum models), nor is it always assumed that the so-called predisposing condition is a necessary cause of the second condition. Thus, these models assume that one set of factors or condition (usually personality) functions as a set of risk factors for the development of the other condition (usually depression). In contrast to the spectrum models, two different pathological processes and/or disorders are assumed— one for the development of the risk factor, the other for the influence of the risk factor, once present, on the other condition—although some functional and conceptual interrelationships may account for the specificity of particular linkages (e.g., between dependency and depression). Although the details are not always stated, these models assume that the second condition develops because the first condition creates risk factors that are specific to the second condition (e.g., an introverted personality fails to get positive social reinforcement and becomes depressed). Another form of the vulnerability model, from genetics, states that the risk factor functions as an "amplifier" of the second condition; that is, it serves as a trigger or lowers the threshold for the more fundamental disorder.

Although most predisposition models focus on personality traits or disorders as the predisposing factors, it is also logically possible to consider depression (particularly chronic depression) as a predisposing factor in the development of certain personality traits, and as an even more likely factor in the evolution of traits into full-fledged personality disorders. When the second condition develops as a result of increasing severity or more general dysfunctional aspects of the first condition, a "complication" model is probably the more appropriate label. This is but one example of the fluidity of the boundary between vulnerability and complication models.

Although vulnerability models seem straightforward and plausible in the abstract, in practice they are complex and difficult to test. Clear and distinct definitions of risk factors and target conditions, longitudinal assessment of each, and explicit statements of any hypothesized linkages between risk factors and target conditions are essential. Once both risk factors and target conditions are present, distinctions between vulnerability, pathoplasty, or complication models become extremely difficult to make.

The assumptions of the vulnerability models outlined above have been elaborated in considerable detail in the growing number of "diathesis–stress" models that propose complex relationships between stress, personality, and depression (e.g., Dohrenwend & Dohrenwend, 1981; Lazarus & Folkman, 1984; Lewinsohn, Hoberman, Teri, & Hautzinger, 1985). These models specify one or more interactions between individual dispositions or vulnerabilities, such as temperament (e.g., Akiskal, 1988; Cloninger, 1987; Siever & Davis, 1991), personality traits (e.g., Brown & Harris, 1978; Ormel & Schaufeli, 1991; Ormel & Wohlfarth, 1991), and cognitive styles or schemas (e.g., Abramson, Metalksy, & Alloy, 1989; Abramson, Seligman, & Teasdale, 1978; Beck et al., 1990; Brewin, 1985), and the occurrence of environmental stressors or chronic strains, which are hypothesized to interact in some fashion with the dispositions as joint causes of symptoms or disorders (e.g., Billings & Moos, 1982; Brown & Harris, 1978; Cohen & Wills, 1985; Monroe, 1983a). Additional complexity is often introduced in the form of other sets of intervening variables, such as mood (Miranda & Persons, 1988; Watson & Clark, 1984), social support (e.g., Aneshensel & Frerichs, 1982; Holahan & Moos, 1991; Monroe & Steiner, 1986; Schradle & Dougher, 1985; Swindle, Cronkite, & Moos, 1989; Thoits, 1983), social skill (Coyne, Aldwin, & Lazarus, 1981; Lewinsohn, 1974), coping styles (Nezu & Ronan, 1985; Thoits, 1986), or other personal resources (e.g., Dienstbier, 1989; Litt, 1988) that are hypothesized to potentiate or buffer these relationships. Thus these models attempt to resolve the "person–situation" issue (Mischel, 1973) by defining personality in terms of the individual's active transactions with important components of the environment, rather than by viewing personality as composed of static traits (Cantor, 1990). The advantages of these models are their integration of many variables, the latitude they provide for individual variations in vulnerabilities and/or strengths, and their specification of multiple determinants and alternative pathways in the actual expression and course of disorders.

As these models increase in complexity, however, they become correspondingly difficult to test. When key intervening variables involve subjective process constructs, such as appraisals, perceptions, or expectations, it is often difficult to distinguish between sets of variables that play different functional roles in the models (e.g., between stress and depression; Depue & Monroe, 1986; Monroe, 1982, 1983b; Monroe & Simmons, 1991). Measures even of distinguishable concepts are prone to confounding (Lazarus, DeLongis, Folkman, & Gruen, 1985), especially from mood and symptom variables, when cross-sectional self-reports are the primary means of assessment (Thoits, 1982; Depue & Monroe, 1986). Rigorous tests require precise definitions of intervening variables and longitudinal assessment of all components of the models; there are few studies in which this has been done in well-defined clinical samples (e.g., Keller, Lavori, Rice, Coryell, & Hirschfeld, 1986; Lewinsohn, Zeiss, & Duncan, 1989; Pilkonis & Frank, 1988; Swindle et al., 1989). Nonetheless, these models hold out great promise for the integration of variables from biological and psychosocial domains, as well as for the conceptualization of different modes of causation and variations in clinical expression of disorders.

## Pathoplasty or Exacerbation Models

"Pathoplasty" or "exacerbation" models assume that personality and depression are etiologically distinct, but that when they occur at the same time, additive effects or interactions between their distinct features influence the presentation *but not the risk* of either. Thus personality may color the specific way in which depressed affect is experienced and expressed; depression may interact with certain personality traits and influence behavior or cognitions. Exacerbation models share the main assumptions of pathoplasty models, but propose more specifically that the presence of one condition influences the severity and/or outcome of the other. In each case, interactions between components of personality and depression are the primary focus, and because they are the primary focus, the mechanisms and process involved in these linkages and interactions must be spelled out and carefully assessed.

Both cross-sectional and longitudinal designs can be used to test these models. A common cross-sectional design has been to compare subgroups of patients with and without the comorbidity; however, few studies have controlled for the general effect of comorbidity with appropriate contrast groups (e.g., subjects with unrelated personality traits or disorders) or by means of data analysis procedures (e.g., controlling for general distress when examining depression–personality relationships). Ideally, all possible combinations of the disorders in question (personality and depression, depression but not personality, personality but not depression, neither personality nor depression) should be examined. The challenge in longitudinal design is both conceptual and procedural: In cases where the onset of one condition has preceded the other, the alternative vulnerability model may be impossible to rule out. It also may be difficult to define and measure pathoplastic interaction effects that are clearly distinguishable from vulnerability effects. If one condition has been a risk factor for a second condition, it follows that it will continue to operate as a risk factor, although it may also exert new and different pathoplastic effects over time. One way to conceptualize the difference between vulnerability and pathoplastic effects is to reserve the vulnerability model for relationships that are central to theories of causal relationships between personality and depression, and to restrict the pathoplasty model to the more peripheral relationships. Another distinction has to do with the specific kind of effect that one variable has on another; thus variables involved in pathoplasty models may be variables that are sufficient only to change the presentation of, but not to trigger the onset of, the concurrent condition. For example, it might be hypothesized that the avoidant and dependent personality disorders are specific risk factors for depression because of their emphasis on attachment concerns, while "Cluster B" disorders such as histrionic disorders function to alter the presentation of depression rather than to directly cause depression. Unless such distinctions are kept in mind and can be made in practice, it would seem that the boundaries between vulnerability and pathoplasty models are too fluid to be meaningful. The difference may be mainly one of temporal focus: Vulnerability factors are associated with the onset of a particular condition; pathoplasty factors are associated with presentation and course during an episode.

## Complication or Scar Models

"Complication" or "scar" models are also close conceptual relatives of vulnerability and pathoplasty models, except that the focus in these models is shifted from onset and course to the residual or recovery phases. As above, the assumption is that the two conditions are distinct, but related in ways that determine clinical status over time. This relationship may take different forms. The most common complication model refers to the situation in which the second disorder develops because of or in the context of the first disorder, and continues *even after* the primary disorder has remitted. In this case, full recovery of mental health is compromised or "complicated," and/or the second condition is a residual effect or "scar" of the first. This form of the model is very difficult to distinguish from the vulnerability model on logical grounds; again, the distinction is mainly one of temporal focus.

Another variant of the complication model applies when the presence of the second disorder (which may or may not have been causally related to the first disorder) interferes in some way with complete recovery from the first disorder. Here too, longitudinal assessment, appropriate contrast groups to control for general comorbidity and severity factors, and careful theoretical specification of interactions are essential for model testing. In addition, some control over the type and quality of treatment is essential if complication effects are to be distinguished from partial recovery or remission of the primary disorder. And as with all follow-up studies, careful descriptions of treatments and tracking of events during the follow-up phase are necessary to rule out alternative models.

## Summary

Even from these descriptions of the models in their abstract and hypothetical forms, it is apparent that the boundaries between types of models may often be quite arbitrary or fluid. In general, the different models that have been proposed capture (1) different hierarchical relationships between personality, depression, and, in some cases, a hypothesized common cause; (2) different temporal relationships; and (3) differences in the directness and/or specificity of relationships. More direct and/or specific effects involve linkages that are central to theories of the development of depression and/or personality—that is, variables that have the status of either necessary or sufficient causal conditions. An example is the link between dependency and depression, which is made by social learning theories (i.e., dependency causes social skill deficits; Lewinsohn, 1974) or interpersonal theories (i.e., dependency leads to negative responses of others; Coyne et al., 1981). Indirect effects or interactions are those in which the relationships are mediated by more general factors of pathology or involve variables that are less central to a causal model of the personality–depression process. Examples would include the pathoplastic effects of histrionic traits on the way an individual experiences and expresses depression, or the residual complication effects of a personality disturbance following a depressed episode, when the same personality disturbance might be found with equal frequency after another condition.

## MODELS IN THE CONTEXT OF SPECIFIC CLINICAL SYNDROMES

Although consideration of the models as abstractions may be useful to highlight their logical premises and implications for testing, it is also essential to consider the models in relation to examples of the clinical syndromes on which they have been developed. As one looks at models in relation to any of the specific clinical syndromes described below, it becomes apparent that the boundaries and distinctions between models readily become blurred, and that principles from more than one model—usually several—can be discerned.

## Subaffective Models

"Subaffective" models share the assumption that personality disturbances are in some way secondary to a primary (i.e., more basic) affective disorder process. This can be because the personality disorder is an alternative form of the affective disorder or because the personality disorder is an earlier stage or subclinical manifestation of the depressive disorder (see Table 1.2 for a summary).

### Akiskal's Subaffective Dysthymic/Cyclothymic Disorder(s)

The basic premise of Akiskal's model is that personality characteristics in certain subgroups represent milder or alternative expressions of a basic and biogenetically determined affective illness process. Thus it is assumed that personality traits and affective episodes are caused by the same factors, through common pathological mechanisms. In a series of papers, Akiskal and colleagues first described a group of "subaffective dysthymics" who, by age 25 or earlier, manifested a cluster of personality traits originally described by Schneider as characteristic of the depressive temperament (see Table 1.2) and some melancholic features (Akiskal, 1980, 1983b; Akiskal et al., 1980, 1983). In this model, both sets of characteristics are attributed to the same biological cause(s), as evidenced by family history, shortened REM latency, and a positive or hypomanic response to tricyclics or lithium. Although a high percentage of these individuals intermittently experienced more severe depressive episodes (i.e., double depression), the model suggests that, but does not explain why, the affective disturbance is generally milder or more attenuated than in other forms of unipolar affective disorder.

This model has also been extended to encompass individuals with cyclothymic personality traits (Akiskal, 1981, 1983a; Akiskal et al., 1977; Akiskal, Khani, & Scott-Strauss, 1979). The prototype was developed on a group of 50 outpatient cyclothymics who showed traits and behaviors that could be attributed both to personality maladjustments and to cyclothymia (e.g., tempestuous relationships, scholastic or

**TABLE 1.2.** Summary of Assumptions of Affective Clinical Models

---

*Subaffective dysthymic disorder (Akiskal)*

Basic assumption: Personality features are caused by the same factors that cause affective disorder, but the affective component of the disorder is milder.

Defined by: Dysthymia and manic or hypomanic response to drugs.

Contrast group(s): Dysthymics not responsive to drugs (character spectrum).

Clinical features:
  Clinical status when studied: Probably dysthymic outpatients.
  Affective: No more than two melancholic features.
  Personality: Schneiderian traits; quiet, passive, unassertive; gloomy, pessimistic, incapable of fun; self-critical, hypercritical, and complaining; conscientious and self-disciplining; brooding and given to worry; preoccupied with inadequacy, failure, and negative events.
  History and course: Onset before 25, continuous or intermittent, may have episodes of major depression.
Other features: Short REM latency, family history of affective disorder.

*Subaffective cyclothymic disorder (Akiskal)*

Basic assumption: Personality features are caused by the same factors that cause affective disorder, but the affective component of the disorder is milder.

Defined by: Behavioral criteria for cyclothymia (see below)—that is, some features of hypomania or depression without full syndrome, never-hospitalized outpatients.

Contrast group(s): Bipolar I with history of mania, "pseudocyclothymics" (personality features of cyclothymia without behavioral indicators).

Clinical status when studied: Outpatients seeking help for "various personality maladjustments." Affective disturbance apparent only after "intensive" investigation.

Clinical features:
  Affective: Irritable periods; explosive, aggressive outbursts followed by guilt, sprees, shifts in work or interests, episodic promiscuity, impulsive joining of cults.
  Personality: Tempestuous relationships; marital failure; drug or alcohol use; emotional instability; hysteric, narcissistic, borderline, sociopathic, or obsessive features noted in history.
  Course: Onset in early or middle teens; more frequent affective (mostly depressed or hypomanic) episodes on follow-up, even when on tricyclics.

*Subaffective borderline disorder*

Basic assumption: Borderline and affective disorders are independent, but with some overlapping risk factors and interactions among depressive symptoms and personality traits.

Defined by: Nonschizotypal borderline personality disorder (DSM-III).

Contrast group(s): Affective disorder (mostly unipolar) without borderline diagnosis; nonborderline personality disorder (mostly histrionic or mixed); normal noncases.

*continued*

TABLE 1.2. *Continued*

Clinical status when studied: In "trait" condition with acute episodes of dysphoria or depression.

Clinical features:
Affective: Dysthymia or cyclothymia, high scores on Beck Depression Inventory, dysphoric arousal.
From Gunderson: Depression marked by sustained feelings of emptiness, inner badness, and destructiveness; also anger.

Personality:
From Akiskal: Consistent instability, vulnerability to object loss, histrionic and sociopathic features, substance abuse.
From Gunderson: Intense, unstable relationships, dependency, manipulativeness, devaluation; self-destructiveness; fear of abandonment; cognitive (nondelusional paranoid, dissociative, or odd distortions in response to unstructured situations); impulsivity, poor role performance.
From Siever: Affective instability, affective sensitivity, impulsive traits, manipulativeness.

vocational problems, emotional instability, irritable periods, etc.; see Table 1.2). However, the "question of specificity of personality to polarity of affective illness" (Akiskal et al., 1983, p. 807) has never been clearly resolved, although greater risks for depression and hypomania than for mania are suggested in some studies (Akiskal et al., 1979; Depue et al., 1981).

In recent elaborations of the affective spectrum concept, Akiskal (1987, 1988) proposes a more complex and integrated model that links genetic, developmental, environmental, and demographic factors as potential risk factors for affective episodes. In this "multicausal etiologial scheme," affective personality traits are considered to be "temperamental disorders" and are given the status of intermediary or mediating variables, linking the various etiological risk factors to clinical manifestations of affective disorder. In this sense, these temperamental disorders are "subclinically active at all times and easily triggered by environmental challenge" (1988, p. 139), and exert an ongoing influence on the course and risk of recurrence of affective episodes.

## Subaffective Borderline Disorders

In subsequent discussions of the subaffective concept, Akiskal and colleagues further broadened the scope of clinical phenomena covered by the subaffective rubric to include a subgroup of borderlines with concurrent affective disorders (most predominantly, dysthymia and/or cyclothymia). For this group, a mixture of common causal factors is proposed (Akiskal et al., 1985a). The subaffective component of the disorder (the "affective border") is attributed to the same set of biological factors as in the subaffective dysthymics, whereas the borderline personality traits are thought to stem from unstable developmental histories and/or histrionic traits (the "personality border"). In addition, further interactions (vulnerability, pathoplasty, complications) between chronic affective disorder and borderline instability are proposed as the illness progresses. That is, recurrent affective episodes early in life are thought to disrupt ego development and relationships; borderline instability is said to heighten sensitivity to affective arousal. Thus, this group may best be thought of as a subgroup within the broader category of subaffective dysthymics who show a "chronic tempestuous course" (Akiskal, Yerevanian, Davis, King, & Lemmi, 1985b, p. 197). Although the causes of affective and personality pathology are seen as independent to some extent, many direct interactions between the borderline and affective pathology are described (e.g., interactions between affective distress and impulsiveness lead to the intense displays of affect, which are characteristic of the so-called borderline condition).

This model has been further developed and reformulated by Gunderson and colleagues to clarify the question of the degree of independence of personality and depressive pathology. In their reviews of the borderline diagnosis, Gunderson and Elliott (1985) and Gunderson and Zanarini (1987) suggest that depression in borderlines is qualitatively different (e.g., feelings of emptiness, inner badness, conflicted dependency, destructive impulses) from classical melancholic depression (e.g., guilt, unconflicted dependency). Because of this and the lack of evidence for alternative models (i.e., primary depression leads to borderline personality disorder; depression is secondary to being borderline; depression and borderline personality disorder are independent), they suggest an expansion of the common-cause hypothesis to include vulnerability and pathoplasty: Concurrent borderline and depressive disorders are attributed to a biological deficit that increases the risk of early developmental impairments; these impairments, in turn, increase vulnerability to either or both disorders; and variations in actual presentation are shaped by temperament and later life experiences. "The key to the overlap and dissimilarities between these two disorders, then may be a constellation of innate and external factors that are inconsequential individually, but combine to shape depression, chronic dysphoria, or borderline behavior—alone or in any possible combinations" (Gunderson & Elliott, 1985, p. 286).

The conception of this borderline subaffective subtype has also been elaborated and extended by Siever (1989). Following Akiskal, Siever posits a common core liability for affective disorder, which is directed by other factors either toward an autonomous affective disorder or in the direction of an affectively related borderline personality disorder. The causal mechanism for the primary affective vulnerability in both forms is a cholinergic dysfunction, as indicated by reduced REM latency and other biological markers for affective disorder. Noradrenergic dysregulation is the mechanism that underlies the classical vegetative symptoms of autonomous endogenous depression. In contrast, a serotonergic dysfunction is the mechanism that underlies the personality disorder variant, through its association with heightened affective instability and the disinhibition of aggressive/impulsive behavior. Thus in this model, Siever hypothesizes a "common core" affective sensitivity (cholinergic cause), which is magnified by its interaction with affective instability, as expressed in the form of impulsive traits and action-oriented or impulsive behavior (serotonergic cause or pathoplastic effect). Those with only the "core" affective sensitivity who do not also have the impulsive trait will instead be dysthymic or cyclothymic. In addition, Siever suggests that psychosocial factors and "adverse environmental circumstances" may also predispose an individual toward personality and/or affective disorder (vulnerability).

This model has been further extended (Siever & Davis, 1991) to specify linkages between a wider range of Axis I and Axis II disorders on dimensions of temperament and behavior that are determined by specific biological systems or substrates. Four psychobiological process dimensions (cognitive organization, affective regulation, impulse control, and anxiety modulation) are posited as core causal factors that contribute, singly or in combination, to the development of personality traits, personality disturbances or disorders, or their more severe Axis I counterparts. Thus an individual's status on a particular core dimension influences his or her development by determining the interplay between childhood experiences and perceptions of the environment, the perceptions and responses of caretakers (also influenced by the caretakers' dispositions on these dimensions), and the development of coping strategies.

In the unfolding of personality–depression linkages, for example, Siever and Davis (1991) outline a developmental sequence in which an infant with an inborn tendency to affective instability shapes interactions with parents who must attempt to comfort and regulate these states. At the same time, the infant's mood states act as a filter for learning and color the way the world is perceived and appraised, and the way the developing self is experienced. Heightened sensitivity to frustration, separation experiences, or punishment, for example, will both exacerbate dysphoria and lead to the development of strategies (e.g., dependency) to avoid this state. Oscillations in mood and negatively toned appraisals of self and others further perpetuate a sense of the self as "defective and caretakers as abandoning or frustrating" (Siever & Davis, 1991 p. 1665)—perceptions that are further exacerbated in individuals whose impulsivity is also heightened. In its present state of development, this model has evolved considerably beyond its original form to incorporate elements of common cause, vulnerability and pathoplasty in a complex and multivariate developmental model.

## Issues and Questions

Although the subaffective models just reviewed cover a fairly wide range of disorders and differ in complexity, a number of common issues and questions are raised. Foremost is the problem of overlapping criteria for affective disorders and certain of the personality disorders. As Widiger (1989) states the issue, it is tautological to draw conclusions about the personality correlates of an affective disorder when affective criteria are also part of the DSM-III or DSM-III-R definition of a given personality disorder; it is also impossible to control for the overlap without destroying the meaning of the constructs involved. A related and equally important question can be raised about the extent to which the so-called personality traits observed in the subaffective disorders (e.g., dysthymic, cyclothymic, borderline) are conceptually or empirically distinguishable from milder affective symptoms or mood states. Both of these problems highlight the boundary problems associated with the distinctions between Axis I and Axis II, and with the difficulty of imposing a categorical system on personality and symptomatic variables that are dimensional in nature (Widiger, 1989). Other difficulties arise because of imbalances in the degree of differentiation within current conceptualizations and measures of depression and personality constructs. At present, more distinctions are made among personality traits than are made among the symptoms of depression. The assumption that depression is a fairly unitary concept may have hampered the development of more differentiated conceptions of the linkages between personality traits and specific subcomponents of depressive symptomatology. In a recent analysis of depressive symptoms, for example, Wiener (1989) provides examples of how the same depressive symptom has different meanings in different interpersonal contexts. For instance, helplessness in the context of a dependent relationship may mean "I can't do anything by myself"; in the context of withdrawal, it may mean "Nothing I do will change these circumstances for me" (Wiener, 1989, p. 311).

An alternative to continuing to look for and draw conclusions from what may be artifactual empirical associations (arising from artificial conceptual distinctions) between affect and personality variables may be to shift the focus to more specifically defined relationships among key variables, while placing less emphasis on efforts to decide what is attributable to personality trait and what is affective state. In some cases this might lead to questions and hypotheses about the conditions in which milder forms of affective disturbance become full-blown affective disorders; questions about when the risk of a serious affective disorder is averted or attenuated by certain traits; questions about when mood states become chronic and trait-like; or attempts to distinguish interactions between traits and states that are closely associated with depressed affect from relationships that arise from other and more general components of pathology. Such efforts would require a shift from what has been the dominant concern with *content-oriented* definitions of personality and pathology to more *process-oriented* formulations. Concepts related to mood (e.g., affective dyscontrol or regulation, pervasiveness or chronicity of affect) and personality-related concepts (e.g., motives, congruence of needs, quality of defenses or coping in relation to goals, and the function and/or organization of self-perceptions and cognitive processes) need to be developed. Further refinement and specification could also be achieved with greater differentiation of the key components of personality (at least into affective and nonaffective categories), and with a comparable differentiation of affective symptoms in terms of adaptive function (e.g., Kupfer & Ehlers, 1989), transactional context (e.g., Wiener, 1989), and/or mode of expression. For example, in research on personality, it would be beneficial to distinguish temperament or affect regulation from variables concerned with interpersonal, cognitive, or self-concept processes; for conceptions of depression, the separation of vegetative or behavioral symptoms from symptoms involving interpersonal process, cognitive process, or self-concept disturbances would be valuable. Such distinctions might make it easier to manage the boundary problems and to investigate more specific linkages between processes without becoming sidetracked by the need to defend what may turn out to be fairly arbitrary distinctions between personality and depression or trait and state. This sort of conceptual development would make it possible to move the field beyond an implied division between psychosocial and biological causes to a more integrated view.

## Cloninger's General Model

One example of such a broader and more integrated perspective on the relationship between personality and depression is provided by the elegant and complex general model proposed by Cloninger (1986,

1987). Although Cloninger still assumes a common causal pathway for personality and affect, these concepts are more clearly integrated and articulated in the context of a more general model that encompasses anxiety and affective disorders, personality at the trait and disorder levels, and a number of mediating variables. The basic assumption is that anxiety, affective, and personality disorders are determined by a more basic set of heritable traits (novelty seeking, harm avoidance, and reward dependence), each of which is associated with a different neuro-biological mechanism/system (dopamaninergic, serotonergic, and noradrenergic, respectively). Combinations of the three sets of heritable traits interact to shape the development of personality by influencing patterns of learning, information processing, mood, reactions to stress, and adaptation over time. Thus personality traits and disorders evolve differently in the context of various combinations of the three core systems/traits in interaction with the environment.

The model also relates each of the three traits and associated neuro-biological systems to different kinds of anxiety and/or dysphoria: Soma-tic anxiety is associated with high novelty seeking, cognitive anxiety with high harm avoidance, and dysphoria with reward dependence. Consistent with the view that those high in reward dependence are most sensitive to external sources of reward, Cloninger conceives of dysphor-ia as being a somewhat more reactive state than are the two forms of anxiety. Specifically, frustration of reward dependence is posited to set off a chain of events in the noradrenergic system, where the core vulnerability is centered (rebound noradrenergic hyperactivity followed by hypercortisolemia, which leads to the dysphoric state). Cloninger distinguishes this more reactive dysphoria from more autonomous forms of mood disorder, in which depressive episodes are not so closely tied to environmental stressors in vulnerable personality types.

In Cloninger's model, different combinations of core traits and personality styles thus function to determine specific patterns of vul-nerability, response, and adaptation to stress. In this respect, the model combines principles of common-cause, predisposition/vulnerability, and pathoplasty models, with greatest emphasis on predisposition. In the case of reactive dysphoria, this form of affective disorder is the response of an individual with the core liability (noradrenergic dysfunction) to certain environmental events to which he or she is specifically sensitive or vulnerable, as colored or shaped by combinations of other traits and experiences. Cloninger suggests that this condition can be distinguished from an autonomous affective disturbance, which is not related to personality and not environmentally responsive. With respect to per-sonality features associated with this vulnerability to dysphoria, the model describes the constellation of personality traits that will be associated with the highest level of reward dependence:

> social vulnerability associated with ready tendency to openly reveal personal intimacies; . . . need for praise and approval of others with excessive tendencies to conform to peer pressures; . . . highly sympathetic and easily exploited by sentimental appeals; . . . intensely driven, frequently pushing self to point of exhaustion; . . . marked persistence in previously rewarded behavior despite frustration of efforts; . . . marked sensitivity to social cues of approval or rejection, loss and frustrative nonreward with persistent craving for gratification; . . . excessive reward seeking behavior in response to rejection or frustration (such as overeating, overworking, increased sexual activity, or unnecessary buying. (Cloninger, 1987, p. 582)

As dysphoria is linked to frustrations in individuals with high reward dependence, the model predicts that this affective disturbance will be most prominent in those personality types with the most unbuffered or unmodulated components of reward dependence (from highest to lowest: cyclothymic, histrionic, passive aggressive, and dependent). Because the core traits determine needs and vulnerability to stress, dysphoric reactions are most likely when specific needs or combinations of needs are frustrated. Most prominent and intense dysphoric reactions and widest mood swings are predicted for cyclothymic disorder, the disorder with the least buffered amount of reward dependence, although sensitivity to specific stressors may be determined by other aspects of personality. In other personality disorders, reward dependence is mediated by either high novelty seeking (histrionic) or high harm avoidance (passive aggressive, dependent), and depressive reactions will be linked to stressors or frustrations in these specific domains (e.g., to monotony in the novelty seeker; aversive events in the harm-avoidant person). Borderline personality disorder shares many traits with histrionic personality disorder, except that in the borderline individual novelty seeking is stronger than reward dependence, which explains the greater impulsivity. Cloninger also posits an autonomous affective disturbance, which is not related to personality and not environmentally responsive.

## Depressive Personality

The notion of "depressive personality disorder" (or "depressive personality") may well represent the crossroads of personality and depression, as the constructs of personality and depression are essentially blended into one clinical and conceptual entity. Depressive mood or features are represented as chronic, stable personality traits; that is, the character structure is depressive. Within this general framework, several conceptualizations of depressive personality have been proposed, with somewhat different clinical features and hypothesized causality (Phillips, Gunderson, Hirschfeld, & Smith, 1990). These include the notion of "depressive temperament" proposed by German psychiatrists, with a heavy emphasis on hereditary factors, and various psychoanalytic conceptions that emphasize developmental factors. Typical features of the depressive personality as described by the different approaches include chronic gloominess, pessimism, low self-esteem, self-criticalness, and guilt. Thus the core deficit in the depressive personality appears to be primarily in the cognitive domain (Hirschfeld, Shea, Gunderson, & Phillips, 1989b). However, this model differs from other cognitive models in the persistence and pervasiveness of the dysfunctional beliefs and styles. That is, the negative beliefs and styles persist across situations and over time, as opposed to being latent or predisposing features that require activation by other agents, as is true in conceptions of neurotic depression and diathesis–stress models.

Akiskal (1983b) and others (e.g., Klein, 1990; Kocsis & Frances, 1987) have speculated that the category of depressive personality may overlap significantly with dysthymia, particularly early-onset dysthymia as recently defined in DSM-III-R (American Psychiatric Association, 1987). Akiskal (1983b) also equates depressive personality with the subaffective variant of dysthymia. Klein (1990), however, has reported only modest overlap (30%) between subjects carefully diagnosed for depressive personality and/or dysthymia, and finds some differences between subjects with depressive personality only (i.e., male sex, milder symptoms of depression, less nonbipolar disorder in relatives) and those with dysthymia. This suggests that depressive personality may indeed be a valid and distinct subtype in which mild depressive symptoms are chronically associated with temperamentally determined dysfunctional personality traits.

## Character Spectrum Models

The same boundary problems that have been noted for the subaffective disorders (which are generally assumed to have a biologically determined affective basis) appear when we consider clinical examples of the disorders in which personality is assumed to be a primary cause of depression. Here again, it is difficult to make or maintain the distinction between personality traits and chronic and/or pervasive affective states. The assumption that the affective disorders are biologically determined to a greater event than personality traits or disorders is as problematic and fallible as the assumption that affective states and disorders are not comparably altered by psychosocial experiences (Widiger, 1989). If neither assumption can be supported on logical or empirical grounds, then the question about relationships between biological and psychosocial determinants of depression and personality can perhaps be more meaningfully reformulated in terms of the processes or mechanisms involved in specific relationships. For example, the link between depression and dependency may be mediated by biologically determined tendencies to withdraw under stress, or by learned helplessness.

## Winokur's Depression Spectrum Disease

Using family history as a criterion for defining subgroups, Winokur and colleagues defined a group of female depressed patients whose family histories were positive for alcoholism and/or sociopathy, while being negative for depression (VanValkenberg, Lowry, Winokur, & Cadoret, 1977; Winokur, 1972; Winokur, Behar, VanValkenberg, & Lowry, 1978; see Table 1.3). When contrasted with depressives with family histories of depression only, this subgroup was found to have somewhat fewer melancholic features (i.e., significantly less loss of interest, a statistical trend for less diurnal variation, and greater anxiety and externalized blame). With respect to personality traits, the spectrum group had more unstable relationship histories; were more irritable, demanding, and nervous; and were more likely to have been diagnosed as neurotic. Although they were reported to have had more past episodes of depression, their current status was less severe, and fewer relapses or rehospitalizations were reported. Winokur has conceptualized this group as a distinct form of neurotic–reactive depression, in which the depression can be seen as secondary to personality characteristics associated with a "chronic, stormy, and disabling life-style" (1985, p. 1119). Winokur also noted some similarities to patients with bipolar disorder that might suggest a link between these two groups, but does not clearly define the specific mechanisms by which these disorders are related (VanValkenberg et al., 1977).

**TABLE 1.3.** Summary of Assumptions of Characterological Clinical Models

---

*Depression spectrum disease (Winokur)*

Basic assumption: Alcoholism and sociopathy cause depression.

Defined by: Family history of alcoholism or sociopathy without affective disorder (major depression and/or bipolar disorder).

Contrast group(s): Family history of affective disorder without alcoholism or sociopathy ("pure depressives").

Clinical features:
  Clinical status when studied: Major depression.
  Affective: Less loss of interest, somewhat less diurnal variation.
  Personality: Unstable relationships, irritable, demanding, nervous.
  History and course: Prior diagnoses of neurosis, current episode less severe, and better recovery.

*Character spectrum dysphoria*

Basic assumptions: Personality (characterological features) causes the affective illness. Personality disturbance caused by childhood parental loss, broken homes, familial alcoholism.

Defined by: Early onset of DSM-III dysthymia, not secondary to major affective disorder; no response to tricyclics; normal REM.

Clinical features:
  Clinical status when studied: Not known.
  Affective: Major depressive episode lacks melancholic features.
  Personality: Unstable traits (substance abuse; dependent, histrionic, antisocial, or schizoid features).
  History and course: Early onset for character disorder; depression intermittent, does not respond to drugs; when major depressive episodes remit, they return to baseline state.

*Pilkonis's prototypes*

Basic assumption: Personality (attachment) conflicts caused by problems in early object relations make individual vulnerable to depression under specific life stresses. Two styles that develop from this conflict: (1) dependent, anxious attachment; (2) excessive autonomy, creating specific vulnerabilities to stress (interpersonal vs. loss of mastery and control)

Defined by: Depressed patients and similarity to prototypes.

Clinical features:
  Clinical status when studied: During and after a depressed episode.
  Affective: Major depression criteria; depression shaped by personality traits; sadness, dependency, passivity in dependent type; defeat, agitation, withdrawal, self-criticism in autonomous subtype.
  History and course: Will respond to different treatments; outcome for more autonomous types may be better.

---

## Character Spectrum Dysphoria

Akiskal (1983b) has described a similar subgroup of patients whose dysphoria was secondary to long-standing characterological problems (Table 1.3). Their personalities were characterized by a "melange" of unstable traits (drug and alcohol abuse; dependent, histrionic, antisocial, or schizoid traits), which are attributed to chaotic developmental experiences at the hands of parents with sociopathic traits and/or other (nonaffective) personality disorders. Although the mode of transmission can be biogenetic, environmental, or a mixture of both, the factors implicated in the development of the personality features and associated pathology are hypothesized to be distinct from the biological or environmental factors involved in the development of affective disorder. Moreover, the affective disorder, which is secondary to the personality component, does not show the biological markers associated with classical endogenous depression. Instead, it is suggested that the depressive features may be more heavily influenced or colored by personality style (pathoplasty).

## Neurotic Depression

The most enduring and classical example of a constellation of clinical conditions in which depression is seen as secondary to personality is the venerable conception of "neurotic depression." In the dynamic literature, many manifestations of depression were thought to be the result of certain neurotic personality subtypes and/or conflicts (e.g., Chodoff, 1972; Klerman, Endicott, Spitzer, & Hirschfeld, 1979). Both dependent (oral) and obsessive (anal) character traits were emphasized as predispositions to depressive episodes. Generally, frustration in early object relations caused by extremes of poor parenting (unresponsive, demanding parents; overly controlling, manipulative parents) was suggested as the primary causal factor in the development of core conflicts in an individual who feels chronically needy, deprived, frustrated, and angry, and whose expressions of anger are turned inward (Laughlin, 1967). In this developmental and motivational context, the symptoms of depression, especially affective and performance deficits, are assumed to be "active" demands for nurturance and/or recognition from important others, demands that simultaneously fulfill needs for revenge and rebellion (Bonime, 1975). To the extent that these needs are partially fulfilled and/or expressed, the depressive character traits may also function as a defense against more severe depressive episodes. In this respect, depressive symptoms may be viewed as defenses or adaptive attempts to maintain control and self-consistency.

As Hirschfeld and Klerman (1979) noted more recently, many of the characteristics of neurotic depression can also be understood within the framework of other contemporary psychosocial theories of depression. Cognitive theories of depression articulate the linkages between specific cognitive characteristics, such as the "cognitive triad," with depression (Beck, 1974, 1976) or between uncontrollable stress and depression (Seligman, 1975), or emphasize perceptions of one's ability to cope with negative events that increase and maintain depression through negative effects on self-esteem (Abramson et al., 1978, 1989). Shustack and West (1985) suggest an alternative view—that many of the symptoms and behaviors of depressed people can be understood as consistent with needs to maintain a negative self-schema. This hypothesis may be particularly important in understanding why depressive symptoms persist. Behavioral analyses of depression focus on the association between deficits in social skill and social reinforcement (Ferster, 1965; Lewinsohn, Biglan, & Zeiss, 1976). Again, the effects of key behavioral variables on depression are mediated by self-esteem. Interpersonal views have identified specific interpersonal problems such as interpersonal disputes, interpersonal deficits, and communication problems (Weissman & Paykel, 1974), or abandonment or attack by significant others (Benjamin, in press). Other current formulations of antecedents to depression suggest that certain coping or defensive styles may be important mediating variables in the development or maintenance of depression (Barnett & Gotlib, 1988; Matussek & Fell, 1983).

## Chronic Depression

The chronic depressions are complex phenomena: All of the possible causal models for personality–depression relationships may explain different subtypes of chronic depression (Kocsis & Frances, 1987). Different models may be at work in the chronic versus the onset phases of depression (e.g., Brewin, 1985; Needles & Abramson, 1990), and conditions may become chronic because more than one model is at work at different phases of the illness (Brewin, 1985; Depue & Monroe, 1986). Some clinical syndromes, such as dysthymia, double depression, and depressive personality, are chronic by definition; most other subtypes have either chronic or recurrent forms. There are several explanations for the persistence of depression. Consistent with vulnerability models, the same environmental and personality risk factors that caused the initial episode may persist. Weissman and others, for example, find that family conflict variables associated with the onset of depression were also associated with nonrecovery at 1 year (Keitner & Miller, 1990;

Sargeant, Bruce, Florio, & Weissman, 1990). Billings and Moos find continuing life stresses, social resource deficits, and patterns of dysfunctional coping to be associated with nonremission at 1- and 4-year follow-up (Billings & Moos, 1985; Swindle et al., 1989). Pre-existing comorbidity in general is associated with chronicity (Keitner, Ryan, Miller, Kohn, & Epstein, 1991); comorbid personality disorders may interfere with the course of recovery by disturbing relationships with important others, including therapists (Pilkonis & Frank, 1988; Shea et al., 1987).

Consistent with complication models, the consequences of depression may create additional risk factors for nonrecovery. Inadequate coping styles or negative behavior in important roles and relationships may convert one-time stressful events into chronic strains (Depue & Monroe, 1986) and further erode social support (Cole & Milstead, 1989; Monroe & Steiner, 1986). Chronic negative affect and related personality variables such as neuroticism or negative appraisal patterns may also lower thresholds for stress (e.g., Ormel & Schaufeli, 1991; Ormel & Wohlfarth, 1991). Family responses to the patient's depression may prolong it (Keitner & Miller, 1990). Interactions between depression and personality may become more frequent or intense when both features are continuously present (e.g., Free & Oei, 1989). Depressed symptoms may also linger as "scars" of the illness; that is, symptomatic patterns, cognitive responses, or interpersonal behavior that first appeared during an acute episode may "convert" into more enduring patterns and take on the characteristics of personality traits. It is interesting that recent examples of this conversion or scarring process suggest that the impact of depression and associated cognitive and/or social deficits on the self-concept or self-schema is crucial to chronicity (e.g., Shustack & West, 1985). Indeed, it may be that the motivation to maintain self-consistency (even of a maladaptive or depressed self) is powerful enough to maintain depressive behavior (e.g., Andrews, 1989).

## Theoretical Perspectives on Personality–Depression Relationships

In most of the so-called "characterological" syndromes described above, it is clear that the effects of personality traits and disorders on the expression of depression can take many different forms, and that features of several models of influence can be identified in each clinical syndrome. An example of a relationship consistent with the predisposition model would be a case when depression arises from the problems in living associated with personality pathology, such as when an individual's passive aggressive, antisocial, or borderline traits provoke interpersonal disputes in areas specific to his or her personality problems. The frequently noted association between histrionic traits and the manner in which depressed affect is experienced and displayed by the depressed person would be consistent with pathoplasty. Another example of pathoplasty and/or complication models would be a case when personality features unrelated to vulnerability to a depressed episode interfere with recovery (e.g., schizoid or paranoid traits may interfere with an individual's ability to establish or maintain a therapeutic relationship, or may prevent the development of positive social contacts).

Considering the fact that the groups of patients with so-called characterological depression are often residual groups, having been defined after individuals with biological markers have been differentiated, it is not particularly surprising to find considerable heterogeneity with respect to personality characteristics—a heterogeneity that has no doubt interfered with the development of meaningful and valid models of personality-based depressive disorders. Some of this heterogeniety may be resolved in recently developed models of personality–depression relationships, which reflect different theoretical perspectives (i.e., dynamic–developmental, interpersonal, cognitive, temperamental).

## Pilkonis's Personality Prototypes

One example of an attempt to resolve the heterogeneity problem is Pilkonis's (1988) effort to define clinically meaningful subtypes within the broad ranges of character pathology that might cause depression. Many features of earlier characterizations of depression as secondary to personality have been integrated into this two-prototype model, which combines elements of common-cause, predisposition, subclinical, and pathoplasty models; predisposition, however, plays the most central role. In Pilkonis's model (Table 1.3), the shared etiological factor in the two subtypes of depression is the individual's failure, because of difficulties with early object relations, to experience "secure attachment" and to develop an appropriate balance over time between adult autonomy and attachment needs (Pilkonis, 1988, p. 149). Two pathways are suggested to predispose an individual to depression: (1) a childhood style of "anxious–avoidant" attachment, leading to a "compulsively self-reliant" pattern and an excessively autonomous adult style in which the risk for depression arises when needs for mastery and control are frustrated by events such as achievement failure; and (2) a contrasting childhood style of "anxious–ambivalent" attachment, leading to an "anxiously attached" adult style characterized by excessive dependency needs and vulnerability to depression when interpersonal stresses and/ or losses occur (Pilkonis, 1988, p. 149). In addition to serving as vulnerability or risk factors, these personality styles also will shape the experience of depression (pathoplasty): The excessively autonomous types, when depressed, are more likely to be high in self-criticism and concerned with failure and defeat; the more dependent types, when depressed, will complain more of sadness, loss, and abandonment. Many of these same traits will also influence treatment outcome and the risk of residual symptoms (complications). With respect to treatment responsiveness, the autonomous subgroup may benefit more from cognitive therapy, the dependent subgroup may benefit more from interpersonal therapy, and the depression in either subgroup may fail to resolve unless key stresses and/or problematic life situations can be resolved. This model overlaps in some respects with Beck's (1983) distinction between sociotropy and autonomy in depression, a distinction which has been validated in some respects by Robins and Luten (1991).

## *Benjamin's Structural Analysis of Social Behavior*

Benjamin's model of depression and personality disorder is based on her general model, the "structural analysis of social behavior" (SASB; Benjamin, 1974). To explain the relationship between personality disorder and depression, the analysis focuses on two key interpersonal and intrapsychic processes, helplessness and self-criticism, as common causes of certain personality traits and depression. In this theory, helplessness, and self-criticism, or both are sufficient to cause depression and shape the development and phenomenology of a subset of the personality disorders. Social withdrawal or disengagement may also be associated with depression, but this is considered a secondary reaction to, or a defense against, the more fundamental tendency to submit. Thus depressive states may be characterized by an alternation between submission and disengagement.

According to Benjamin, the most important influences on personality in general are early interactions and social learning experiences with parents and significant others. Areas of learning that are especially important in the development of the adult interpersonal patterns corresponding to the personality disorders (which Benjamin views as qualitatively different from normal personality processes) are (1) development of the sense of instrumental or interpersonal competence (i.e., how others react when one does well); (2) learning about what happens if one is sick, needy, or disabled (i.e., how others respond to the sick role); (3) identity development (i.e., relationship of self-concept to one's actual behavior and potential); and (4) learning about the interpersonal consequences of the expression of affect. Helplessness, conceptualized and measured in Benjamin's (1974) SASB by submissiveness, can be caused either by parental neglect or abandonment, which induce helplessness in the object, or by an excess of parental dominance or control. Self-criticism arises from the internalization of criticism and attack from parents and important others. Thus, helplessness/ submission and internalized self-criticism are common causes of personality and depressive pathology, so that the relationship of depression to personality disorders is determined by the degree to which the common causal factors have been present in the individual's development.

Some personality disorders are more heavily programmed for helplessness and/or self-criticism; it is those in which depression should be most prominent. In Benjamin's (in press) recently articulated interpersonal models for each of the personality disorders, the disorders involving the largest amounts of helplessness/submission are dependent, borderline, compulsive, schizotypal, avoidant, and passive aggressive, in that order. Although histrionics and schizoids also behave submissively on occasion, their submission is in the service of control and therefore may buffer depression. The dependent personality has the heaviest concentration of submissiveness and would be expected to be most vulnerable to depression. Self-criticism is hypothesized to be high in borderline, narcissistic, histrionic, avoidant, and passive aggressive personality disorders and would account for experiences of depression in these cases. Other personality features may also interact to determine how criticism is experienced. Thus the narcissist will be depressed specifically when admiration from others is lost; the histrionic will be depressed when efforts to get a response from others fail.

*Cognitive Models*

Various cognitive models of depression have been suggested; these propose pathological beliefs or attributional styles as predisposing factors or vulnerabilities to depression. Generally, these cognitive features are presumed to be stable "traits," and thus function as aspects of personality. Beck's theory, for example, postulates underlying irrational beliefs or "schemas," which are the products of early developmental experiences (Beck, Rush, Shaw, & Emery, 1979). Two types of core beliefs are described (Beck, 1983): sociotropy, in which the dysfunctional beliefs are centered around the need for love and approval (e.g., "I am worthless if everyone doesn't love me"), and autonomy, characterized by perfectionistic beliefs (e.g., "If I make a mistake, I am a worthless person"). Under certain circumstances, these dysfunctional beliefs are activated, resulting in depression. As representations of self–other interactions figure prominently in these schemas, these models can be said to integrate cognitive and interpersonal perspectives (Safran, 1990). Recently, other investigators have gone further to integrate cognitive and interpersonal perspectives into models of social cognition of object relations (Westen, 1991) or person schemas (Horowitz, 1991).

Beck et al. (1990) have also extended this theory directly to the development of the personality disorders, and have developed a taxonomy of the core problems and underlying schemas for most of the personality disorders. This view provides for multiple links between personality disorders and depression: In some cases, the links between the personality disorder and depression are attributable to the presence of overlapping cognitive schemas, consistent with a common-cause model of influence. What distinguishes personality disorders from depression is that the schemas are more continuously operative in the information processing of individuals with personality disorders, but are more intermittent or latent in individuals with depression. For example, although the schema "I need help" will be prominent only during an episode of depression for individuals without a personality disorder, this schema is part of the normal, everyday information processing for individuals with a dependent personality disorder. This overlap of schemas would seem to be most characteristic of dependent personality disorder, in which the content of schemas and beliefs appears to be the most similar to those in depression. The overlap concerns primarily beliefs and feelings of helplessness and needs for approval and support from others. A real or perceived loss of approval or support is associated with feelings of worthlessness, pessimism, and so on.

In addition to the effect of common elements of schemas and beliefs as common determinants of personality disorders and clinical depression, each of the personality disorders is also characterized by unique schemas, beliefs, and related behaviors that operate as vulnerability or risk factors for depression under specific circumstances. For example, narcissistic personality disorder is characterized by grandiose beliefs and expectations; when these beliefs are challenged by large discrepancies with reality, the ensuing sense of loss and humiliation may be a precipitant for depression. Narcissistic entitlement or insensitivity in relationships may result in repeated losses or interpersonal conflicts that lead to depression. For obsessive compulsive personality disorder, characteristic schemas are concerned with perfectionism and needs for control; circumstances that threaten the sense of control may result in depression. In other personality disorders, behaviors associated with characteristic schemas may also heighten vulnerability to depression through their effects on life circumstances, including loss of relationships, occupational failures, and so forth, that generally precipitate depression. For example, the manipulative and exploitative behavior of the person with antisocialy personality disorder or the tempestuous rage of the borderline individual are likely to destroy relationships and result in repeated losses.

More recent cognitive models of depression have shifted the emphasis from schemas to *styles* of cognition. For example, both learned helplessness (Abramson et al., 1978) and learned hopelessness (Abramson et al., 1989) theories hypothesize certain attributional styles as stable factors that predispose individuals to depression. Such states are characterized by the tendency to make internal, stable, and/or global attributions regarding the cause of negative life events and about one's inability to alter negative outcomes, as well as the development of hopeless expectations about the future.

Research on cognitive factors and depression has not consistently supported the hypothesis that dysfunctional attitudes and attributions are stable traits that precede or persist beyond depressive episodes (Barnett & Gotlib, 1988). Persons and Miranda (1990), however, have developed the "mood-state hypothesis" to interpret and integrate the pattern of negative findings in a framework that is still consistent with the original vulnerability hypotheses of the cognitive models. They propose that the dysfunctional attitudes and beliefs are stable but *latent;* that is, they are not accessible to the individual unless they are activated by a negative mood state. Research using mood induction studies has supported this view (Persons & Miranda, 1990; Miranda & Persons, 1988; Miranda, Persons, & Byers, 1990).

## Tellegen's Dimensions of Mood and Personality

Tellegen's (1985) model of the relationship of depression and personality arises from his empirical efforts to identify the primary dimensions of personality and mood. Reanalyses of previous factor-analytic studies of mood have consistently revealed two primary orthogonal mood dimensions that Tellegen and his colleagues refer to as "positive affect" and "negative affect" (Tellegen, 1985; Watson & Tellegen, 1985; Zevon & Tellegen, 1982). Positive affect is considered a state of pleasurable engagement that is characterized by descriptors such as "elated," "active," and "enthusiastic," but not "drowsy," "sleepy," or "sluggish." Negative affect is viewed as a state of unpleasurable engagement reflected by high ratings on adjectives such as "distressed," "fearful," and "hostile," but low ratings for "relaxed" and "calm."

These positive and negative affect systems, and their parallel trait forms, positive and negative affectivity, are posited by Tellegen to give rise to and influence the basic dimensions of personality. For example, several studies have demonstrated that positive and negative affectivity are highly correlated with extraversion and neuroticism, respectively (Costa & McCrae, 1980; Meyer & Shack, 1989; Tellegen, 1985). Moreover, given the relationship of extraversion to specific interpersonal dispositions, such as assuredness, dominance, and warmth (McCrae & Costa, 1989), such personality variables may be construed as mediators between affective experience and interpersonal behavior.

Although Tellegen's model has not been studied specifically with depressed individuals, he has suggested that depression is associated with low levels of positive affectivity (Tellegen, 1985). It may be further hypothesized, based on the pattern of empirical findings (e.g., McCrae & Costa, 1989; Watson & Tellegen, 1985), that the depressed individual would display a particular combination of affect (low positive affect), personality traits (introversion), and interpersonal dispositions (low assuredness, low dominance, and low warmth). Clearly, this model highlights the structural commonalities among these different conceptual perspectives and describes significant relationships of affective and personality variables. Thus, this approach suggests that personality and psychopathology are organized by and around common affective processes, and suggests that concepts of affect are central to the experiences of both personality and depression, which in our experience are best viewed as inextricably entwined.

## REFLECTIONS AND RECOMMENDATIONS

Several different types of models for relationships between personality and depression have been discussed, and many different clinical subgroups and/or theoretical developments have been reviewed. Despite the diversity of the models, clinical conditions, and perspectives, certain common issues can be identified that may provide useful guidelines for ongoing model development. These reflections and recommendations are not intended to serve as a comprehensive summary of model development or research findings to date, but rather to summarize conceptual and methodological points that are important to consider in the development and refinement of models in the future.

## Integration of Models of Causality and Modes of Influence

In Figure 1.2 we outline the scaffolding for an integrated conception of personality–depression relationships that combines the different causal models reviewed above (row headings) with modes of influence corresponding to some of the conceptual domains that have held promise for understanding personality–depression relationships (column headings). This grid is offered as an alternative to attempts that have been made to define specific subgroups conforming to only one model of causality or mode of influence. It is our opinion that the field is better served by models that attempt to integrate these domains than by research that attempts to make sharp distinctions between biological and psychosocial variables or one causal model.

## Integration of Different Conceptually Based Modes of Influence

In the proposed grid, psychosocial approaches are further subdivided into interpersonal, cognitive, and dynamic domains to reflect the past

THEORETICAL PERSPECTIVE

| TYPE OF PERSONALITY–DEPRESSION RELATIONSHIP | Cognitive | Interpersonal | Dynamic | Biological |
|---|---|---|---|---|
| Predisposition | | | | |
| Prodromal or subclinical form | | | | |
| Pathoplasty or interaction | | | | |
| Complication or scar | | | | |

FIGURE 1.2. Framework for the integration of theoretical modes of influence and models of causality.

and current contributions from these perspectives. While one column is provided for biological influences, greater differentiation might also be developed (e.g., sleep or neuroendocrine processes). Although there have been some tendencies in the past to view these biological and psychosocial perspectives as competing models, the current tendency is toward greater and greater integration (e.g., Akiskal, 1988; Cloninger, 1987; Free & Oei, 1989; Siever & Davis, 1991). Concepts have also become more differentiated within the psychosocial realm. Lazarus's (1991) theoretical analysis of the role of cognitive appraisals in emotion and Westen's (1991) integration of cognitive and object relation theories are but two examples. Given the potential richness and complexity of the theoretical, empirical, and clinical phenomena covered, we suggest that efforts to understand personality–depression relationships must transcend attempts to decide which mode of influence (biological or psychosocial, interpersonal or cognitive) has more explanatory power and press instead to develop and test the models that will establish how the many linkages function. The suggested perspective, encompassing a range of theoretical domains, variables within domains, and models of transmission, is a first requirement for this shift of focus.

## Integration of Different Causal Models

Considering the degree of conceptual overlap among the models, and the complexity of the clinical phenomena they are intended to characterize, it is equally important to develop a framework for theory that considers and integrates the different causal relationships outlined in Table 1.1 and in the row headings in Figure 1.2. These headings correspond roughly to different ways in which variables or sets of variables can be hypothesized to contribute to a given pathological process. The concepts represented can be restated in terms of propositions about whether a given variable is a cause of, contributor to, concomitant of, or antecedent of the clinical condition of interest (see Barnett & Gotlib, 1988, for an excellent review of these issues for psychosocial variables). For variables thought to be causal, further consideration of their relative importance is necessary, that is, whether they are necessary but insufficient or necessary and sufficient conditions/ causes. For variables thought to be contributory but not causal, questions about the nature of this contribution, whether it is in the form of a main effect or interaction, must be resolved: Is the variable alone sufficient to have the specified effect, or must it be combined with other variables? For variables thought to be concomitants or antecedents of a given condition, it is important to specify whether and how these variables influence future course and outcome: As complications, do they acquire causal or contributory status with respect to future episodes, or do they remain as more stable but "benign" markers of a former episode?

## Temporal Complexity and Chronicity

All of the models that have been reviewed have considered to some degree, dimensions of time and conceptions of course and/or outcome. Causal and vulnerability models are most concerned with onset (most specifically with first-episode onset). Pathoplasty and interaction models are generally, but not exclusively, concerned with symptom and response patterns during an episode; complication models are concerned with the recovery or residual phase. These time perspectives, however, are often very difficult to untangle in cross-sectional research on clinical samples, where principles of several models may apply.

Many models have been guided by the implicit assumption that personality variables are more "chronic" or enduring than are the symptoms or syndrome of depression. This assumption may have led investigators to believe that hypotheses about the personality causes of first episodes of depression could be tested in clinical samples. Apart from the difficulties of assessing personality variables in individuals in a depressed state, current conceptions and methods of diagnosing depression may also obscure the possibility that in many individuals, mood disturbances may be as chronic and enduring as personality traits or disturbances. Evidence has grown in recent years to suggest that a high number of adults who are first *treated* for depression have had some degree of long-standing mood disturbance or have had prior episodes of depression that have not necessarily been diagnosed or treated (e.g., Billings & Moos, 1984; Keller, Lavori, Endicott, Coryell, & Klerman, 1983; Shea et al., 1987). The results of recent treatment studies indicate that the majority of patients treated for depression, either by drugs or psychotherapy, will relapse or experience new episodes unless they receive maintenance or booster treatment (e.g., Belsher & Costello, 1988; Frank et al., 1990; Keller et al., 1984; Keller & Shapiro, 1981; Kupfer & Frank, 1987; Lewinsohn et al., 1989; Shapiro & Keller, 1981). High rates of nonrecovery have also been found in community studies (e.g., Sargeant et al., 1990). This calls into question the often implicit assumption that depression symptoms are more acute or transient phenomena than personality traits. It also provides further evidence for the importance of developing different models for first and subsequent episodes.

## Process Conception of the Linkages

Many of the models that we have examined have dealt with what might be considered the content of relationships among traits (e.g., between a noradrenergic deficit and psychological dependency) or between traits and states (e.g., between a noradrenergic deficit and vegetative symptoms of depression; between introversion and brooding). These models have not, however, always been very clear about the specific processes involved in these linkages, nor have they consistently spelled out the assumptions involved in the relationships suggested or observed. An essential step in model development will be to shift away from hypotheses limited to "content" relationships to clear statements of the processes involved in such relationships. Unless and until the specific processes involved in the linkages in various models can be specified, it will be impossible to overcome the limitations of correlational studies and to design the kind of research that will shed light on the processes involved in the development of the various pathological conditions of interest to us.

Some steps have been taken in this direction, particularly by models that detail various maladaptive responses to stress, interpersonal transactions, self-appraisals, or self-regulatory processes that heighten depression. Behavioral analyses of depression have focused on the function of negative reinforcement from others for social skills deficits in the onset and maintenance of depression, and have suggested that the social skills deficits that result from depression may contribute further to the cycle of negative reinforcement (Cole & Milstead, 1989). Hops, Biglan, and colleagues have hypothesized that some depressive symptoms have the effect of reducing family members' negative responses (Hops et al., 1987). Hammen and colleagues (Hammen, Davila, Brown, Ellicott, & Gitlin, 1992) propose a model that suggests ways in which adverse early experiences interact with family history to create a vicious cycle of poor coping and depression. Howoritz details how the self-derogations of the depressed person sustain and reinforce dominance–submission cycles (Horowitz et al., 1991). Oatley and Bolton (1985) conceptualize the disruptive effect of life events in terms of their impact on self-defining role schemas, setting off a chain of reactions including dejection, negative inner dialogue, and negative patterns of social interaction. Similar conceptions highlight heightened self-awareness (Lewinsohn et al., 1985), negative self-perseveration (Pyszczynski & Greenberg, 1987), negative self evaluation (Dent & Teasdale, 1988), or negative self-confirmation (Andrews, 1989) as processes that precipitate and/or sustain depressed affect. Allred and Smith (1989) link negative self-statements to the lack of appropriate autonomic responses to stress.

Dienstbier (1989) associates psychological vulnerability with different patterns of maladaptive neuroendocrine responses to sudden and ongoing stress. It is interesting that a common element of these process theories is their focus on the self and on adaptation and vicious cycles. While depression is generally characterized as a maladaptive response to stress, it can also be viewed as an attempt to adapt and maintain equilibrium, once negative external circumstances and psychological states are established.

## The Structure of Depression and Personality

It has already been noted that the development of conceptions and instrumentation within the domain of personality has led to a much wider array of variables and a number of suggestions about the structure of personality traits or disorders (e.g., Tellegen, 1985; Livesley & Jackson, 1986). Although some attempts have been made to develop more differentiated conceptions of affect and depressive symptoms, these conceptions are not yet as fully developed as in the personality domain (e.g., Goldberg, 1990; Watson & Tellegen, 1985). Although conceptual parsimony may facilitate theoretical development and make research less cumbersome (by requiring fewer and less complex measures), the choice of concepts in both areas of concern (depression, personality) must ultimately be based on the most fully-developed and empirically grounded models possible. This has been done for interpersonal behavior (e.g., Benjamin, 1974), for cognitive variables (e.g., Beck et al., 1990), and for personality and mood inventories (e.g., Tellegen, 1985), but comparable exploration for biological variables and affective symptoms would seem essential to further specification of the linkages and processes involved. One example of such refinement is the distinction made by Kupfer and Ehlers (1989) between patterns of biological markers associated with hypothalamic–pituitary–adrenal axis disturbances accompanying acute episodes of depression (type 2) and patterns associated with more chronic disturbances in the regulatory process (type 1).

## Specificity versus Generality of Relationships

The problem of the specificity of relationships has been particularly vexing for psychopathology research. Most models propose relationships between variables that are intended to be fairly specific to depression or personality. When these models are put to empirical test in selected clinical subgroups, however, variables that reflect pathology at a more general level (*g* factors) are not always carefully differentiated from more specific relationships (*s* factors) that are of more particular theoretical interest. It has been suggested, for example, that the frequently found relationship between neurotic personality traits and depression may be more attributable to general distress than to factors more specific to the development of depression (Tellegen, 1985). Although these *g* factors may indeed play an important role in the pathological processes involved in personality–depression relationships, their contributions may not necessarily take the same form or involve the same processes as those that are more specific to personality–depression relationships. Moreover, variance from the *g* factors may obscure relationships between the very *s* factors that are the real focus of models. In developing models and research, we must attempt to differentiate these factors in advance, to measure each, and to choose control groups or data analysis methods that control appropriately for *g* factor variance.

## A Framework for Integrated Model Development

As a first step in the development of an integrated multivariate model for personality–depression relationships, we offer for consideration the models outlined in Figures 1.3 and 1.4. Rather than suggesting a series of opposing models corresponding to each of the different personality–depression relationships that have been proposed, this approach integrates variables from the different theoretical domains involved as modes of influence (biological, psychological, social) in a temporal framework that also incorporates the models of causal relationships reviewed above (e.g., core cause, vulnerability, pathoplasty, etc.). In line with the growing body of interest in processes involved in chronic and recurrent depression, slightly different variations of the model are suggested for first and repeated episodes.

### First Episode of Disorder

Figure 1.3 outlines the model for a hypothetical first episode of a disorder. The first three columns of the model suggest a developmental sequence and define alternative patterns of interaction among variables that contribute to the development of the clinical condition in column 4, which may consist of varying blends of depressive and personality features. Variables selected for the boxes are only examples of some of the many variables that may be important for personality–depression

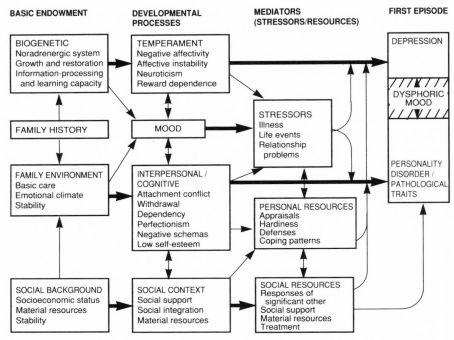

**FIGURE 1.3.** Integrated model of personality–depression relationships: First episode. Bold arrows indicate stronger or more direct effects.

relationships; because of space limitations, this list is representative but by no means exhaustive.

The first column, "basic endowment," refers to the "givens"—that is, to basic background variables or, in a model of pathology, actual or potential deficits in essential capacities over which the individual has no initial control. (The "family history" box is placed midway between the "biogenetic" and "family environment" boxes to highlight its two possible avenues of influence, genetic and environmental.) The second column, "developmental processes," defines the developmental processes that are directly influenced by the basic endowments, and thus characterizes their impact on the individual's baseline development. Taken together, concepts in the "temperament" and "interpersonal/cognitive" boxes correspond to two conceptions of the developing personality trait structure of the individual. The "mood" box is placed in an intermediate position between the "temperament" and "interpersonal/cognitive" boxes in the "developmental processes" column to indicate its complex

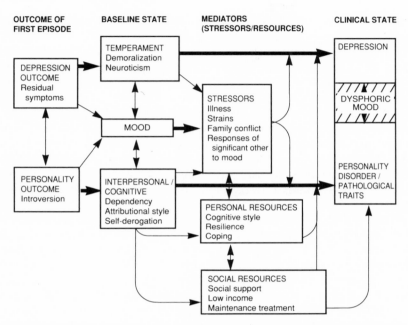

FIGURE 1.4. Integrated model of personality–depression relationships: Subsequent episodes.

relationships with both of these domains. Mood is clearly influenced by temperament and psychosocial factors; mood serves as an intervening variable or mediator of relationships between the two domains; mood can mediate the relationships between baseline traits and other effects in the model. For example, self-schemas that enhance mood may offset the negative effect of stress in an individual with an unstable temperament. Variations in mood are also provided in the shaded area of the box in the fourth column, which corresponds to the clinical outcome. An individual's "baseline mood" may heighten or buffer his or her vulnerability to stress; this level of stress will, in turn, determine the severity of the mood disturbance in a clinical episode.

Because the model is concerned with the development of pathology, entries for specific variables refer to the disturbed forms of the basic developmental processes involved, and the constructs in the "developmental process" column may be thought of as representing chronic and ongoing biobehavioral or personality strains.

Variables within each of the three major domains of the "basic endowment" column ("biogenetic," "family environment," "social background") are hypothesized to exert direct effects on developmental processes within each of the corresponding domains, as indicated by the connections from "biogenetic" to "temperament," from "family environment" to "interpersonal/cognitive," and from "social background" to "social context," respectively. Thus the direct and bold arrows between boxes on the same plane indicate relatively strong causal connections between the initial endowments and their expression in the developmental process. Several types of cross-domain interactions are also defined. First, an endowment variable can exert an indirect effect across domains through its direct effect on a related process in the same plane, which in turn will influence a variable in a different domain through its impact on mood. For example, parental failure to meet an infant's basic emotional needs will cause attachment conflicts; attachment conflicts will lower mood and increase neuroticism over time, and so on. Second, an endowment variable can also influence the interaction between process domains through its direct influence on mood, as indicated in Figure 1.3 by the arrows from the "basic endowment" boxes to the "mood" box. These alternatives are provided mainly to allow for three-way interactions among variables as alternative pathways of influence. It is important, however, that no *direct* cross-domain effects are specified; family environment, for example, does not directly affect neuroticism, except through its influence on mood. This limitation is intended to underscore our view that process linkages must be specified for all hypothesized core causal or vulnerability factors. Although this model employs mood as a major mediating variable, many other processes, such as neuroendocrine function, information processing, and behavior, could also be substituted.

Direct arrows between boxes in the same plane suggest relatively strong or highly likely causal relationships. Thus the continuing direct and bold arrows from basic endowment, through developmental processes, to the disorder boxes are consistent with the hypothesis that certain deficits and associated disturbances, if strong enough, are sufficient conditions for the development of certain clinical disorders. Certain biological deficits, if strong enough, may be sufficient to cause pathology solely through their influences on temperament. The same principle will hold for the effects of highly toxic family environments through their effects on the psychological structure.

It is also important to note that the clinical outcome is defined so as to incorporate the symptoms of depression, dysphoric mood (in the shaded area), and personality pathology/disorders. Although researchers have often attempted to distinguish among them, our model deliberately places each of these components of the clinical outcome within a single box to suggest that trait and state, or affective syndrome and personality components of disorder, cannot be pulled apart in the real world of clinical phenomena. However, the depression and personality features are placed at the corresponding ends of the clinical condition box to suggest that there may be direct relationships between biological determinants and the symptoms of affective disorder and between psychosocial factors and personality disturbances. That is, the links between biologically determined neuroendocrine deficits, affective instability, and vegetative symptoms of depression, or links between a punitive emotional climate, negative schema, and low self-esteem or guilt, will be particularly strong. Other arrows, however, provide for many other possible interactions among the domains that may operate in cases when direct when direct effects are weaker.

In contrast to the endowment and baseline variables, the "mediators" column depicts factors that are not in themselves sufficient to cause a clinical condition, but that operate primarily in interaction with causal or vulnerability factors. Stressors can be thought of as variables that disturb the baseline adaptation or further heighten process disturbances; resources can be thought of as factors that buffer the effect of stressors. These relationships are represented by the arrows touching the arrows between the processes and clinical states. Arrows from processes to mediators also indicate possible interactions between vulnerabilities or baseline disturbances on the one hand, and stressors or resources on the other (e.g., individuals with specific interpersonal conflicts or temperaments may precipitate certain life events, self-concept or appraisals may shape coping abilities, etc.). Arrows from the "social resources" box to the clinical episode are also intended to indicate the effects of these external variables, including treatment, on outcome.

As diagrammed, this model includes variables that are relatively specific to the connections between personality and depression. Other boxes in the "basic endowment," "developmental processes," and "mediators" columns could be added to indicate more complex interaction and/or pathoplasty effects.

The "first episode" column has been designed to encompass a variety of clinical mixtures of depression and personality, and also to reflect pathoplastic and complication effects that have been proposed. By placing symptoms of depression and personality pathology in separate areas, the model also provides for interactions within the clinical condition. As in the "developmental processes" column, mood is the mediator between the "more biological" symptoms of depression and the "more psychological" traits. Conditions such as depressive personality and/or dysthymia are also thought to fall within the shaded area of greatest overlap, for in these conditions depressive and personality traits are blended into one clinical entity.

What is the correspondence between this integrated model and thedifferent models of causality outlined in Figure 1.2? By definition, this model specifies a number of relationships that fall in the pre-disposition/vulnerability domains. Common-cause models involving biogenetic and family influences are also possible, provided that the cross-mode influences are mediated by mood or by some other process that might be substituted in the "mood" box. What Figure 1.3 suggests, however, is that common-cause models are extremely unlikely; effects from other domains would have to be weak or neutral in order for influences from only one endowment or developmental domain to predominate. With respect to subaffective models, Figure 1.3 would point the way toward specification of variables that might explain why full expression of the pathological process did not take place. A full-blown affective disorder might not result from certain endowment–developmental variables if other mediating influences were present (e.g., if psychosocial factors were to offset the influences of biogenetic and/or temperamental factors; if stresses were low or if resources were high). Finally, complication models are suggested by the relationships within the clinical condition box. Again, it is our belief that efforts to demonstrate how different models of causality interdigitate in a given clinical condition will prove more fruitful than efforts to support one model over another.

## Subsequent Episodes of Disorder

Figure 1.4 is intended to capture the effect of prior episodes on subse-quent functioning and to outline risk factors for subsequent episodes. The quality of recovery from a prior episode can be thought of as establishing a new baseline or process state; this may include new or heightened levels of personality traits, such as dependency or introver-sion, which develop as complications from prior episodes and continue as risk factors for future episodes. As Barnett and Gotlib (1988) indicate in their review of the role of psychosocial variables in depression, there is growing evidence that many variables that have previously been assumed to cause or contribute to depression, such as an internal, stable, global attributional style or dependency, are more likely to be residual factors from prior episodes that increase risk of subsequent episodes than to be causes of first episodes. Because most biological and psy-chosocial research has been focused on acute and/or remitted samples, it is likely that the conclusions about biological and psychosocial pre-dictors of depression reflect relationships depicted in Figure 1.4 rather than in Figure 1.3.

## Conclusion

How can these recommendations for an integrated model of personality–depressions relationships be implemented? The models in Figures 1.3 and 1.4 are intended simply to indicate general directions for research development. In order to define realistically testable models, the next step will be to fill in the boxes in either model with relevant variables, and to shift our conceptual and design strategy to more completely capture the processes that are important at all stages of the development of relationships between personality and/or depressive disorders. A number of methodological and assessment issues will also need to be addressed before these models can be tested in existing or new data bases. A minimum requirement would be that most variables be assessed longitudinally and that reliable clinical diagnoses be available, along with detailed measures of affective and personality variables. These and other issues related to data collection and data analysis strategies will be discussed in other chapters in this volume.

## ACKNOWLEDGMENTS

This chapter was written with the support of the MacArthur Foundation Research Network on the Psychobiology of Depression and Other Affective Disorders. We are especially grateful to David Kupfer for his encouragement and support; to Hermi Rojahn for her nurturance; and to members of the Personality and Depression Working Groups—Lorna Benjamin, Robert Cloninger, Paul Crits-Cristoph, Robert Hirschfeld, Steven Hollon, Phillip Lavori, Christopher Perry, Paul Pilkonis, Larry Siever, Auke Tellegen, and Thomas Widiger—for their many substantive contributions to the development of the models.

## REFERENCES

Abramson, L. Y., Metalsky, G. I., & Alloy, L. B. (1989). Hopelessness depression: A theory-based subtype of depression. *Psychological Review, 96,* 358–372.

Abramson, L. Y., Seligman, M. E. P., & Teasdale, J. D. (1978). Learned helplessness in humans: Critique and reformulation. *Journal of Abnormal Psyychology, 87,* 49–74.

Akiskal, H. S. (1980). External validating criteria for psychiatric diagnosis: Their application in affective disorders. *Journal of Clinical Psychiatry, 41,* 6–15.

Akiskal, H. S. (1981). Subaffective disorders: Dysthymic, cyclothymic, and bipolar II disorders in the "borderline" realm. *Psychiatric Clinics of North America, 4,* 25–47.

Akiskal, H. S. (1983a). Dysthymic and cyclothymic disorders: A paradigm for high-risk research in psychiatry. In J. M. Davis & J. W. Maas (Eds.), *The affective disorders* (pp. 211–231). Washington, DC: American Psychiatric Press.

Akiskal, H. S. (1983b). Dysthymic disorder: Psychopathology of proposed chronic depressive subtypes. *American Journal of Psychiatry, 140,* 11–20.

Akiskal, H. S. (1987). Overview of biobehavioral factors in the prevention of mood disorders. In R. F. Munoz (Ed.), *Depression prevention: Research directions* (pp. 263–280). Washington, DC: Hemisphere.

Akiskal, H. S. (1988). Personality as a mediating variable in the pathogenesis of mood disorders: Implications for theory, research, and prevention. In T. Helgason & R. J. Daly (Eds.), *Depressive illness: Prediction of course and outcome* (pp. 131–146). Berlin: Springer-Verlag.

Akiskal, H. S., Chen, S. E., Davis, G. C., Pusantian, V. R., Kashgarian, M., & Bolinger, J. M. (1985a). Borderline: An adjective in search of a noun. *Journal of Clinical Psychiatry, 46,* 41–48.

Akiskal, H. S., Djenderedjian, A. H., Rosenthal, R. H., & Khani, M. K. (1977). Cyclothymic disorder: Validating criteria for inclusion in the bipolar affective group. *American Journal of Psychiatry, 134,* 1227–1233.

Akiskal, H. S., Hirschfeld, R. M. A., & Yerevanian, B. I. (1983). The relationship of personality to affective disorders. *Archives of General Psychiatry, 40,* 801–810.

Akiskal, H. S., Khani., M. K., & Scott-Strauss, A. (1979). Cyclothymic temperamental disorders. *Psychiatric Clinics of North America, 2,* 527–554.

Akiskal, H. S., & McKinney, W. T. (1975). Overview of recent research in depression: Integration of ten conceptual models into a comprehensive clinical frame. *Archives of General Psychiatry, 32,* 285–305.

Akiskal, H. S., Rosenthal, T. L., Haykal, R. F., Lemmi, H., Rosenthal, R. H., & Scott-Strauss, A. (1980). Characterological depressions: Clinical and sleep EEG findings separating "subaffective dysthymias" from "character spectrum disorders." *Archives of General Psychiatry, 37,* 777–783.

Akiskal, H. S, Yerevanian, B. I., Davis, G. C., King, D., & Lemmi, H. (1985b). The nosologic status of borderline personality: Clinical and polysomnographic study. *American Journal of General Psychiatry, 142,* 192–198.

Allred, K. D., & Smith, T. W. (1989). The hardy personality: Cognitive and physiological responses to evaluative threat. *Journal of Personality and Social Psychology, 56,* 257–266.

American Psychiatric Association. (1987). *Diagnostic and statistical manual of mental disorders* (3rd. ed., rev.). Washington, DC: Author.

Aneshensel, C. S., & Frerichs, R. R. (1982). Stress, support, and depression: A longitudinal causal model. *Journal of Community Psychology, 10,* 363–376.

Andrews, J. D. W. (1989). Psychotherapy of depression: A self-confirmation model. *Psychological Review, 96,* 576–607.

Barnett, P. A., & Gotlib, I. H. (1988). Psychosocial functioning and depression: Distinguishing among antecedents, concomitants, and consequences. *Psychological Bulletin, 104,* 97–126.

Beck, A. T. (1974). *Depression: Theory and research.* New York: Wiley.

Beck, A. T. (1976). *Cognitive therapy and the emotional disorders.* New York: International Universities Press.

Beck, A. T. (1983). Cognitive therapy of depression: New perspectives. In P. J. Clayton & J. E. Barrett (Eds.), *Treatment of depression: Old controversies and new approaches* (pp. 265–290). New York: Raven Press.

Beck, A. T., Freeman, A., & Associates. (1990). *Cognitive therapy of personality disorders.* New York: Guilford Press.

Beck, A. T., Rush, A. J., Shaw, B. F., & Emery, G. (1979). *Cognitive therapy of depression.* New York: Guilford Press.

Belsher, G., & Costello, C. G. (1988). Relapse after recovery from unipolar depression: A critical review. *Psychological Bulletin, 104,* 84–96.

Benjamin, L. S. (1974). Structural analysis of social behavior. *Psychological Review, 81,* 392–425.

Benjamin, L. S. (in press). *Interpersonal diagnosis and treatment of the DSM personality disorders.* New York: Guilford Press.

Billings, A. G., & Moos, R. H. (1982). Psychosocial theory and research on depression: An integrative framework and review. *Clinical Psychology Review, 2,* 213–237.

Billings, A. G., & Moos, R. H. (1984). Treatment experiences of adults with unipolar depression: The influence of patient and life context factors. *Journal of Consulting and Clinical Psychology, 52,* 119–131.

Billings, A. G., & Moos, R. H. (1985). Psychosocial processes of remission in unipolar depression: Comparing depressed patients with matched community controls. *Journal of Consulting and Clinical Psychology, 53,* 314–325.

Block, J. H., Gjerde, P. E., & Block, J. H. (1991). Personality antecedents of depressive tendencies in 18-year-olds: A prospective study. *Journal of Personality and Social Psychology, 60,* 726–738.

Bonime, W. (1975). The psychodynamics of neurotic depression. *Journal of the American Acadamy of Psychoanalysis, 4,* 301–326.

Brewin, C. R. (1985). Depression and causal attributions: What is their relation? *Psychological Bulletin, 98,* 297–309.

Brown, G. W., & Harris, T. (1978). *Social origins of depression.* New York: Free Press.

Cantor, N. (1990). From thought to behavior: "Having" and "doing" in the study of personality and cognition. *American Psychologist, 45,* 735–750.

Charney, D. S., Nelson, J. C., & Quinlan, D. M. (1981). Personality traits and disorder in depression. *American Journal of Psychiatry, 138,* 1601–1604.

Chodoff, P. (1972). The depressive personality: A critical review. *Archives of General Psychiatry, 27,* 666–673.

Cloninger, C. R. (1986). A unified biosocial theory of personality and its role in the development of anxiety states. *Psychiatric Developments, 3,* 167–226.

Cloninger, C. R. (1987). A systematic method for clinical description and classification of personality variants. *Archives of General Psychiatry, 44,* 573–588.

Cohen, S., & Wills, T. A. (1985). Stress, social support, and the buffering hypothesis. *Psychological Bulletin, 98,* 310–357.

Cole, D. A., & Milstead, M., (1989). Behavioral correlates of depression: Antecedents or consequences? *Journal of Counseling Psychology, 36,* 408–416.

Coyne, J. C., Aldwin, C., & Lazarus, R. S. (1981). Depression and coping in stressful episodes. *Journal of Abnormal Psychology, 90,* 439–447.

Costa, P. T., & McCrae, R. R. (1980). Influence of extraversion and neuroticism on subjective well-being: Happy and unhappy people. *Journal of Personality and Social Psychology, 38,* 668–678.

Dent, J., & Teasdale, J. D. (1988). Negative cognition and the persistence of depression. *Journal of Abnormal Psychology, 97,* 29–34.

Depue, R. A., & Monroe, S. M. (1986). Conceptualization and measurement of human disorder in life stress research: The problem of chronic disturbance. *Psychological Bulletin, 99,* 36–51.

Depue, R. A., Slater, J. F., Wolfstetter-Kausch, H., Klein, D., Goperlud, E., & Farr, D. (1981). A behavioral paradigm for identifying persons at risk for bipolar depressive disorder: A conceptual framework and five validation studies [Monograph]. *Journal of Abnormal Psychology, 90*(5), 381–437.

Dienstbier, R. A. (1989). Arousal and physiological toughness: Implications for mental and physical health. *Psychological Review, 96,* 84–100.

Dohrenwend, B. S., & Dohrenwend, B. P. (Eds.). (1981). *Stressful life events and their contexts.* New York: Prodist.

Farmer, R., & Nelson-Gray, R. O. (1990). Personality disorders and depression: Hypothetical relations, empirical findings, and methodological considerations. *Clinical Psychology Review, 10,* 453–476.

Ferster, C. B. (1965). Classification of behavioral pathology. In L. Krasner & L. P. Ullmann (Eds.), *Research in behavior modification* (pp. 2–26). New York: Holt, Rinehart & Winston.

Frances, A. (1980). The DSM-III personality disorders section: A commentary. *American Journal of Psychiatry, 137,* 1050–1054.

Frances, A. (1982). Categorical and dimensional systems of personality diagnosis: A comparison. *Comprehensive Psychiatry, 23,* 516–527.

Frank, E., Kupfer, D. J., Perel, J. M., Cornes, C., Jarrett, D. B., Mallinger, A. G., Thase, M. E., McEachran, A. B., & Grochocinski, V. J. (1990). Three-year outcomes for maintenance therapies in recurrent depression. *Archives of General Psychiatry, 47,* 1093–1099.

Free, M. L., & Oei, T. P. S. (1989). Biological and psychological processes in the treatment and maintenance of depression. *Clinical Psychology Review, 9,* 653–688.

Goldberg, L. R. (1990). An alternative "description of personality": The "big-five" factor structure. *Journal of Personality and Social Psychology, 6,* 1216–1229.

Gunderson, J. G., & Elliott, G. R. (1985). The interface between borderline personality disorder and affective disorder. *American Journal of Psychiatry, 142,* 277–288.

Gunderson, J. G., & Zanarini, M. C. (1987). Current overview of the borderline diagnosis. *Journal of Clinical Psychiatry, 48,* 5–11.

Hammen, C., Davila, J., Brown, G, Ellicott, A., & Gitlin, M. (1992). Psychiatric history and stress: Predictors of severity of unipolar depression. *Journal of Abnormal Psychology, 101,* 45–52.

Hirschfeld, R. M. A., & Klerman, G. L. (1979). Personality attributes and affective disorders. *American Journal of Psychiatry, 136,* 67–70.

Hirschfeld, R. M. A., Klerman, G., Clayton, P. J., Keller, M. B., McDonald-Scott, P., & Larkin, B. H. (1983). Assessing personality: Effects of depressive state on trait measurement. *American Journal of Psychiatry, 140,* 695–699.

Hirschfeld, R. M. A., Klerman, G. L., Lavori, P., Keller, M. B., Griffith, P., & Coryell, W. (1989a). Premorbid personality assessments of first onset of major depression *Archives of General Psychiatry, 46,* 345–352.

Hirschfeld, R. M. A., Shea, M. T., Gunderson, J. G., & Phillips, K. A. (1989b). *Proposal for a depressive personality disorder.* Unpublished manuscript, DSM-IV Work Group in Personality Disorder.

Holahan, C. J., & Moos, R. H. (1991). Life stressors, personal and social resources, and depression: A 4-year structural model. *Journal of Abnormal Psychology, 100,* 31–38.

Hops, H., Biglan, A., Sherman, L., Arthur, J., Friedman, L., & Osteen, V. (1987). Home observations of family interactions of depressed women. *Journal of Clinical and Consulting Psychology, 55,* 341–346.

Horowitz, M. J. (1991). Person schemas. In M. J. Horowitz (Ed.), *Person schemas and maladaptive interpersonal patterns* (pp. 13–31). Chicago: University of Chicago Press.

Horowitz, L. M., Locke, K. D., Morse, M. B., Waikar, S. V., Dryer, D. C. D., Tarnow, E., & Ghannam, J. (1991). Self-derogations and interpersonal theory. *Journal of Personality and Social Psychology, 61,* 68–79.

Keitner, G. I., & Miller, I. W. (1990). Family functioning and major depression: An overview. *American Journal of Psychiatry, 147,* 1128–1137.

Keitner, G. I., Ryan, C. E., Miller, I. W., Kohn, R., & Epstein, N. B. (1991). 12-month outcome of patients with major depression and comorbid psychiatric illness (compound depression). *American Journal of Psychiatry, 148,* 345–350.

Keller, M. B., Klerman, G. L., Lavori, P. W., Coryell, W., Endicott, J., & Taylor, J. (1984). Long-term outcome of episodes of major depression. *Journal of the American Medical Association, 252,* 788–792.

Keller, M. B., Lavori, P. W., Endicott, J., Coryell, W., & Klerman, G. L. (1983). "Double depression": Two-year follow-up. *American Journal of Psychiatry, 140,* 689–694.

Keller, M. B., Lavori, P. W., Rice, J., Coryell, W., & Hirschfeld, R. M. A. (1986). The persistent risk of chronicity in recurrent episodes of nonbipolar major depressive disorder: A prospective follow-up. *American Journal of Psychiatry, 143,* 24–28.

Keller, M. B., & Shapiro, R. W. (1981). Major depressive disorder: Initial results from a one-year prospective naturalistic follow-up study. *Journal of Nervous and Mental Disease, 169,* 761–768.

Kernberg, O. F. (1984). *Severe personality disorders: Psychotherapeutic strategies.* New Haven: Yale University Press.

Klein, D. N. (1990). Depressive personality: Reliability, validity and relation to dysthymia. *Journal of Abnormal Psychology, 99,* 412–421.

Klein, D. N., Taylor, E. B., Dickstein, S., & Harding, K. (1988). The early–late onset distinction in DSM-III-R dysthymia. *Journal of Affective Disorders, 14,* 25–33.

Klerman, G. L., Endicott, J., Spitzer, R., & Hirschfeld, R. M. A. (1979). Neurotic depressions: A systematic analysis of multiple criteria and meanings. *American Journal of Psychiatry, 136,* 57–61.

Kocsis, J. H., & Frances, A. J. (1987). A critical discussion of DSM-III dysthymic disorder. *American Journal of Psychiatry, 144,* 1534–1542.

Kupfer, D. J., & Ehlers, C. L. (1989). Two roads to rapid eye movement latency. *Archives of General Psychiatry, 46,* 945–948.

Kupfer, D. J., & Frank, E. (1987). Relapse in recurrent unipolar depression. *American Journal of Psychiatry, 144,* 86–88.

Laughlin, H. P. (1967). *The neuroses.* London: Butterworths.

Lazarus, R. S. (1991). Progress on a cognitive–motivational–relational theory of emotion. *American Psychologist, 46,* 819–834.

Lazarus, R. S., DeLongis, A., Folkman, S., & Gruen, R. (1985). Stress and adaptational outcomes: The problem of confounded measures. *American Psychologist, 40,* 770–779.

Lazarus, R. S., & Folkman, S. (1984). *Stress, appraisal, and coping.* New York: Springer.

Lewinsohn, P. M. (1974). A behavioral approach to depression. In R. M. Freidman & M. Katz (Eds.), *The psychology of depression: Contemporary theory and research* (pp. 157–185). New York: Wiley.

Lewinsohn, P. M., Biglan, A., & Zeiss, A. M. (1976). Behavioral treatment of depression. In P. O. Davidson (Ed.), *The behavioral management of anxiety, depression, and pain* (pp. 91–146). New York: Brunner/Mazel.

Lewinsohn, P. M., Hoberman, H., Teri, L., & Hautzinger, M. (1985). An integrative theory of depression. In S. Reiss & R. Bootzin (Eds.), *Theoretical issues in behavior therapy* (pp. 331–359). New York: Academic Press.

Lewinsohn, P. M., Zeiss, A. M., & Duncan, E. M. (1989). Probability of relapse after recovery from an episode of depression. *Journal of Abnormal Psychology, 98,* 107–116.

Litt, M. D. (1988). Cognitive mediators of stressful experience: Self-efficacy and perceived control. *Cognitive Therapy and Research, 12,* 241–260.

Livesley, W. J., & Jackson, D. N. (1986). The internal consistency and factorial structure of behaviors judged to be associated with DSM-III personality disorders. *American Journal of Psychiatry, 143,* 1473–1474.

Matussek, P., & Fell, W. B. (1983). Personality attributes of depressive patients. *Archives of General Psychiatry, 40,* 783–790.

McCrae, R. R., & Costa, P. T. (1989). The structure of interpersonal traits: Wiggins's circumplex and the five factor model. *Journal of Personality and Social Psychology, 56,* 586–595.

Mellsop, G., Varaghese, F., Joshua, S., & Hicks, A. (1982). The reliability of Axis II of DSM-III. *American Journal of Psychiatry, 139,* 1360–1361.

Meyer, G. J., & Shack, J. R. (1989). Structural convergence of mood and personality: Evidence for old and new directions. *Journal of Personality and Social Psychology, 57,* 691–706.

Miranda, J., & Persons, J. B. (1988). Dysfunctional attitudes are mood-state dependent. *Journal of Abnormal Psychology, 97,* 76–79.

Miranda, J., Persons, J. B., & Byers, C. N. (1990). Endorsement of dysfunctional beliefs depends on current mood state. *Journal of Abnormal Psychology, 99,* 237–241.

Mischel, W. (1973). Toward a cognitive social learning reconceptualization of personality. *Psychological Review, 80,* 252–283.

Monroe, S. M. (1982). Life events and disorder: Event–symptom associations and the course of disorder. *Journal of Abnormal Psychology, 91,* 4–24.

Monroe, S. M. (1983a). Major and minor life events as predictors of psychological distress: Further issues and findings. *Journal of Behavioral Medicine, 6,* 189–205.

Monroe, S. M. (1983b). Social support and disorder: Toward an untangling of cause and effect. *American Journal of Community Psychology, 11,* 81–97.

Monroe, S. M, & Simmons, A. D. (1991). Diathesis–stress theories in the context of life stress research: Implications for the depressive disorders. *Psychological Bulletin, 110,* 406–425.

Monroe, S. M., & Steiner, S. C. (1986). Social support and psychopathology: Interactions with preexisting disorder, stress, and personality. *Journal of Abnormal Psychology, 95,* 29–39.

Needles, D. J., & Abramson, L. Y. (1990). Positive life events, attribuational style, and hopefulness: Testing a model of recovery from depression. *Journal of Abnormal Psychology, 99,* 156–165.

Nezu, A. M., & Ronan, G. F. (1985). Life stress, current problems, problem solving and depressive symptoms: An integrative model. *Journal of Consulting and Clinical Psychology, 53,* 693–697.

Oatley, K., & Bolton, W. (1985). A social-cognitive theory of depression in reaction to life events. *Psychological Review, 92,* 372–388.

Ormel, J., & Schaufeli, W. B. (1991). Stability and change in psychological distress and their relationship with self-esteem and locus of control: A dynamic equilibrium model. *Journal of Personality and Social Psychology, 60,* 288–299.

Ormel, J., & Wohlfarth, T. (1991). How neuroticism, long-term difficulties, and life situation change influence psychological distress: A longitudinal model. *Journal of Personality and Social Psychology, 60,* 744–755.

Persons, J. B., & Miranda, J. (1990). *Cognitive theories of depression: Reconciling negative evidence.* Unpublished manuscript.

Pfohl, B., Stangl, D., & Zimmerman, M. (1984). The implications of DSM-III personality disorders for patients with major depression. *Journal of Affective Disorders, 7,* 309–318.

Phillips, K. A., Gunderson, J. G., Hirschfeld, R. M. A., & Smith, L. E. (1990). A review of the depressive personality. *American Journal of Psychiatry, 147,* 830–837.

Pilkonis, P. A. (1988). Personality prototypes among depressives: Themes of dependency and autonomy. *Journal of Personality Disorders, 2,* 144–152.

Pilkonis, P. A., & Frank, E. (1988). Personality pathology in recurrent depression: Nature, prevalence, and relationship to treatment response. *American Journal of Psychiatry, 145,* 435–441.

Pyszczynski, T., & Greenberg, J. (1987). Self-regulatory perseveration and the depressive self-focusing style: A self-awareness theory of reactive depression. *Psychological Bulletin, 102,* 122–138.

Robins, C. J., & Luten, A. G. (1991). Sociotropy and autonomy: Differential patterns of clinical presentation in unipolar depression. *Journal of Abnormal Psychology, 100,* 74–77.

Safran, J. D. (1990). Towards a refinement of cognitive therapy in light of interpersonal theory: I. Theory. *Clinical Psychology Review, 10,* 87–106.

Sargeant, J. K., Bruce, M. L., Florio, L. P., & Weissman, M. M. (1990). Factors associated with 1-year outcome of major depression in the community. *Archives of General Psychiatry, 47,* 519–526.

Schradle, S. B., & Dougher, M. J. (1985). Social support as a mediator of stress: Theoretical and empirical issues. *Clinical Psychology Review, 5,* 641–661.

Seligman, M. E. P. (1975). *Helplessness: On depression, development, and death.* San Francisco: W. H. Freeman.

Shapiro, R. W, & Keller, M. B. (1981). Initial 6-month follow-up of patients with major depressive disorder. *Journal of Affective Disorders, 3,* 205–220.

Shea, M. T., Glass, D., Pilkonis, P., Watkins, J., & Docherty, J. (1987). Frequency and implications of personality disorders in a sample of depressed outpatients. *Journal of Personality Disorders, 1,* 27–42.

Shea, M. T., Hirschfeld, R. M. A., & Lavori, P. (1989, November). *Familial transmission models of personality disorder and depression.* Paper presented at the meeting of the MacArthur Foundation Research Network on the Psychobiology of Depression and Other Affective Disorders, Network Task Force on Personality and Depression, Alexandria, VA.

Shustack, B., & West, M. (1985). Chronic depression reconsidered: Maladaptive competence as an explanatory concept. *Clinical Psychology Review, 5,* 569–579.

Siever, L. J. (1989, November). *Model of personality disorder and depression.* Paper presented at the meeting of the MacArthur Foundation Research Network on the Psychobiology of Depression and Other Affective Disorders, Network Task Force on Personality and Depression, Alexandria, VA.

Siever, L. J., & Davis, K. L. (1991). A psychobiologic perspective on the personality disorders. *American Journal of Psychiatry, 148,* 1647–1658.

Swindle, R. W., Cronkite, R. C., & Moos, R. H. (1989). Life stressors, social resources, coping and the 4-year course of unipolar depression. *Journal of Abnormal Psychology, 98,* 468–477.

Tellegen, A. (1985). Structures of mood and personality and their relevance to assessing anxiety, with an emphasis on self-report. In A. H. Tuma & J. D. Maser (Eds.), *Anxiety and the anxiety disorders* (pp. 681–706). Hillsdale, NJ: Erlbaum.

Thoits, P. A. (1982). Conceptual, methodological, and theoretical problems in studying social support as a buffer against life stress. *Journal of Health and Social Behavior, 23,* 145–159.

Thoits, P. A. (1983). Dimensions of life events that influence psychological distress: An evaluation and synthesis of the literature. In H. B. Kaplan (Ed.), *Psychological stress: Trends in theory and research* (pp. 33–103). New York: Academic Press.

Thoits, P. A. (1986). Social support as coping assistance. *Journal of Consulting and Clinical Psychology, 54,* 416–423.

VanValkenberg, C., Lowry, M., Winokur, G., & Cadoret, R. (1977). Depression spectrum disease versus pure depressive disease. *Journal of Nervous and Mental Disease, 165,* 341–347.

von Zerssen, D. (1982). Personality and affective disorders. In E. S. Paykel (Ed.), *Handbook of affective disorders* (1st ed., pp. 212–228). New York: Guilford Press.

Watson, D., & Clark, L. A., (1984). Negative affectivity: The disposition to experience aversive emotional states. *Psychological Bulletin, 96,* 465–490.

Watson, D., & Tellegen, A. (1985). Toward a consensual structure of mood. *Psychological Bulletin, 98,* 219–235.

Weissman, M. M., Leaf, P. J., Bruce, M. L., & Florio L. (1988). The epidemiology of dysthymia in five communities: Rates, risks, cormobidity, and treatment. *American Journal of Psychiatry, 145,* 815–819.

Weissman, M. M., & Paykel, E. S. (1974). *The depressed woman: A study of social relationships.* Chicago: University of Chicago Press.

Westen, D. (1991). Social cognition and object relations. *Psychological Bulletin, 109,* 429–455.

Widiger, T. A. (1989). The categorical distinction between personality and affective disorders. *Journal of Personality Disorders, 3,* 77–91.

Widiger, T. A., & Frances, A. (1985a). Axis II personality disorders: Diagnostic and treatment issues. *Hospital and Community Psychiatry, 6,* 619–627.

Widiger, T. A., & Frances, A. (1985b). The DSM-III personality disorders: Perspectives from psychology. *Archives of General Psychiatry, 42,* 615–623.

Widiger, T. A., & Hyler, S. E. (1987). Axis I/Axis II interactions. In R. Michels & J. Cavenar (Eds.), *Psychiatry* (Vol. 1, Ch. 29). Philadelphia: J.B. Lippincott.

Widiger, T. A., & Kelso, K. (1983). Psychodiagnosis of Axis II. *Clinical Psychology Review, 3,* 491–510.

Wiener, M. (1989). Psychopathology reconsidered: Depressions interpreted as psychosocial transactions. *Clinical Psychology Review, 9,* 295–321.

Winokur, G. (1972). Depression spectrum disease: Description and family study. *Comprehensive Psychiatry, 13,* 3–8.

Winokur, G. (1985). The validity of neurotic–reactive depression. *Archives of General Psychiatry, 42,* 1116–1122.

Winokur, G., Behar, D., VanValkenberg, C., & Lowry, M. (1978). Is a familial definition of depression both feasible and valid? *Journal of Nervous and Mental Disease, 166,* 764–768.

Zevon, M. A., & Tellegen, A. (1982). The structure of mood change: An idiographic/nomothetic analysis. *Journal of Personality and Social Psychology, 43,* 111–122.

# Commentary

LARRY J. SIEVER
*Mount Sinai School of Medicine*
*Department of Veterans Affairs Medical Center, Bronx, New York*

Marjorie Klein, Stephen Wonderlich, and M. Tracie Shea are to be commended for tackling a very difficult task: attempting to organize and present current models of the relationship between personality and depression, and to confer some conceptual clarity on an area that is currently confusing. By defining such models in terms of those that emphasize (1) independent causes; (2) common causes; (3) personality and depression as related but differing manifestations of the same process (subclinical or spectrum models); (4) personality as providing a predisposition of vulnerability to depression, or vice versa; (5) personality as influencing the expression of depression, or vice versa (pathoplasty or exacerbation models); and (6) the residual effects of personality as influencing the development of depression, or vice versa (complication or scar models), Klein and her coauthors set a context for evaluating current models of depression and personality.

It is clear in Chapter One that although some models of depression and personality started as more or less "pure" examples of one type of model (e.g., a subclinical model or a common-cause model), most models that have been more fully developed and elaborated contain elements of several of these types. Ultimately, our understanding of the relationship of affective and personality disorders will be advanced by models invoking specific mechanisms that can be formulated in testable hypotheses. To the extent that we can move from vague notions of relationships to more conceptually crystallized specific models, we will be better able to formulate research strategies for future investigation. Klein, Wonderlich, and Shea's articulation of the types of models

55

that have been proposed should provide a basis for more sophisticated hypothesis testing.

Part of the problem in conceptualizing the relationship between personality and depression is our tendency to reify these constructs, which have come to carry considerable conceptual baggage in their common usuage. "Depression" is considered a mood disorder with biological underpinnings that is usually episodic in nature and responsive to medication treatment; "personality" is considered a collection of traits that are largely psychological or behavioral in nature, arise developmentally, and are not easily modifiable. Yet "depression" can be a transient state or an enduring feeling tone in one's experience that may have psychological–developmental antecedents, whereas "personality" may develop from temperamental underpinnings with biological roots and be responsive to medication. Thus, our stereotypic notions regarding the nature of these disorders may color our conceptualization of them.

If one confines oneself to a consideration of major depressive disorder (defined by current diagnostic systems as a relatively sustained alteration in mood) and personality disorder (defined as a relatively enduring and persistent set of traits and behaviors that are maladaptive), the task of relating these two domains becomes more circumscribed and feasible. It is then clear that individuals may have either diagnosis alone or both, and that the definition of "primacy" may largely depend on the filter or lens through which the observers view the disorders. Clinicians and investigators focusing primarily on the affective disorders, such as Donald Klein and Hagop Akiskal, began to recognize that many patients in their affective disorder clinics presented with long-standing trait disturbances that might be diagnosed as personality disorder by many clinicians, yet appeared to have an underlying affective component that was treatable by antidepressant medication. On the other hand, psychosocially oriented clinicians working in long-term treatment with personality disorder patients have noted the frequent emergence of depressive mood when habitual defenses and coping strategies fail to relieve the patients' inner turmoil. These may represent partially distinct populations or overlapping populations viewed from different perspectives.

Although transient feelings of depression may be observed in everybody, one dimension that potentially distinguishes patients suffering from major depressive disorder from those suffering from the vicissitudes of mood associated with many of the personality disorders is the degree of autonomy versus reactivity of the depressed mood. In episodes of major depression, the depressed mood becomes relatively autonomous from environmental influence once initiated, and is often accompanied by vegetative disturbances such as sleep and appetite loss. On the other hand, the altered affective states of personality disorder patients, such as those with borderline personality disorder, are marked by excessive sensitivity or reactivity to the environment. Affective shifts are often transient and dramatic. Because individuals with personality disorder are so affectively responsive to the environment, they may respond more sensitively to separations, frustrations, or losses. This reactivity over the course of their development may serve to influence the development of their personalities.

The ways in which affective sensitivity manifests itself will depend on other concomitant psychobiological predispositions. For example, affective sensitivity coupled with impulsivity may result in affective instability (extreme reactions to disappointment, as well as feelings of excitement and euphoria after personal gain). Impulsive people may tend to use action-oriented strategies that appear to others to be manipulative to maintain their self-esteem and buffer themselves against disappointment—for example, "acting out" by engaging in promiscuous behavior or abusing alcohol or drugs when a therapist goes on vacation (Siever & Davis, 1991). These actions are sometimes palliative: They may immediately relieve the stress, and they often serve to attract the attention of the person who has "abandoned" the patient, in an effort on the patient's part to restore equilibrium by getting the "abandoning" person to return. However, they usually have long-term negative consequences.

On the other hand, individuals with affective sensitivity and anxiety may respond to transient disappointment and frustration by withdrawal and inhibition (Kalus & Siever, in press). This withdrawal may be a precursor to more full-blown depressive episodes with vegetative symptoms. Thus, one might predict (and some evidence supports the hypothesis) that individuals prone to more endogenous major depressive episodes with vegetative symptoms would be more likely to have "Cluster C" anxiety-related personality disorders (Shea, Glass, Pilkonis, Watkins, & Docherty, 1987). In contrast, major depressive episodes, when they do occur in patients with prominent impulsivity and affective instability, might be expected to be more atypical and less endogenous; this is also consistent with current evidence.

In summary, this model of a distinction between major depressive disorder and the affect-related traits of personality disorder is based on the reactivity and environmental sensitivity of personality disorder patients' affective states, which are often intense and transient. In contrast, classical depressive episodes are relatively autonomous and often are accompanied by vegetative symptoms. The co-occurrence of impulsivity in these affectively reactive personality disorder patients may confer a predisposition to behaviors associated with borderline personality disorder, whereas affective sensitivity coupled with inhibition or anxiety may lead to an anxiety-related personality disorder marked by avoidance, submissiveness, dependence, or compulsivity. Patients who do develop serious major depressive disorders would be more likely to have personality traits on a continuum with the anxiety-related personality disorders. Such a model fits with many of the available data regarding the relationship with the personality disorder traits and major depressive disorder. It remains to be determined how specific biological factors may predispose an individual to one or the other or both.

Elsewhere, my colleagues and I have proposed some heuristic starting points for investigation into the biochemical substrates of these personality traits (Siever & Davis, 1991; Kalus & Siever, in press). Only limited evidence is available regarding the biological substrates of personality disorder at this time, but evidence to date suggests that there are both biological commonalities and differences between patients suffering from major depressive disorder and patients with personality disorder traits who suffer from depression. It is still unclear what the biological underpinnings of the predisposition to affective disturbance, broadly defined, may be. Some data hint at alterations in the cholinergic system in borderline personality disorder (Akiskal, Yerevarian, Davis, King, & Lemmi, 1985; McNamara et al., 1983; Bell, Grummet, Lycaki, & Sitaram, 1983), as well as in patients with major depressive disorder (Nurnberger, Berrettini, Mendelson, Sack, & Gershon, 1989). Whether these commonalities may be reflective of a common core affective vulnerability in the cholinergic system across these disorders, or whether other biological systems as yet uncharacterized confer a broad affective vulnerability across diagnostic categories, is an area that invites further research. More evidence suggests that reduction in serotonergic activity underlies a dimension of impulsivity associated with affective instability (Brown et al., 1982; Linnoila et al., 1983; Coccaro et al., 1989).

A third biological system that may be implicated in the modulation of the expression of an underlying affective vulnerability is the activity of the noradrenergic system. Dysregulation of the noradrenergic system may be associated with the endogenous symptoms of depression (Siever & Davis, 1985; Siever, 1987), whereas increased reactivity of the noradrenergic system may mediate reactivity to the environment in relation to irritable/impulsive/aggressive behaviors (Siever & Davis, 1991). An affective vulnerability coupled with a hyperactive noradrenergic system may be more likely to manifest itself in transient but dramatic affective swings and impulsive behavior, whereas reductions in noradrenergic activity may be more closely associated with autonomous major depressive disorders. These hypotheses must still be considered as speculative and only as starting points for further research, but they are eminently testable.

As Klein and her colleagues note, the testing of any of these hypotheses will be complicated and difficult. Ultimately, for any of the models elaborated by these authors, longitudinal high-risk studies would be desirable. However, to test hypotheses such as those noted above, cross-sectional studies of patients with major depressive disorder and patients with personality disorder that measure specific biological variables should detect commonalities and differences between these patient groups. Furthermore, specific biological measures could be correlated dimensionally with such variables as degree of depressive symptoms; relative autonomy of depressive symptoms; and stability of affect, impulsivitiy, and reactivity to the environment. This may enable us to begin to chart neurotransmitter–behavior relationships, which should allow us to develop more realistic models of the ways in which biological variables may influence the expression of underlying affective vulnerabilities—either toward discrete depressive episodes or toward affect-related personality traits.

Of course, such biological vulnerabilities are going to be manifested and channeled in various ways, depending on the nature of environmental influences throughout the course of development. Affectively unstable and impulsive children who learn early from parents to view their activity as "dangerous aggression" may develop a negative self-image, marked by feelings of self-loathing in relation to angry or aggressive feelings (Siever & Davis, 1991; Siever, Klar, & Coccaro, 1985). Combined biological–developmental models may be the most difficult to test; they are likely to bear more fruit at such time as biological underpinnings are more clearly delineated, so that interactions may be measured in more homogeneous subgroups of vulnerable individuals. Thus, the richest and most realistic of models may be the last to be tested. However, any model must have an identifiable starting point from which it can be investigated. Klein, Wonderlich, and Shea highlight the need for further research and provide an informative framework by which models of various types can be conceptualized and eventually (let us hope) integrated into the richer, more elaborated patterns that we see in our clinical experience.

# REFERENCES

Akiskal, H. S., Yerevarian, B. I., Davis, G. C., King, D., & Lemmi, H. (1985). The nosologic status of borderline personality: Clinical and polysomnographic study. *American Journal of Psychiatry, 142,* 192–198.

Bell, J., Grummet, M., Lycaki, H., & Sitaram, N. (1983). The effect of borderline personality disorder on sleep EEG state and trait markers of depressions. In *Abstracts of the 38th Meeting of the Society of Biological Psychiatry.* Los Angeles: Society of Biological Psychiatry.

Brown, G. L., Ebert, M. H., Goyer, P. F., Jimerson, D. C., Klein, W. J., Bunney, W. E., & Goodwin, F. K. (1982). Aggression, suicide, and serotonin: Relationships to CSF amine metabolites. *American Journal of Psychiatry, 139,* 741–746.

Coccaro, E. F., Siever, L. J., Klar, H. M., Maurer, G., Cochrane, K., Cooper, T. B., Mohs, R. C., & Davis, K. L. (1989). Serotonergic studies in patients with affective and personality disorders: Correlates with suicidal and impulsive aggressive behavior. *Archives of General Psychiatry, 46,* 587–599. (Correction, 1990, *47,* 124.)

Kalus, O., & Siever, L. J. (in press). The biology of personality disorders. In J. J. Mann & D. J. Kupfer (Eds.), *The biology of depressive disorders: An examination of illness subtypes, state versus trait and cormorbid psychiatric disorders.* New York: Plenum Press.

Linnoila, M., Virkkunen, M., Scheinin, M., Nuutila, A., Rimon, R., & Goodwin, F. K. (1983). Low cerebrospinal fluid 5-hydroxyindoleacetic acid concentration differentiates impulsive from nonimpulsive violent behavior. *Life Sciences, 33,* 2609–2614.

McNamara, E., Reynolds, C. F., III, Soloff, P. H., Mathias, R., Rossi A., Spiker, D., Coble, P. A., & Kupfer, D. J. (1984). EEG sleep evaluation of depression in borderline patients. *American Journal of Psychiatry, 141,* 182–186.

Nurnberger, J., Jr., Berrettini, W., Mendelson, W., Sack, D., & Gershon, E. S. (1989). Measuring cholinergic sensitivity: I: Arecoline effects in bipolar patients. *Biological Psychiatry, 25,* 610–617.

Shea, M. T., Glass, E. R., Pilkonis, P. A., Watkins, J., & Docherty, J. (1987). Frequently and implications of personality disorders in a sample of depressed outpatients. *Journal of Personality Disorders, 1,* 27–42.

Siever, L. J. (1987). The role of noradrenergic mechanisms in the etiology of affective disorders. In H. Y. Meltzer (Ed.), *Psychopharmacology: The third generation of progress.* New York: Raven Press.

Siever, L. J., & Davis, K. L. (1985). Towards a dysregulation hypothesis of depression. *American Journal of Psychiatry, 142,* 1017–1031.

Siever, L. J., & Davis, K. L. (1991). A psychobiologic perspective on the personality disorders. *American Journal of Psychiatry, 148,* 1647–1658.

Siever, L. J., Klar, H., & Coccaro, E. F. (1985). Psychobiologic substrates of personality. In H. Klar & L. J. Siever (Eds.), *Biologic response styles: Clinical implications.* Washington, DC: American Psychiatric Press.

# Commentary

C. ROBERT CLONINGER
*Washington University School of Medicine*

The model of the relationships between personality and depression described by Klein, Wonderlich, and Shea has important heuristic implications for investigators of both personality and depression. They have presented several novel insights about the nature of the theoretical problem and about opportunities and obstacles to progress. I believe that these important insights were stimulated by the authors' integration of information about both personality and depression from multiple perspectives. These perspectives include biological, cognitive, interpersonal, and developmental considerations about both personality and affective disorders.

After reviewing a wide variety of models about the temporal and causal relationships between personality and depression, Klein and colleagues describe their own complex integrative model. This new integrative model includes basic endowment variables (biogenetic, family environment, social background), developmental processes related to personality and mood, and mediating variables of stress and support influencing the development of either first episodes or recurrences. This biopsychosocial–developmental model allows them to point out several opportunities and obstacles to future progress. I comment here on the significance of some of their key points. These points include what I believe to be important observations about (1) the measurement of personality, (2) the measurement and classification of mood disorders, (3) the measurement of other intervening variables, and (4) the necessity of precise longitudinal measures in systematically ascertained samples. The important implications of their insightful observations for future research strategies are emphasized.

# MEASUREMENT OF PERSONALITY

Klein and her colleagues make at least four observations about the measurement of personality that have seldom been so clearly recognized and stated. First, they emphasize the distinction between temperament variables (e.g., neuroticism and introversion) and interpersonal/ cognitive variables (e.g., self-esteem, perfectionism, and dependency). Second, they suggest that measures of temperament and emotionality are closely related to one another and to biogenetic aspects of susceptibility to mood disturbances. (A corollary to the correspondence between personality and emotionality is that some aspects of personality disorders and mood disorders can only be distinguished artificially.) Third, they suggest that interpersonal/cognitive variables such as self-esteem are strongly influenced by family environment, and in turn influence the effectiveness of social skills and coping strategies, which are critical in the development of personality disorders. Fourth, they note that the measurement of personality variables is more highly differentiated and adequate for research purposes than is the measurement of depression.

The distinction between temperament and what Klein and colleagues label "interpersonal/cognitive" variables is particularly important, because it has often been overlooked or neglected by personality researchers. Depression research has a long tradition of focusing on either biogenetic factors, such as affect regulation and temperament, or on cognitive styles and schemas, as Klein and her colleagues note. However, personality research has often overlooked the difference between these two sets of variables. For example, in Costa and McCrae's (1990) five-factor model of personality, variables from the interpersonal/cognitive domain (e.g., agreeability and conscientiousness) are treated as comparable to variables in the temperament domain (e.g., neuroticism and extraversion). Likewise, Tellegen (1985) lists such traits as empathy and alienation along with distress reaction, and combines these into higher-order traits such as negative affectivity.

However, my recent work in personality assessment has led me to distinguish between temperament and character variables (Cloninger & Svrakic, 1992). As suggested here by Klein and colleagues, temperament variables (e.g., novelty seeking, harm avoidance, and reward dependence) are closely related to automatic emotional reactions (e.g., loss of temper, fear, and sentimental crying at loss of attachments), which are moderately heritable and not influenced appreciably by family environment (Cloninger, 1987). In contrast, the character domain includes factors called self-directedness, cooperativeness, and self-transcendence, reflecting different levels of identification of self as an individual, as a member of society, and as part of the universe, respectively. Self-directedness includes measures of self-esteem, resourcefulness, and purposefulness, which appear to be influenced by family environment (Coopersmith, 1967). Frankel (1978) has suggested that variables such as this are critical in the distinction between neurotic and autonomous depressions. Cooperativeness includes measures of social acceptance, empathy, and helpfulness, which have a major impact on interpersonal interactions (Rogers, 1961). In recent work we have shown that these characterological variables are distinct from temperament variables, supporting the distinction made by Klein and associates. Our working hypothesis is that the character variables distinguish whether or not an individual is classified as having a personality disorder; the temperament variables characterize the subtype of personality disorder and suceptibility to emotional disorders on Axis I of the *Diagnostic and Statistical Manual of Mental Disorders,* third edition, revised (DSM-III-R) (Cloninger & Svrakic, 1992). These findings about our model of personality strongly support the model suggested by Klein and associates.

Klein and her associates also suggest that available methods for measurement of personality are more highly differentiated and adequate than those for depression. Given all the controversy in the field of personality about the preferred model, this may be the nicest thing anyone has ever said about personality research, but provides little consolation for depression research. Personality investigators disagree about the optimal scales for measuring personality, but the alternative methods are highly correlated with one another. In contrast, in depression research, there is essentially no consistently validated method for distinguishing even neurotic/reactive from endogenous/autonomous depression, and much difficulty even in distinguishing depressive and anxiety states (Maser & Cloninger, 1990).

## MEASUREMENT OF DEPRESSION

Klein and her colleagues review the major ways in which psychiatrists have subdivided depression, but in their model they emphasize the distinction in etiology between first and subsequent episodes. The absence of a validated nosology of depressive subtypes has been a major obstacle in delineating relationships between particular personality traits and particular depressive subgroups or components. One improvement, not mentioned by Klein and colleagues, could be to restrict work to individuals with "primary depression"—that is, those who have no other psychiatric disorder preceding the onset of depression, as suggested by Robins and Guze originally (Cloninger, 1989). However, differences even among primary depressives exist: Some individuals have prominent personality traits that distinguish them from the average, and others are unremarkable in their personality profile. It is uncertain whether this variation in personality distinguishes neurotic/ reactive from endogenous/autonomous depressives, because the subtyping of depression is difficult and comorbidity with other psychopathology has seldom been taken into account.

## MEASUREMENT OF MODERATOR VARIABLES

A major strength of the Klein et al. model is the inclusion of such variables as stress and social supports as moderators in a multivariate developmental framework. Many investigators of stress and social support have tended to ignore differences between individuals in the significance and salience of different environmental events. The same external event (e.g., death of an acquaintance) has a different meaning and significance, depending on the personality of the individual and the social context of the occurrence. Accordingly, little understanding can be achieved without simultaneous measurement of personality, mood, and putative moderating or intervening variables, such as stress and social supports. If both individual differences in personality and learning are understood as biases in response to different types of stimuli (e.g., threats, rewards, social approval), then variation in state can be related systematically to the interaction of personality with specific types of provocative stimuli, mediated further by concepts regarding the significance of those stimuli for an individual's particular self-image. The result is inevitably a biopsychosocial–developmental model similar to that described by Klein and her associates. Although the general form of the model may be similar for different types of depressives (e.g., depressed bipolars, depressed borderline personalities, etc.), the relevant variables and their importance may be different for each subtype and its phase of illness.

## LONGITUDINAL DEVELOPMENTAL MODELS

Klein and her associates emphasize that testing of the model will ultimately require repeated measures of a large number of biological, cognitive, social, and clinical variables over extended periods of time in large, systematically ascertained samples. As they note, the requirements for resolution and testing of the model are stringent. An effort to initiate a large-scale study of all relevant variables in a broadly defined sample could easily degenerate into an expensive fishing expedition that would lead to arguable conclusions. Longitudinal studies are often handicapped by changes in the field, as different measures are validated and different concepts need to be tested. How, then, shall we proceed?

## IMPLICATIONS FOR FUTURE RESEARCH STRATEGIES

Klein and her colleagues have offered several thoughtful suggestions for future studies. In addition, a broadly stated sequential strategy for resolution of the model should include four phases, in my opinion.

### Phase One: Measurement Development

Each conceptual domain requires empirical measures that are practical, reliable, and (one hopes) validated to some extent. Demonstration that different investigators or sites can obtain consistent results is obviously necessary. Furthermore, if a measure is ultimately going to be used repeatedly in a large-scale study of many variables, efforts must often be made to shorten it for such use. Tests of alternative measures of personality, emotionality, depression, social environment are currently underway in the MacArthur Foundation Research Network on the Psychobiology of Depression and Other Affective Disorders. The measurement of DSM-III-R personality disorder categories is highly problematic at the moment, because appropriate structured interviews take over 90 minutes and yield many overlapping diagnoses; cross-validation of self-reports or orthogonal personality dimensions with categorical interview diagnoses is likewise underway.

### Phase Two: Validation and Tests of Strength of Association

Before a long-term study with many variables is undertaken, it will be crucial to measure the strength of association between different variables (e.g., the association of personality with depression, or of social stress and supports with depression). At the same time this will serve to validate the measures and show the strength of their relevance to the etiology or course of depressive disorders. Individuals with the most interest and expertise in measurement of particular variables can undertake such studies before a more comprehensive test of the model is conducted. In particular, little work using measures of both personality and social stress has been carried out. Some work in Australia (A.

Heath, personal communication, 1991) suggests that self-report measures of social stress actually behave more like personality tests than like measures of environmental precipitants; accordingly, more labor-intensive interviews may be unavoidable if transient social factors are to be validly assessed.

## Phase Three: Tests of the Risk of Depressive Disorders in Different Personality Types

At Phase Three, we face a choice of whether to begin with samples selected for their personality profiles and follow them for risk of depression, or vice versa. There are two strong reasons to begin with personality as the initial selection basis. First, mood disorders complicate the measurement of personality, so the only sure way to measure pre-depressive personality is to measure personality before the onset of mood disorder. Second, the measurement of personality is more highly differentiated and adequate than that of depressive disorders, as noted by Klein and colleagues. Accordingly, it would be ideal to begin with a general population sample of individuals with measured personality and follow them up for risk of depression—or, alternatively, to do stratified sampling of different personality profiles, including individuals hypothesized to be at high and at low risk for depression. A compromise strategy would be to identify probands with mood disorder and follow their relatives prospectively before and after onset of depression; however, the adequacy of this design depends on the adequacy of the selection of depressive probands, who may or may not have disorders related to particular personality profiles. Clinical, background, and moderating variables would all have to be assessed repeatedly over time (even "background" variables change when adult parents have late onset of psychopathology). Such follow-up leads to estimates of the risk of depression with specific combinations of personality and environmental features. Although this is a logical third phase, it is remarkable that there has been little prospective work beginning before the first episode of depression. Yet such observations are critical and should be both practical and fruitful.

## Phase Four: Validation of Model by Assessing Personality in Individuals with Depression

After the relative risk of depression is quantified according to personality profile and environment, this can be tested by trying to predict the personality correlates of depression associated with particular environmental factors. Beginning with samples of depressive probands or their relatives at high risk for depression, the interaction of environmental and personality variables can be studied before onset of depression (in relatives only), and for recurrences of episodes.

## CONCLUDING COMMENTS

Klein, Wonderlich, and Shea have contributed a particularly valuable developmental model of the relationships between personality and depression. Their well-balanced synthesis should stimulate research in both personality and depression, in addition to helping us understand the relationships.

## REFERENCES

Cloninger, C. R. (1987). A systematic method for clinical description and classification of personality variants. *Archives of General Psychiatry, 44,* 573–588.

Cloninger, C. R. (1989). Establishment of diagnostic validity in psychiatric illness: Robins and Guze's method revisited. In L. N. Robins & J. E. Barrett (Eds.), *The validity of psychiatric diagnosis* (pp. 9–18). New York: Raven Press.

Cloninger, C. R., & Svrakic, D. M. (1992). Personality dimensions as a conceptual framework for explaining variations in normal, neurotic, and personality disordered behavior. In G. Burrows, M. Roth, & R. Noyes, Jr. (Eds.), *Handbook of anxiety* (Vol. 5, pp. 79–104). Amsterdam: Elsevier.

Coopersmith, J. (1967). *The antecedents of self-esteem.* San Francisco: W. H. Freeman.

Costa, P., & McCrae, R. (1990). Personality disorders and the five factor model of personality. *Journal of Personality Disorders, 4,* 362–369.

Frankel, V. E. (1978). *The unheard cry for meaning: Psychotherapy and humanism.* New York: Washington Square Press.

Maser, J. D., & Cloninger, C. R. (Eds.). (1990). *Comorbidity of mood and anxiety disorders.* Washington, DC: American Psychiatric Press.

Rogers, C. (1961). *On becoming a person.* Boston: Houghton Mifflin.

Tellegen, A. (1985). Structures of mood and personality and their relevance to assessing anxiety, with an emphasis on self-report. In A. H. Tuma & J. Maser (Eds.), *Anxiety and the anxiety disorders* (pp. 681–706). Hillsdale, NJ: Erlbaum.

# Commentary

PETER A. BARNETT

*Victoria Hospital, London, Ontario, Canada*

Klein, Wonderlich, and Shea have written an integrative review of some of the models of relations among personality traits and depressive disorders. They have delineated abstract models of these relations, identified problems with some existing theories, made recommendations intended to guide future research, and offered an etiological model of their own. In this commentary, I discuss specific strengths and weaknesses of their chapter. Overall, Klein et al. provide a useful overview of a complex area of heterogeneous theories and raise many important questions. My major criticism concerns the relative absence of detailed discussion of these issues. It may be simply that Klein et al. have chosen to emphasize synopses of selected theories of personality and depression at the expense of an expanded presentation of their original ideas. However, in so doing, they perpetuate some of the problems they identify in this area of research, particularly in their formulation of an integrated model. As part of this commentary, then, I make some suggestions for developing the kind of research program the authors appear to be calling for.

There are a number of strengths to this chapter. Klein et al. have identified fundamental issues and problems in the area of personality and depression that cut across individual theories and research approaches. Chief among these is the lack of clarity that permeates not only multivariate theories but definitions of individual variables. This represents such a pervasive problem that the authors themselves are guilty at times of not properly clarifying their terms. For example, they describe a neurochemical deficit as a "trait" (p. 37) and refer to personality as a "condition" (p. 4). A more substantive example that provides a segue to a series of issues is the authors' suggestion that for the purposes of their discussion, "personality" can be read as either "personality trait" or "personality disorder." Similarly, "depression" may refer to either a mood disturbance or an episode of affective disorder. These may be attempts to avoid repetitious or awkward writing, but they do highlight the lack of precision often encountered in definitions of both independent and dependent variables.

The difficulty of defining and distinguishing dependent variables receives considerable attention in this chapter. It has been debated in the literature in terms of both the relative merits of a categorical versus dimensional nosology for personality disorders (Widiger, 1989; Widiger & Kelso, 1983) and the difficulties involved in classifying affective disorders on the basis of phenomenology (Craighead, 1980; Farmer & McGuffin, 1989). Klein et al. address a number of aspects of this general issue. They comment on the overlap of aspects of affective and personality disorders, suggest exploring subcomponents of each disorder rather than assuming unitary categories, and recommend teasing out affective from other components of personality to minimize both conceptual overlap and artificially inflated correlations. But their most important contribution is their call for a change in focus from content or descriptive variables to process or explanatory variables. This change presumably would be a shift away from describing "diseases" and toward greater research emphasis on the pathogenic processes underlying psychological distress in general and depression in particular.

This recommendation is useful and promising. Klein et al. even identify some of the variables that might be included in a process-oriented approach. For example, they state, "Concepts related to mood (e.g., affective dyscontrol or regulation, pervasiveness or chronicity of affect) and personality-related concepts (e.g., motives, congruence of needs, quality of defenses or coping in relation to goals, and the function and/or organization of self-perceptions and cognitive processes) need to be developed" (p. 19). However, little more is said of either the nature of these variables or how they might be developed. If these variables are central to a new model or framework for research, then it would be helpful to review what is known of them: how they are defined, operationalized, measured, and researched presently, and how these aspects might be improved in the future. Furthermore, general recommendations for developing such constructs in an adequate way would be useful. Klein et al. comment on the way in which the unitary conceptualization of depression may have impeded more creative research. Similarly, inadequare attention to demonstrating the construct validity of independent variables may have led to spurious empirical data. What is needed, then, is greater emphasis on understanding the nature of individual constructs or variables.

As an example of the need for better definition and operationalization of independent variables, consider the research on self-esteem and
depression. A number of recent theories of depression have implicated,
directly or indirectly, the contingency of self-esteem on limited external
sources as a risk factor for depression (Blatt, 1974; Hirschfeld, Klerman,
Chodoff, Korchin, & Barrett, 1976; Kuiper & Olinger, 1986; Linville,
1985; Oatley & Bolton, 1985: Pyszczynski & Greenberg, 1987). Furthermore, individuals who are vulnerable to a loss of self-esteem, and thus
to the development of depression, are thought to possess higher
amounts of various indicators of labile or contingent self-esteem. These
vulnerabilities include a tendency to make internal attributions for
negative events (Abramson, Seligman, & Teasdale, 1978), high numbers
of dysfunctional attitudes (Kuiper & Olinger, 1986), low cognitive complexity (Linville, 1985), and high amounts of dependency and self-
criticism (Blatt, 1974; Hirschfeld et al., 1976).

Interestingly, despite the centrality of self-esteem in these theories
of depression, little research has investigated the contingency of vulnerable individuals' self-esteem on external sources. One reason may be the
lack of not just consensus about, but attention to something as basic as,
a definition of "self-esteem." This construct is complex and multifaceted. Previous attempts to measure self-esteem in research on depression have ranged from the use of a few self-descriptive adjectives (e.g.,
"ambitious," "assertive"; Billings & Moos, 1985) to interviewer-rated
attitudes toward the self (Brown, Bifulco, Harris, & Bridge, 1986). Few
researchers have provided a discussion of the construct of self-esteem
and their choice of measure. Given the apparent lack of interest in the
construct validity of this independent variable, it is not surprising that
research has been inconsistent in demonstrating, for example, that
formerly depressed probands have lower self-esteem than nondepressed
people (Altman & Wittenborn, 1980; Billings & Moos, 1985; Cofer &
Wittenborn, 1980; Lewinsohn, Steinmetz, Larson, & Franklin, 1981).

Klein et al. do not appear as concerned with the construct validity
of individual variables as with hypothesized relations among these
variables and depression. Their primary criticism of many existing
theories is that the processes or mechanisms by which variables affect
one another and lead to psychological disorders have not been clearly
described. The authors make a number of recommendations with respect to theory development, two of which are particularly apparent in
the model they present. They underscore the need to integrate the
plethora of models that have been developed during the last two decades. They suggest that integration take place at the level of both
conceptual domain (e.g., psychosocial and biological) and causal model
(e.g., predisposition and pathoplasty). In addition, they state that "pro-

cess linkages must be specified for all hypothesized core causal or vulnerability factors" (p. 42).

There is no question that an integrated and precise model would advance the field enormously. It is questionable, however, whether enough is currently known to enable us to develop such a comprehensive theory. With their model, Klein et al. appear to put the cart before the horse in a number of ways, most of which can be reduced to one shortcoming: There is no theory apparent in their model. The authors argue for an integration of existing theory, but this seems lacking in their formulation. Instead, domains of variables are culled from various models and are described as having certain causal relations with either affective or personality disorders, but not both. There may be data to support these hypothesized relations among domains, but as presented in this chapter, the causal model appears to comprise somewhat arbitrary assertions by the authors. For example, it is not clear why neuroticism or reward dependence can not directly influence the development of a personality disorder. Nor is it clear why introversion is hypothesized to be a direct consequence of the family environment, when Eysenck (Eysenck & Eysenck, 1985) posits that this trait is a reflection of the degree of cortical arousal. The authors have not provided compelling arguments for delineating two causal lines leading to either depression or personality disorder, not have they justified their selection of variables comprising each line.

Despite the authors' emphasis on the need for greater precision in describing mechanisms and processes, there is little clarity in their model concerning these issues. Although certain main effects are specified, the relations among vulnerabilities, moderators, and triggers have been left quite vague. The assumptions of different diathesis–stress models (see Monroe & Simons, 1991), such as the critical threshold of a diathesis, the stress-inducing nature of certain diatheses, and specificity between vulnerability and trigger, are not described. It is understood that this model is intended to be a framework and not a finished product; however, it is not clear in what ways this framework will promote novel research. In short, Klein et al. do not appear to be proposing an integrated theory of the etiology of depression or personality disorder, but simply describing some possible interrelations among variables or sets of variables.

To some extent, the weaknesses evident in the integrated model of Klein et al. may be inherent in all models of this kind. Large-scale models cast extremely broad nets that almost by definition do not have the fine precision of smaller-scale theories. Mapping out the entire terrain of depression research can be helpful for discovering areas that have received little research attention, or for highlighting a missing turn in a well-trodden path to the onset of depression. However, the model in question is like a map to places that are still under construction or in the planning stage. We simply do not know enough about the individual variables in his model, let alone their interrelations. To focus now on complex, multivariate interactions before a great deal of work has been done on elucidating the nature of individual constructs seems premature. Furthermore, without an internally consistent theory to guide model development, hypotheses about the processes involved are likely to remain vague.

Research on personality and depression will benefit from incorporating some of the recommendations made by Klein et al., particularly those concerning a shift in focus away from atheoretical descriptions and toward theoretically driven hypotheses concerning underlying processes and mechanisms. In addition, the authors' call for the integration of different theories is timely, but this must be qualified. It makes sense to integrate similar theories that use different terms to describe closely related phenomena, and to encourage greater uniformity among research groups in their use of variable definitions, measures, and subject selection. Thus, variables and processes can be studied and understood in the context of a somewhat broader but nevertheless specific theoretical orientation. Similarly, integration could occur through the elaboration of the definition of important constructs, making the variables multifaceted (with cognitive *and* interpersonal aspects, for example).

Building on the recommendations of Klein et al., I might describe the direction for future research that I have in mind as a "construct validity" approach. This approach was adopted by Jackson (1970, 1971) for developing questionnaires; it is based on the work of Cronbach and Meehl (1955) and Loevinger (1957) on the importance of theory for personality assessment. As it might pertain to research on personality and depression, this approach would focus on a very small number of key constructs or variables at a time. Clear and specific descriptions of these variables and their relations with each other would be required. As suggested above, constructs could be defined as multifaceted, with unconscious, conscious, affective, interpersonal, behavioral, and biological aspects where appropriate. The nomological network of these constructs would be explored as part of the demonstration of the construct validity of the operationalized variables. In this way, relations among small groups of variables would be discovered and elucidated in theory-driven research. As these relations become reliably demonstrable, it might be possible to link two bodies of research data and begin to piece together the jigsaw puzzle. As the pieces are linked, theoretical integration could occur to generate new, empirically based, yet theory-driven research questions.

An example of this kind of thinking is evident in the paper by Hirschfeld et al. (1975) on the trait of interpersonal dependency. By reviewing many theorists' ideas concerning orality, dependency, and fragile self-esteem, Hirschfeld et al. identified a single trait that itself represented an integration of ideas on the depressogenic personality. The trait was defined; its dynamic, affective, and interpersonal aspects were described; and its relations with self-esteem and depression were discussed and specified. Finally, a measure was developed to assess the trait (Hirschfeld et al., 1977), and studies were conducted with currently and previously depressed probands (see review by Barnett & Gotlib, 1988). Despite all of this effort, however, the nomological network of this trait has not been systematically explored. Specifically, the diathesis–stress aspects of this integrated model have rarely been addressed empirically. The loss of self-esteem among dependent people subsequent to the breaking of an affectional bond could be investigated to determine the etiological role of these factors in triggering a depressive episode. Many untested aspects of this model remain to be explored in empirical research that might employ alternative methods, such as direct observation or family interviews, to measure interpersonal dependency.

Furthermore, the elegant, small-scale model of Hirschfeld et al. (1976) is but one of a number of theories, as noted above, that have identified contingent or vulnerable self-esteem as an important etiological construct. An integration of these theories, using fragile self-esteem as an organizing focus, might lead to a greater understanding of self-esteem, its relation with depression, and its relations with other variables identified in these theories. Similarly, the traits of dependency, self-criticism. and autonomy have been given different names and descriptions by different theorists, but are nevertheless central to several theories linking personality and depression (Arieti & Bemporad, 1980; Beck, 1983; Blatt, 1974; Hirschfeld et al., 1976). An integration of these theories might generate a more useful research effort than would any one theory alone. Perhaps similar examples can be found in the biological literature, in which different models emphasize one or two highly similar organic constructs or mechanisms that putatively lead to or maintain depression. In fact, a construct validity approach could be applied to the dependent variables as well, as suggested by Klein et al. and elaborated by Craighead (1980). For example, Craighead suggested that different symptom clusters or "presenting problems" among unipolar depressives may have different etiological diatheses, triggers, and paths. Although some work has been done to investigate theoretically predicted subtypes of depression (Blatt, Quinlan, Chevron, McDonald, & Zuroff, 1982; Klein, Harding, Taylor, & Dickstein, 1988; Robins, Block, & Peslow, 1989), much remains to be done.

In summary, Klein et al. have made some useful recommendations to help shape future research on personality and depression. However, it does not seem that their integrated model will provide an optimally focused research program. This program might better proceed by seeking points of overlap among promising theories and attempting to integrate similar aspects of these theories. Research should emphasize the construct validity of operationalized key variables; demonstrate these constructs' nomological networks in studies with manageable numbers of variables; and test the validity of theoretically relevant hypotheses, particularly those concerning the underlying pathological processes involved in affective and personality disorders. No one research program can investigate the universe of variables thought to be associated with these disorders. It may be more fruitful to examine smaller pieces more thoroughly before attempting to assemble the whole puzzle.

## REFERENCES

Abramson, L. Y., Seligman, M. E. P., & Teasdale, J. (1978). Learned helplessness in humans: Critique and reformulation. *Journal of Abnormal Psychology, 87,* 49–74.

Altman, J. H., & Wittenborn, J. R. (1980). Depression-prone personality in women. *Journal of Abnormal Psychology, 89,* 303–308.

Arieti, S., & Bemporad, J. (1980). The psychological organization of depression. *American Journal of Psychiatry, 136,* 1369.

Barnett, P. A., & Gotlib, I. H. (1988). Psychosocial functioning and depression: Distinguishing among antecedents, concomitants, and consequences. *Psychological Bulletin, 104,* 96–127.

Beck, A. T. (1983). Cognitive therapy of depression: New perspectives. In P. J. Clayton & J. E. Barrett (Eds.), *Treatment of depression: Old controversies and new approaches* (pp. 265–290). New York: Raven Press.

Billings, A. G., & Moos, R. H. (1985). Psychosocial processes of remission in unipolar depression: Comparing depressed patients with matched community controls. *Journal of Consulting and Clinical Psychology, 53,* 314–325.

Blatt, S. J. (1974). Level of object representation in anaclitic and introjective depression. *Psychoanalytic Study of the Child, 29,* 107–157.

Blatt, S. J., Quinlan, D., Chevron, E., McDonald, C., & Zuroff, D. (1982). Dependency and self-criticism: Psychological dimensions of depression. *Journal of Consulting and Clinical Psychology, 50,* 113–124.

Brown, G. W., Bifulco, A., Harris, T., & Bridge, L. (1986). Life stress, chronic subclinical symptoms, and vulnerability to clinical depression. *Journal of Affective Disorders, 11,* 1–19.

Cronbach, L. J., & Meehl, P. E. (1955). Construct validity in psychological tests. *Psychological Bulletin, 52,* 281–302.

Cofer, D. H., & Wittenborn, J. R. (1980). Personality characteristics of formerly depressed women. *Journal of Abnormal Psychology, 89,* 309–314.

Craighead, W. E. (1980). Away from a unitary model of depression. *Behavior Therapy, 11,* 122–128.

Eysenck, H. J., & Eysenck, M. W. (1985). *Personality and individual differences: A natural science approach.* New York: Plenum Press.

Farmer, A., & McGuffin, P. (1989). The classification of depressions: Contemporary confusion revisited. *British Journal of Psychiatry, 155,* 437–443.

Hirschfeld, R. M. A., Klerman, G. L., Chodoff, P., Korchin, S., & Barrett, J. (1976). Dependency–self-esteem–clinical depression. *Journal of the American Academy of Psychoanalysis, 4,* 373–388.

Hirschfeld, R. M. A., Klerman, G. L., Gough, H. G., Barrett, J., Korchin, S. J., & Chodoff, P. (1977). A measure of interpersonal dependency. *Journal of Personality Assessment, 41,* 610–618.

Jackson, D. N. (1970). A sequential system for personality scale development. In C. D. Spielberger (Ed.), *Current topics in clinical and community psychology* (Vol. 2, pp. 61–96). New York: Academic Press.

Jackson, D. N. (1971). The dynamics of structured personality tests: 1971. *Psychological Review, 78,* 229–248.

Klein, D. N., Harding, K., Taylor, E. B., & Dickstein, S. (1988). Dependeny and self-criticism in depression: Evaluation in a clinical population. *Journal of Abnormal Psychology, 97,* 399–404.

Kuiper, N. A., & Olinger, L. J. (1986). Dysfunctional attitudes and a self-worth contingency model of depression. In P. C. Kendall (Ed.), *Advances in cognitive-behavioral research and therapy* (Vol. 5, pp. 115–142). New York: Academic Press.

Lewinsohn, P. M., Steinmetz, J. L., Larson, D. W., & Franklin, J. (1981). Depression related cognitions: Antecedent or consequence? *Journal of Abnormal Psychology, 91,* 213–219.

Linville, P. (1985). Self-complexity and affective extremity: Don't put all your eggs in one cognitive basket. *Social Cognition, 3,* 94–110.

Loevinger, J. (1957). Objective tests as instruments of psychological theory. *Psychological Reports, 3,* 635–694.

Monroe, S. M., & Simons, A. D. (1991). Diathesis–stress theories in the context of life stress research: Implications for the depressive disorders. *Psychological Bulletin, 110,* 406–425.

Oatley, K., & Bolton, W. (1985). A social-cognitive theory of depression in reaction to life events. *Psychological Review, 92,* 372–388.

Pyszczynski, T., & Greenberg, J. (1987). Self-regulatory perseveration and the depressive self-focusing style: A self-awareness theory of reactive depression. *Psychological Bulletin, 102,* 122–138.

Robins, C. J., Block, P., & Peselow, E. D. (1989). Relations of sociotropic and autonomous personality characteristics to specific symptoms in depressed patients. *Journal of Abnormal Psychology, 98,* 86–88.

Widiger, T. A. (1989). The catgeorical distinction between personality and affective disorders. *Journal of Personality Disorders, 3,* 77–91.

Widiger, T. A., & Kelso, K. (1983). Psychodiagnosis of Axis II. *Clinical Psychology Review, 3,* 491–510.

# CHAPTER TWO

# Personality and Depression: Assessment Issues

THOMAS A. WIDIGER
*University of Kentucky*

The interaction of personality and personality disorders with depression has been of substantial theoretical and clinical interest for some time (Akiskal, Hirschfeld, & Yerevanian, 1983; Barnett & Gotlib, 1988; Chodoff, 1972; Docherty, Fiester, & Shea, 1986; Farmer & Nelson-Gray, 1990; Gorton & Akhtar, 1990; Hirschfeld, Klerman, Clayton, & Keller, 1983a; Millon & Kotik, 1985; Nietzel & Harris, 1990; Widiger & Hyler, 1987). The purpose of this chapter is to discuss issues pertaining to the assessment of personality (and depression) that are of particular importance when their interaction is considered.

Personality (disorder) and depression can interact in four fundamental ways: (1) Personality can contribute to the development of depression (predisposition or vulnerability); (2) personality can be fundamentally altered by the occurrence of depression (complication); (3) personality and depression can affect each other's manifestation or presentation (pathoplasty); or (4) personality and depression can represent overlapping manifestations of a common, underlying etiology (spectrum). These various forms of interaction are not the focus of this chapter; they are discussed in Chapter One by Klein, Wonderlich, and Shea. However, it is necessary to be cognizant of these relationships in this chapter, since the difficulty in distinguishing among them is the fundamental assessment problem.

I begin with an overview of the difficulties in distinguishing between mood states and personality traits. This is followed by a discussion of various approaches for addressing their differentiation, including the use of (1) semistructured interviews versus self-report inventories,

(2) longitudinal versus cross-sectional designs, (3) specific acts versus trait constructs, (4) dimensional versus categorical assessments, (5) idiographic versus nomothetic assessments, and (6) indirect assessments and probes. The chapter concludes with a set of explicit recommendations for future research.

## PERSONALITY TRAITS VERSUS MOOD STATES

The distinction between personality and depression is in some respects a distinction between traits and states. Various studies have suggested that the assessment of dependency, introversion, neuroticism, and other personality traits may have involved instead an assessment of depressed mood. It may not have been the case that neuroticism resulted in the person's becoming depressed (predisposition), but rather that the degree of neuroticism assessed in the subject represented either (1) an effect of the depressed mood of the subject at the time of the assessment of neuroticism (pathoplasty), or (2) a manifestation of a chronic, sub-affective depressive temperament (spectrum). Each of these alternative explanations involves the distinction between a (depressed) state and a (personality) trait.

### Pathoplastic State Effects

An extensive number and wide variety of studies have documented that the assessment of both a personality trait and a personality disorder is affected substantially by the mood of the subject (e.g., Boyce et al., 1989; Eaves & Rush, 1984; Hamilton & Abramson, 1983; Hirschfeld et al., 1983b; Hollon, Kendall, & Lumry, 1986; Joffe & Regan, 1988, 1989; Klein, Harding, Taylor, & Dickstein, 1988a; Klein, Taylor, Harding, & Dickstein, 1988b; Lewinsohn, Steinmetz, Larson, & Franklin, 1981; Libb et al., 1990; Liebowitz, Stallone, Dunner, & Fieve, 1979; Persons & Rao, 1985; Piersma, 1986, 1989; Reich, Noyes, Hirschfeld, Coryell, & O'Gorman, 1987; Schotte, Cools, & Payvar, 1990; Silverman, Silverman, & Eardley, 1984; Wetzler, Kahn, Cahn, van Praag, & Asnis, 1990; Zimmerman & Coryell, 1990; Zimmerman, Pfohl, Coryell, Stangl, & Corenthal, 1988). Persons who are depressed tend to describe themselves as being more dependent, introverted, self-conscious, vulnerable, pessimistic, and self-critical than they would prior to or subsequent to the occurrence of a depressive episode (Barnett & Gotlib, 1988). Depression tends to shade one's self-description in a negative manner. Hopelessness, helplessness, low self-esteem, and negativism are typical manifestations of a depressed mood (Johnson & Magaro, 1987), and it should then be expected that there will be an inaccurate and distorted description of the personality when the person is depressed. Instructing subjects to describe their usual selves prior to their depression (or any similar instruction) does not appear to mitigate the distorting effects of the depressed mood. The consistency and robustness of this state effect make it questionable whether a valid assessment of the personality can be obtained when the subject is in a depressed mood (Hirschfeld et al., 1983b; Reich, 1985; Widiger & Frances, 1987).

## Biological Markers and State Effects

It is also worth noting that biological markers are not immune to the confusion of states and traits. For example, an early appeal of the dexamethasone suppression test (DST) was that it might be able to serve as a trait marker for depression, diagnosing the presence of the depressive pathology in persons who are currently subclinical with respect to the mood disorder. However, it is now evident that although the DST is a useful and valid indicator for the presence of depression, it is neither infallible nor pathognomonic; nor is it a trait marker. Positive DST results will occur with severe dieting, alcohol withdrawal, and various medical illnesses, as well as in a proportion of cases with obsessive compulsive anxiety disorder, mania, and schizophrenia (Arana, Baldessarini, & Ornstein, 1985; American Psychiatric Association [APA] Task Force on Laboratory Tests in Psychiatry, 1987). "Thus, the particular behavioral dimension of depression associated with dexamethasone nonsuppression or hypercortisolemia may relate to a more global construct such as severity or central nervous system arousal" (Kupfer & Thase, 1989, p. 189).

The hypothalamic–pituitary–adrenal (HPA) axis abnormalities assessed by the DST do not appear to be specific to depression and may have a more nonspecific association with stress and arousal. The APA Task Force therefore recommended that "in a screening situation, such as in a general medical clinic, a positive test is likely to be a false positive result rather than a reflection of the presence of major affective disorder because of possible artifacts" (1987, p. 1259). If there are other reasons to believe that the person is depressed, the DST could be used as a confirmatory measure, analogous to the psychometric tradition of seeking convergent (and discriminant validity) data across methodologies that do not share a common measurement error (Campbell & Fiske, 1959).

Similar concerns have also been raised for another biological marker of depression: the shortening of the time from sleep onset to the beginning of the first rapid eye movement (REM). REM latency has attracted almost as much attention as the DST, but the research has again yielded ambiguous results with respect to its sensitivity and specificity (Buysee & Kupfer, in press). Positive REM latency findings occur more frequently during the first few weeks of a depressive episode and more frequently among inpatients (Kupfer, Frank, Grochocinski, Gregor, & McEachran, 1988). They will also occur in samples of schizophrenic patients (e.g., Zarcone, Benson, & Berger, 1987). Kupfer and Ehlers (1989) suggest that two separate mechanisms may be responsible for shortened REM latency. In one (Type 2), REM sleep occurs earlier in the night because of increased REM pressure (Vogel, Vogel, McAbee, & Thurmond, 1980). This Type 2 REM latency is also said to be mediated by the HPA axis and may be "more closely related to changes in arousal" (Kupfer & Ehlers, 1989, p. 946). "It appears to be episode-related and may also be associated with the severity of the depression or acute stresses that the patient is experiencing" (p. 946).

## State-Dependent Traits

In response to the suggestion that dysfunctional attitudes are simply a result of depression, rather than providing a trait vulnerability, it has been argued that cognitive trait vulnerabilities to depression require a particular state or situation to be manifested (Segal, 1988; Teasdale, 1983). Miranda and Persons (1988), for example, have proposed a "mood-state hypothesis," whereby "dysfunctional attitudes are stable vulnerability factors for depression but that an individual's ability to access and report these attitudes is mood-state dependent" (p. 76).

Miranda and her colleagues have demonstrated that the mood-state dependency of dysfunctional attitudes occurs primarily in subjects with a history of depression (Miranda & Persons, 1988; Miranda, Persons, & Byers, 1990). For subjects without a history of depression, dysfunctional attitudes remain low, regardless of mood. Miranda and Persons (1988) therefore concluded that "dysfunctional attitudes are mood-state dependent traits and that accessibility of these attitudes varies as a function of mood" (p. 78).

> The mood-state hypothesis predicts that those who will later develop a depression or who have been depressed but are not currently depressed do in fact have more dysfunctional attitudes than less vulnerable persons, but the differences are evident only when subjects are in a negative mood. Similarly, dysfunctional beliefs appear to remit as

> depressive symptoms remit because these cognitions are activated only when the formerly depressed patient is dysphoric. . . . According to the mood-state hypothesis, vulnerable persons who are experiencing a negative mood state, for whatever reason, are more likely to recall and report dysfunctional beliefs. Activation of dysfunctional beliefs may then precipitate a clinical depression. (Miranda et al., 1990, p. 239)

Miranda suggests that the mood-state hypothesis accounts for the state-dependent data that have been traditionally viewed as damaging to the trait vulnerability model. The findings that (1) dysfunctional beliefs do not distinguish persons who will become depressed later from those who will not (e.g., Lewinsohn et al., 1981); (2) dysfunctional attitudes do not distinguish recovered depressives from normals (e.g., Hamilton & Abramson, 1983); and (3) dysfunctional attitudes remit as depression remits (e.g., Eaves & Rush, 1984) are consistent with the mood-state hypothesis.

However, if a trait vulnerability cannot identify normal persons who will subsequently become depressed, does not distinguish remitted depressives from normals, and requires a mood state to be evident, one perhaps should ask what it can do. Finding that dysfunctional attitudes can be induced by a depressed mood only in persons with a history of depression is equally consistent with the hypothesis that the cognitive attitudes are artifacts of a mood state. The findings of Miranda and colleagues could suggest that the presence of dysfunctional attitudes requires not only a depressed mood but also the presence of a mood disorder. The dysfunctional attitudes would then not represent a personality trait vulnerability to depression, but rather a manifestation of depression in persons with a mood disorder, comparable to a Type 2 REM latency.

## Spectrum Relationships

### Trait–State Overlap

There is some irony in seeking a trait marker for the assessment of depression (e.g., Kupfer & Thase, 1989), while at the same time depression is considered to be an artifactual state in the assessment of personality traits (e.g., Hirschfeld et al., 1983a). Personality is typically interpreted as a trait that is at times confused with (depressive) states (Reich, 1985; Widiger & Frances, 1987), but the more valid markers for depression are said to be those that assess traits rather than states (Kupfer & Thase, 1989).

This apparent paradox does not actually involve an inconsistency. It simply reflects the fact that traits and states are not mutually exclusive, distinct constructs. They are instead prototypal categories that provide meaningful distinctions but lack distinct boundaries (Chaplin, John, & Goldberg, 1988). Some cases can be classified as either states or traits. Depression is a disorder involving a trait vulnerability that is at times expressed in circumscribed episodes (or states) of depressed mood. A person with major depression is considered to possess this vulnerability (trait predisposition) whether or not he or she is depressed at the time, just as a person with schizophrenia is said to be vulnerable to episodes of psychosis. A person can have the disorder of schizophrenia even though he or she currently lacks any overt signs or symptoms (Meehl, 1986; Moore, 1975), just as a person with diabetes can be symptom-free and an extraverted person can at times be withdrawn, placid, and un-assertive. A person with the trait disposition of extraversion need not be extraverted at all times or in all situations, but will display characteristic episodes (states) of extraverted behavior.

The distinction between personality and depression is thus not an absolute distinction of traits versus states. In fact, some disorders of mood involve a chronic (trait) expression of the depressed mood and are therefore indistinguishable from the concept of a personality trait. Early-onset dysthymia, for example, begins in childhood, adolescence, or early adulthood and is usually chronic in its expression. When it is chronic, "the mood disturbance cannot be distinguished from the person's 'usual' functioning" (APA, 1987, p. 231). A characteristic of the person that is present since childhood, is chronic, and represents the person's usual manner of functioning is a manifestation or expression of the personality. Keller (1989) has in fact acknowledged that "early onset dysthymia corresponds to characterological depression or depressive personality, which emphasizes the temperamental traits of dysphoria, the tendency towards despair, and depressive personality traits as opposed to depressive states" (p. 158).

Negative affectivity (NA) and neuroticism are personality traits that explicitly include trait depression (Digman, 1990; McCrae, 1983; Tellegen, 1985; Watson & Clark, 1984). NA is conceptualized by Watson and Clark as a "broad and pervasive personality trait" (1984, p. 465), yet it is also a "mood-dispositional dimension" (p. 465). It is "a dimension of stable and pervasive individual differences in mood and self-concept" (p. 483).

> High-NA subjects are more introspective and honest with themselves, dwelling particularly on their failures and shortcomings. They also tend to focus on the negative side of others and the world in general.

> Consequently, they have a less favorable view of self and other people
> and are less satisfied with themselves and with life. (Watson & Clark,
> 1984, p. 483)

Persons who are characterized by high levels of neuroticism tend to be hopeless, blue, guilty, depressed, tense, worried, apprehensive, easily frustrated, angry, ashamed, easily embarrassed, easily rattled, panicked, and unable to deal with stress (Costa & McCrae, 1985). Because NA is a disposition to experience aversive emotional states, "trait NA scales have a consistently strong relation with state measures of anxiety and general negative affect" (Watson & Clark, 1984, p. 483). This correlation does not question the validity of the trait construct; it is in fact predicted by the trait construct.

In sum, it is perhaps best to conceptualize personality and mood as overlapping constructs. Personality traits are relatively stable, chronic, and enduring dispositions of a person to behave in a characteristic or consistent manner across time and situations (Levy, 1983). Mood is distinct from personality to the extent that it is not characteristic of long-term functioning; however, many personality traits involve mood dispositions, and in these cases there may be no meaningful distinction between the concepts of personality and mood. Trait depression and NA are personality trait dispositions to experience temporary states of depression and/or to feel consistently depressed (McCrae, 1983; Watson & Clark, 1984).

## Personality Disorder versus Mood Disorder

The failure to recognize that the constructs of personality and mood overlap has contributed to efforts to make what are perhaps artifactual distinctions. Akiskal (1983), for example, distinguished between "character spectrum" and "subaffective dysthymic" chronic depression. The character spectrum variant had an onset during adolescence or childhood; an intermittent course; a lack of melancholic features; a developmental history of parental separation or divorce; a family history of alcoholism; parental assortative mating for personality disorders or alcoholism; normal REM latency; a lack of appreciable response to tricyclics, monoamine oxidase inhibitors, or lithium carbonate; and a predominance of "unstable" personality traits, with dependent, histrionic, antisocial, and/or schizoid features. The subaffective variant had an indeterminant onset with cardinal manifestations obvious by the age of 25; a continuous or an intermittent course; at least two melancholic manifestations (e.g., psychomotor inertia, hypersomnia, anhedonia, and diurnal variation); an unremarkable developmental history; a family history of unipolar or bipolar affective disorder; a shortened REM latency; and a positive response to tricyclics or lithium.

These two subtypes, however, were based in part on an artifactual biogenetic distinction (Gunderson & Pollack, 1985; Widiger, 1989), with the personality disorder having a psychosocial etiology and the mood disorder having a biogenetic one. "Childhood parental loss and broken homes seem to provide the developmental roots of the characterological disturbance" (Akiskal, 1983, p. 17), whereas the subaffective dysthymia was thought to share a biogenetic association with depressive mood disorders. This distinction is unnecessary and misleading, since personality is in part biogenetic (Tellegen et al., 1988), and mood is not solely nor in some cases even primarily biogenetic (Abramson, Metalsky, & Alloy, 1989; Rehm, 1989; Segal, 1988).

The artifactual nature of the distinction explains in part why Akiskal's (1983) character spectrum subtype involved a heterogeneous, nonspecific mixture of dependent, histrionic, sociopathic, and schizoid personality traits. There was no descriptive validity to the character spectrum variant; it was simply a wastebasket collection of personality traits that would predispose a person to depressive episodes. The subaffective variant was more internally consistent and more consistent with the construct of a depressive personality, involving Schneider's (1958) "depressive psychopath" traits: (1) quiet, passive, and nonassertive; (2) gloomy, pessimistic, and incapable of fun; (3) self-critical, self-reproaching, and self-derogatory; (4) skeptical, hypercritical, and complaining; (5) conscientious and self-disciplining; (6) brooding and given to worry; and (7) preoccupied with inadequacy, failure, and negative events.

Akiskal (1989), however, has more recently blurred the artifactual distinction. He now considers "the subaffective dysthymic pattern [to be] one type of depressive personality" (p. 222), while still making the distinction between an "acquired character pathology" and a "subaffective temperament" (p. 223). "The subaffective depressive personality is a less penetrant form of cyclothymic disorder, representing a subtle expression of central affective dysregulation that is manifest predominantly in phasic 'minidepressions' which form part of the habitual self of the individual" (p. 223). The "depressive types . . . are defined by their habitual traits rather than by state-dependent symptomatologic clusters" (p. 224). The subaffective variant is a less penetrant form of cyclothymic mood disorder, but it is also a personality disorder and belongs "on Axis II because [the] affective dysregulation is woven into the habitual self, probably on a lifelong basis with origin typically in childhood or adolescence" (p. 225).

A diagnosis of a depressive personality has in fact been proposed for the upcoming fourth edition of the *Diagnostic and Statistical Manual of Mental Disorders* (DSM-IV) (Phillips, Gunderson, Hirschfeld, & Smith, 1990). However, for it to be recognized in DSM-IV, it is likely that the diagnosis would have to be distinguished from dysthymia (Hirschfeld & Shea, 1990), which might be as realistic as trying to distinguish the schizotypal personality and latent schizophrenia spectrum variants of schizophrenic pathology (Widiger & Shea, 1991). Any such distinction will probably be artifactual and often misleading, as the concepts not only lack a clear boundary but share most of their features. There is probably more shared than unique variance in the concepts of early-onset dysthymia and depressive personality, and any effort to distinguish them could be more distorting than clarifying.

One of the more problematic areas of research in this respect is the interaction of borderline personality disorder (BPD) and mood disorder. Various studies have been concerned with the relationship of BPD to mood disorders, addressing course, family history, pharmacotherapy, and biological markers (Gunderson & Elliott, 1985). The interpretation of this research has been complicated by the overlap in the constructs of BPD and mood disorder. Some of the DSM-III-R diagnostic criteria directly or indirectly concern affective dysregulation, including affective instability, physically self-damaging acts, chronic feelings of emptiness, and intense, unstable relationships (APA, 1987). BPD may represent in part a characterological variant of mood pathology, comparable to schizotypal personality disorder's representing a characterological variant of schizophrenic pathology (McGlashan, 1987; Widiger, 1989). The observation of a relationship between BPD and mood disorders would then be to some extent tautological (Kroll & Ogata, 1987), comparable to identifying an association of the personality trait of neuroticism with early-onset dysthymia.

One approach to this overlap in the constructs is to attempt to distinguish the affectivity that is observed in BPD from the affectivity that is observed in mood disorders. Gunderson and Elliott (1985), for example, suggest that the depression seen in borderlines is characterized primarily by feelings of loneliness, emptiness, boredom, inner sense of badness, and deprivation, whereas the depression seen in a mood disorder is more likely to involve feelings of guilt, remorse, and acute failures in self-esteem. An additional proposal being considered for DSM-IV is to emphasize that the affectivity of borderlines tends to be reactive (Gunderson, 1992). However, to the extent that the constructs of (borderline) personality and mood disorders do in fact overlap, these proposed distinctions may again be artifactual.

## APPROACHES TO DIFFERENTIATING
## PERSONALITY AND MOOD

The confusion of personality and mood is clearly problematic to the assessment of their interaction. Various approaches can be taken to this problem. Discussed in this chapter are the uses of (1) semistructured interviews versus self-report inventories, (2) longitudinal versus cross-sectional assessments, (3) specific acts versus trait constructs, (4) dimensional versus categorical assessments, (5) idiographic versus nomothetic assessments, and (6) indirect assessments and probes.

### Interviews versus Inventories

The effect of a depressed state on personality trait assessment has been most clearly established with self-report (or self-administered) instruments. It has therefore been suggested that when the subject is depressed, peer (informant) or observer (clinician) ratings based on semistructured interviews will offer a more valid assessment of the personality than will self-report inventories (Reich, 1985; Widiger & Frances, 1987). The descriptions of the subject by a peer, a spouse, or a clinical interview are not filtered through the distorting lens of a depressed mood. Clinicians and informants are not likely to be overly critical, pessimistic, or negativistic as a result of the depressed mood of the subject.

Informants, however, are not immune to state effects. Zimmerman et al. (1988), for example, compared personality disorder interviews of depressed patients and close informants. Agreement with respect to the personality disorder ratings was poor, with correlations ranging from .17 (compulsive) to .61 (antisocial). If depression was inflating the descriptions by the patients, one would have expected more personality disorder pathology from the patient interviews than from the informant interviews, but the opposite finding was obtained: The informants identified significantly more dependent, avoidant, narcissistic, paranoid, and schizotypal traits than the patients themselves. Zimmerman et al. suggested that "patients were better able to distinguish between their normal personality and their illness" (1988, p. 737). "Many of the items reported significantly more frequently by informants reflect aspects of depressive disorder (low self-esteem, lack of self-confidence, overreaction to minor events . . .). Thus, the patient's depressed state may have had a greater effect on the informant's perception" (p. 737).

Farmer and Nelson-Gray (1990), however, suggested that the patients may have described their ideal selves or their highest level of functioning when asked to describe their "usual" selves. The distortion would then have been provided by the patient interviews rather than the informant interviews. This alternative explanation for the Zimmerman et al. (1988) findings could be addressed in future studies by including a measure of depressed mood to provide an assessment of which rating is more closely associated with the mood of the subjects, and by comparing informants and patients when the patients are no longer depressed.

O'Boyle and Self (1990) assessed the test–retest reliability of personality disorder ratings of depressed subjects provided by two semistructured interviews, the Personality Disorder Examination (PDE; Loranger, 1988) and the Structured Clinical Interview for DSM-III-R Personality Disorders (SCID-II; Spitzer, Williams, Gibbons, & First, 1990). The authors concluded that "PDE dimensional scores were consistently higher (more symptomatic) when subjects were depressed" (O'Boyle & Self, 1990, p. 90). The results were statistically significant for the borderline and obsessive compulsive ratings. The findings are somewhat qualified by the low sample size ($n = 18$), but similar effects of depressed mood on the PDE semistructured interview have also been reported by Ames-Frankel, Walsh, Devlin, and Oldham (1990).

The results of Ames-Frankel et al. (1990), O'Boyle and Self (1990), and Zimmerman et al. (1988) should not be interpreted as suggesting that interviews of informants and interviews of depressed patients are as strongly affected by patients' mood as self-report inventories are. Comparisons of interview and self-report inventory assessments have consistently demonstrated that the self-report inventories provide more elevated assessments of maladaptive personality traits than are provided by semistructured (and unstructured) clinical interviews (e.g., Hyler, Skodol, Kellman, Oldham, & Rosnick, 1990), in part because of the depressed mood of the subjects (Hurt, Hyler, Frances, Clarkin, & Brent, 1984; Zimmerman & Coryell, 1990). Self-report inventories may have a distinct advantage over semistructured interviews with respect to long-term test–retest reliability, but across the brief time span of a single hospitalization semistructured interviews appear to be more resilient to the distortion of mood states. It is not surprising that an interview will be affected less by transient state effects, particularly when the interviewers have been instructed to distinguish between mood and personality. However, it is also not surprising that state effects would still occur during a semistructured interview, since the information available to the interviewer is provided by a depressed subject. The interviewer may attempt to distinguish between current state and long-standing trait, but the verbal description of the patient's history will also be affected by his or her current mood. Further research on the use of informants when patients are depressed is clearly needed. One approach that is often used in personality trait assessment (Costa & McCrae, 1985; Digman, 1990), but that has not yet been explored in personality disorder research, is the use of informants (peers) with self-administered inventories (i.e., peer report inventories). Peer reports may be particularly relevant for assessing maladaptive interpersonal traits (Kiesler, 1991; Wiggins, 1982).

## Cross-Sectional versus Longitudinal Assessment

The advantages of a longitudinal over a cross-sectional design in the assessment of the relationship between personality and depression are apparent. Determining whether a personality trait (disorder) represents a predisposition to, a complication of, a pathoplastic effect of, or a spectrum variant of depression is difficult if not impossible to assess with a cross-sectional design (Farmer & Nelson-Gray, 1990).

### An Illustration

Consider as an illustration the effort of Swartz et al. (1989) to develop an index for the diagnosis of BPD from the Diagnostic Interview Schedule (DIS). The DIS assesses the presence of Axis I symptoms (e.g., anxiety and mood disorders) that have occurred during the past year. Swartz et al. (1989) judged a subset of 24 DIS items to involve BPD symptomatology (e.g, suicide attempts, hitting a partner in a fight, and worthlessness). Using a cutoff score of 11 on these DIS items and a diagnosis of BPD by the Diagnostic Interview for Borderlines (DIB) as the criterion, Swartz et al. identified 18 of 21 DIB borderlines and 50 of 58 nonborderlines (kappa = .67). The authors concluded that the DIS BPD index performed well and was a promising extension of the DIS.

However, one might also interpret their results as suggesting some concern regarding the validity of the DIB criterion diagnoses. The sample included 32 consecutive inpatients, 17 of whom were diagnosed with BPD by the DIB (i.e., 53%), compared to only 4 of the 28 outpatients (14%). The prevalence of BPD among inpatients is high and certainly higher than among outpatients, but the prevalence obtained in this study might suggest a confusion of Axis II with Axis I disorders. As support for the validity of the DIB and DIS diagnoses of BPD, Swartz et al. (1989) indicated a significant association of BPD with various Axis I disorders, including major depression (81% of the borderlines had major depression, vs. 11% of the nonborderlines), generalized anxiety

(86% vs. 31%), panic disorder (62% vs. 21%), dysthymia (52% vs. 21%), and alcohol abuse/dependence (24% vs. 0%). One could interpret these results as indicating substantial comorbidity, but they may indicate substantial confusion of Axis I and II disorders as well.

DIS symptoms occurring during the past year that were used to make the BPD diagnosis included anxiety attacks, anxiety for 1 month or more, tenseness or jumpiness, thoughts of death, suicide attempt, fear of being alone, and three or more depressive symptoms. All of these symptoms would probably be seen in a borderline patient during the past year, but inferring the presence of BPD on the basis of Axis I symptoms that have been evident for only 1 year creates ripe conditions for a confusion of BPD with the respective Axis I disorders. To the extent that BPD can be diagnosed on the basis of a variety of Axis I symptoms that have been evident within the past year, BPD becomes no more than another name for (nonspecific) Axis I symptomatology.

It would be particularly problematic to use DIS cross-sectional data based on an assessment of Axis I symptomatology to make inferences regarding the comorbidity of BPD with the respective Axis I disorders. However, this did occur in a subsequent study by Swartz, Blazer, George, and Winfield (1990). Swartz et al. applied the BPD algorithm to DIS data and found substantial comorbidity of BPD with the various Axis I disorders that had been diagnosed by the DIS. No fewer than 97.8% of the borderlines were given at least one Axis I diagnosis, and the authors concluded that "respondents with the [borderline] disorder are much more likely to [be] diagnose[d] with other DIS/DSM-III diagnoses than nonborderline respondents, and particular comorbidity is found among anxiety and depressive disorders" (p. 270).

> The most common concurrent diagnoses among borderline respondents are generalized anxiety disorder (56.4%), simple phobia (41.1%), major depression (40.7%), agoraphobia (36.9%), social phobia (34.6%), posttraumatic stress disorder (34.4%), alcohol abuse and dependence (21.9%), bipolar (14.1%), panic disorder (13.1%), schizophrenia/schizophreniform (12.9%), mania (9.6%), somatization disorder (8.3%), obsessive-compulsive disorder (6.1%), and antisocial personality disorder (2.7%). All relationships between borderline and these disorders are significant. (Swartz et al., 1990, p. 262)

The authors suggested that their results were not artifactual, since "our findings of extensive comorbidity are consistent with the literature" (Swartz et al., 1990, p. 263). However, this may be all the worse for the literature if the Swartz et al. findings could be attributed in large part to confusing Axis I and Axis II disorders.

## Duration of Time Assessed

Most semistructured interviews specify a minimal period of time for the symptom to have been evident in order to be attributed to a personality disorder, but the duration requirements are not always stringent. The PDE (Loranger, 1988) has the most explicit and perhaps the most stringent criteria:

> If the behavior or trait has not been present for a span of five years it does not receive a positive score, even though it meets all the requirements concerning frequency, intensity, subjective distress, and social or occupational impairment. A positive score is *not* given when the behavior has not occurred at all during the past year. (Loranger, 1988, p. 11)

In other words, evidence for the criterion must be present during the past year and over a 5-year period. However, there is no requirement for the trait to be evident every year of the 5 years, or even for most of the time across the 5 years. In addition, exceptions to this threshold are provided for 19 of the personality disorder criteria, including two borderline items: (1) unstable, intense relationships and (2) recurrent suicidal threats, gestures, or self-mutilating behavior (APA, 1987). These items can receive a maximal positive score "even when they have occurred only once" (Loranger, 1988, p. 11) over the 5-year period.

The exceptions are for "those behaviors that may occur relatively infrequently, yet have considerable clinical significance, e.g., suicidal gestures, arrests, etc." (Loranger, 1988, p. 11). The exceptions are perhaps necessary results of using specific behavioral manifestations of a trait as diagnostic criteria, rather than the trait itself. A personality trait need not be evident all of the time and across all situations, but it certainly should be evident at least once during each year of a person's life. Particular acts or behavioral manifestations of a trait, on the other hand, can vary substantially in the frequency of their occurrence, and some may be quite infrequent (Block, 1989).

For example, displaying no emotion when meeting a long-lost friend at an airport is a prototypic act for introversion (Buss & Craik, 1981); however, one can hardly rely on this act to assess the presence of introversion, since it may never occur in the lives of most introverts—let alone at least one time each year. The likelihood that an introvert would meet a long-lost friend, and would meet this long-lost friend at an airport, is very low. Similarly, self-mutilation may be a prototypic act for BPD, but it may not occur once during each year and/or even 5 years. Some borderlines may never self-mutilate.

Nevertheless, recurrent suicidality as a personality trait should be evident (however it is assessed) more than just once over a 5-year period. It is the recurrence of the suicidal behavior that suggests the presence of a borderline personality trait rather than simply an episode of a mood disorder. One occurrence of a suicidal gesture, no matter how intense or dramatic, could easily be attributable to a mood and/or anxiety disorder rather than to a personality disorder. Unstable, intense relationships should likewise be evident throughout a 5-year period. A relationship that was unstable or intense only once during the past 5 years could simply have been so because of situational or transient factors.

Gunderson (1987) makes the compelling argument that "many of the changes in a borderline person's manifest psychopathology can be understood in terms of his or her relationship to a primary object" (p. 49). "When a primary object is present and supporting, the depressive, masochistic, bored, and lonely features predominate" (p. 49). "When a primary object is frustrating to the borderline person, or the spectre of loss is raised . . . the angry devaluative, and manipulative features predominate" (p. 51). "When a borderline person feels the absence or lack of a primary object, then . . . the clinical phenomena during such periods include the occurrence of brief psychotic episodes, panic states, or impulsive efforts to avoid such panic" (p. 54). One may disagree with the particular clinical symptomatology emphasized by Gunderson, but the point that the symptomatology will vary across situations and time is well taken. A borderline person may not display recurrent suicidality in the context of a supportive relationship. If this relationship were to be maintained over 5 years, then one might not observe any episodes of suicidal behavior.

On the other hand, it would (or should) be difficult to diagnose BPD in someone who has maintained a relationship without suicidality and intense instability over a 5-year, or even a 3-year, period. Gunderson's (1987) cautions regarding the fluctuation of borderline symptomatology relative to the interpersonal situation, in fact, constitute a further argument against a cross-sectional assessment. Borderlines may appear quite different at particular points in time. It is only when their behavior is observed across time and situations that the personality pattern becomes evident.

In sum, a fruitful area for future research would concern the maximal duration of time that is necessary for adequate assessment of a personality trait, and whether the variation in the duration of time covered is helpful in differentiating personality trait and mood-state variables. It would also be of interest to include and compare comparable instructions in self-report inventories (e.g., Spielberger, Jacobs, Russell, & Crane, 1983).

## LEAD Standard

Spitzer (1983) has proposed a LEAD criterion for evaluating the validity of semistructured interviews. "LEAD" is an acronym that refers to a "longitudinal expert assessment using all data."

> Since the core of personality disorder is maladaptive behavior or traits that are characteristic of an individual's recent and long-term functioning, are present in a variety of contexts, and are not limited to episodes of illness, a longitudinal approach to validating cross-sectional personality disorder assessments seems especially appropriate. (Skodol, Rosnick, Kellman, Oldham, & Hyler, 1988, p. 1297)

Skodol et al. (1988) compared LEAD diagnoses of DSM-III-R personality disorders to diagnoses obtained with the SCID-II (Spitzer et al., 1990). The findings were encouraging for some personality disorders (e.g., antisocial and schizotypal) and discouraging for others (e.g., narcissistic and self-defeating). The authors concluded that the LEAD "shows promise as a procedure to validate instruments for diagnosing personality disorders" (pp. 1298–1299) and "that cross-sectional assessments have some potential for diagnosing the long-term personality dysfunction characteristic of personality disorders" (p. 1298).

However, there are substantial limitations to the LEAD standard. The LEAD standard used by Skodol et al. (1988) consisted of a conference

> conducted by the senior ward psychiatrist . . . with representatives from psychiatry, nursing, social work, and occupational therapy . . . They rated each criterion of every DSM-III-R personality disorder by consensus on the basis of patient behaviors during daily living on the ward, community meetings and activities, and group, family, and individual psychotherapy. (p. 1297)

The conference was held "after a period of inpatient observation and treatment sufficiently long for a clear pattern of characteristic functioning to emerge and for Axis I symptoms to subside" (p. 1297). Their procedure was clearly a sincere and concerted effort to obtain a valid personality disorder diagnosis, but even this best effort may have fallen short of the original LEAD prototype. For example, Spitzer (1983) had described the LEAD conference as involving expert clinicians who had conducted comprehensive and independent interviews. The interviews in Skodol et al. (1988) were not independent, nor were they necessarily extensive or conducted by expert clinicians. A risk of the LEAD standard is that it can readily degenerate into a euphemism for unstructured, unsystematic, and unreliable clinical interviews (Zimmerman & Coryell,

1989). In the validation of the Diagnostic Interview for Narcissism (DIN), Gunderson, Ronningstam, and Bodkin (1990) simply indicated that the criterion diagnosis was "a well-informed clinical diagnosis based on extended knowledge (i.e., the 'LEAD' . . . standard)" (p. 677), with no documentation that the clinicians were experts, that the interviews were extensive or systematic, or that a conference among the clinicians was conducted to arrive at a consensus diagnosis. The LEAD standard in this case may have simply been the diagnostic impression by the patients' therapists.

It would be of interest in future studies to compare the diagnoses and item ratings from each of the participants of a LEAD conference (prior to their discussions) to assess interrater reliability, and to determine whether one particular person (e.g., the psychiatrist leading the conference in Skodol et al., 1988) is the major source of the ratings. Most importantly, it would be informative to assess the test–retest and interrater reliability of the LEAD standard. It is quite possible that a cross-sectional semistructured interview would obtain better test–retest and interrater reliability than the results of two LEAD conferences obtained at two independent units of the same hospital, across two separate hospitalizations, or across two different hospitals.

Skodol, Oldham, Rosnick, Kellman, and Hyler (1991) are less sanguine regarding the validity of cross-sectional diagnosis in a subsequent report. "Overall, personality disorders diagnosed by structured interviews administered at a single point in time do not correspond well to the diagnoses that an expert clinician would make, given an opportunity to closely observe patients over a considerable amount of time" (p. 22).

> Even though interviewers are charged with attempting to make state–trait distinctions in psychopathology and the period of longitudinal observation was judged sufficiently long to disentangle symptoms of acute disorder from manifestations of stable personality, no retrospective approach can guarantee clearcut separation of state from strait. Only a prospective study of high risk, never ill persons could adequately distinguish premorbid personality from personality changes resulting from acute or chronic Axis I disorders. (Skodol et al., 1991, p. 22)

## Longitudinal Studies

Longitudinal studies of the nature suggested by Skodol et al. (1991), however, can also be problematic. One of the better-designed studies was that by Hirschfeld et al. (1989). Subjects were obtained from a pool of 1,179 persons who were free of any mental disorder at the time of personality testing, with 943 being at risk (since they were first-degree relatives of patients with a major affective disorder). Of the 1,179, 473 had no prior history of any clinical significant mental disorder, and 29 of these experienced a major depression over the follow-up period of 6 years. The index self-report personality scores of these 29 subjects were then compared to those from 370 of the 444 who had continued to be free of *any* mental disorder over the 6-year period (i.e., the never-ill group). There were significant differences on the scales assessing neuroticism, emotional stability, and ego control. Hirschfeld et al. concluded that "the personality features most predictive of first onset were those indicating decreased emotional strength" (1989, p. 348).

Hirschfeld et al. (1989) were somewhat disappointed in the results, however, as they found no differences with respect to dependency or introversion. They in fact concluded that their prior findings on these dimensions using fully recovered depressives might have been artifactual. The introversion and dependency scores for these fully recovered depressives were consistently higher than those for the never-ill and first-onset groups. "Our results strongly suggest that the experience of depression *does* adversely affect personality" (p. 350), although they were not clear whether this effect was an artifactual distortion of the self-reports because of the depressed mood of the subjects (i.e., pathoplastic state effect) or an actual change in the personality of the subjects secondary to the depression (i.e., complication).

More important, however, was the ambiguity regarding the neuroticism (emotional strength) findings. Hirshfeld et al. (1989) suggested that many of their subjects' elevated neuroticism scores may not have in fact represented a personality predisposition, but rather a prodromal phase of subsyndromal depression:

> Some of them may in fact reflect subsyndromal affective states in the process of becoming syndromal. Since the Emotional Strength item pool contains many emotionally sensitive items, it is likely that subsyndromal subjects would score in the abnormal range. . . . This raises the difficult question of what premorbid really means. Since subsyndromal states are likely to be long lasting, how can these states be separate conceptually and operationally from abnormalities of personality? (Hirschfeld et al., 1989, p. 350)

It may indeed be impossible to distinguish a "long-lasting state" from a trait, as these constructs could have no meaningful distinction. To the extent that a trait of neuroticism includes depressive mood symptomatology, or a depressive mood disorder is characteristic of long-term functioning and has an early onset, there may not be any meaningful distinction.

The blurring of the distinction between personality and mood is evident in a more recent longitudinal study by Zonderman, Herbst,

Schmidt, Costa, and McCrae (1992). Zonderman et al. reported that mild depressive symptoms predicted subsequent occurrence of clinical depression (with a time span of approximately 8 years on the average). However, the relationship was not specific to depression, as the depressive symptom scales also predicted a wide variety of other disorders; the symptom scales also predicted long-term as well as more immediate disorders; the relationship between the symptom scales and the subsequent disorders was graded rather than discontinuous (i.e., there was no cutoff point below which the depressive symptoms posed no risk); and much of this relationship was explained by the relationship of the depressive symptom scales to a measure of general neuroticism. Zonderman et al. therefore suggested that the depressive symptom scales were assessing the personality trait of neuroticism rather than simply a mild depressive mood disorder. They acknowledged that a few of the subjects may have been in the early stages of a clinical depression (as suggested by Hirschfeld et al., 1989), but they noted that the long-term prediction of a variety of disorders would be inconsistent with this interpretation. They argued therefore that "measures of depression predict future psychiatric conditions in large part because they reflect neuroticism."

> The association of clinical depression and other disorders with the personality dimension of neuroticism seems to blur the distinction between the Axis I and Axis II disorders of the DSM-III-R. Disorders of personality are assigned to Axis II; if depression is related to neuroticism, should it not also be considered a personality disorder? (Zonderman et al., 1992)

In sum, even if one assesses personality in fully recovered depressives or someone with a history of depression, the trait scores cannot then be said to indicate a predisposition to future episodes, since they may themselves represent simply a complication (or pathoplastic effect) of the prior episode. The only study that could resolve this dilemma is one that follows persons throughout their entire life course, or at least from the beginning of their lives. And even if a person has no history of depression, to the extent that the personality trait overlaps in content with the mood disorder (e.g., neuroticism or negative affectivity), elevated scores could still represent a (spectrum) subsyndromal manifestation rather than a predisposition.

## Behaviors, Acts, and Traits

It has been suggested earlier that a reliance on the use of specific acts to assess the presence of personality traits may complicate the distinction between personality traits and depressive mood, as specific acts may not occur frequently enough to differentiate the two constructs. However, the artifactual state effect of mood on trait assessment may also be decreased somewhat by relying less on the self-report of traits and more on the self-report of acts, incidents, and specific behaviors.

The substantial improvement in interrater reliability provided by the use of specific diagnostic criteria can be attributed to the curtailment of clinical inference and judgment (Widiger & Frances, 1985). Idiosyncratic biases and mood states will influence a rating to the extent that a subject is given latitude in how to interpret or define what is being assessed. It is no coincidence that the one personality disorder diagnosis (antisocial) that has consistently obtained acceptable levels of interrater reliability in clinical practice, and among the highest levels when semi-structured interviews are used, is the diagnosis that has the most be-haviorally specific and explicit criteria (Hanada & Takahashi, 1983; Mellsop, Varghese, Joshua, & Hicks, 1982; Skodol et al., 1991). The specificity of the antisocial criteria set has been the subject of some controversy (Widiger, Frances, Spitzer, & Williams, 1988), but it may be the criteria set that is also the most resistant to the effects of mood states.

Persons who are depressed (or anxious) may be more likely to exaggerate the extent to which they are irresponsible in caring for their children than in the frequency with which they have failed to obtain medical care for a seriously ill child. They may describe themselves as failing to plan ahead or as acting impulsively when they are depressed or anxious, but they may not distort how often they have traveled from place to place without a prearranged job or how often they have lacked a fixed address for at least a month. The same finding could occur for other personality disorder criteria. Subjects may describe themselves as being easily hurt by criticism or disapproval when they are depressed, but they may not distort how frequently over the past 5 years they have cried in response to criticism by a close friend. In sum, decreasing inference and judgment may not only increase interrater reliability; it may also decrease the distorting influence of depressed mood on self-report descriptions.

Livesley (1986) has generated prototypic acts for all of the per-sonality disorders, and many of these could provide mood-resistant indicators of personality disorder pathology. Some, however, may not yet be sufficiently specific to be resistant to mood effects. For example, one of the prototypic acts for histrionic personality disorder, "expressed feelings in exaggerated way" (Livesley, 1986, p. 731), is no more specific than the diagnostic criterion of "expresses emotion with in-appropriate exaggeration" (APA, 1987, p. 349). More specific prototyp-ic acts and incidents could be readily generated, though (Buss & Craik,

1987). Despite the apparent limitations of specific acts for the assessment of personality traits (Block, 1989) and personality disorders (Widiger, Freiman, & Bailey, 1990), their potential utility as mood-resistant indicators of personality disorder pathology is worth further exploration. It would be of interest, for example, to assess whether prototypic acts obtain better test–retest reliability across changes in the mood of a subject than the current self-report and semistructured interview assessments.

## Personality Traits versus Personality Disorders

This discussion has vacillated between a consideration of personality traits and personality disorders. This is intentional, as the distinction is particularly arbitrary when the relationship of personality to depression is being considered. "It is . . . when personality traits are inflexible and maladaptive and cause either significant functional impairment or subjective distress that they constitute Personality Disorders" (APA, 1987, p. 335). To the extent that a personality trait provides a predisposition or vulnerability to depression, it can be said to be maladaptive, causing functional impairment and therefore constituting a disorder of the personality. A discussion of personality traits that result in mood disorders is a discussion of maladaptive personality traits.

Many of the personality traits that have been considered in this area of research, such as introversion, dependency, and neuroticism, bear a close resemblance to DSM-III-R personality disorders. The dependency constructs of Beck (1983) and Blatt, Quinlan, Chevron, McDonald, and Zuroff (1982) closely resemble the DSM-III-R dependent personality disorder diagnosis; the autonomy and introversion constructs closely resemble the diagnoses of avoidant and schizoid personality disorder; and the constructs of neuroticism and negative affectivity resemble the BPD diagnosis (Pilkonis, 1988; Wiggins & Pncus, 1989; Widiger & Trull, 1992). It is likely that there is substantial redundancy among the personality constructs being related to depression. It would be of interest in future research to assess the extent to which the variety of personality constructs that predispose individuals to depression can be subsumed within a more parsimonious yet comprehensive model. It is conceivable, for example, that an association of avoidant, dependent, and self-critical traits to depression may result not so much from the presence of traits of introversion, submissiveness (agreeableness), or self-criticism, but rather from their sharing facets of neuroticism (e.g., vulnerability) or negative affectivity.

This hypothesis could be addressed by including a measure of the five-factor model of personality (Costa & McCrae, 1985) in future studies, and by assessing the extent to which the variance in such commonly used scales as the Depressive Experiences Questionnaire (DEQ; Blatt et al., 1982), the Sociotropy–Autonomy Scale (SAS; Beck, 1983), the Interpersonal Dependency Inventory (IDI; Hirschfeld et al., 1977), the various measures of the DSM-III and DSM-III-R personality disorders (Widiger & Frances, 1987), and the more recently developed scales to assess dependency and achievement (Pilkonis, 1988), NA (Tellegen & Waller, in press), and other constructs could all be subsumed within this single model. (Tellegen and Waller, however, suggest that an adequate model for the description of both normal and abnormal personality traits will require seven dimensions.) This not only would contribute to an integration of diverse and seemingly distinct findings and research programs, but it would also simplify the implementation of future studies (e.g., only one multiscale inventory would need to be administered). It is unnecessarily redundant, inefficient, and confusing to generate new constructs and measures that overlap substantially with existing constructs and measures. Future studies should at least include scales from alternative models, in order to assess whether there is any incremental validity to the constructs and measures they are proposing.

The relationship among some of the existing constructs is not readily apparent. For example, the self-criticism construct of Blatt et al. (1982) resembles narcissism in some respects, in that both involve a high need for achievement and a vulnerability to failure and defeat (Nietzel & Harris, 1990). But the devotion to achievement and productivity and the ruminative doubts and worries of the self-critical person may suggest a closer resemblance to obsessive compulsive personality disorder. In any case, no published study has yet related empirically the constructs of Blatt et al. (1982) and Beck (1983) to the DSM-III-R personality disorder diagnoses. An integration of these areas of research is likely to be fruitful. It may be the case, for example, that the DSM-III-R taxonomy does not provide the traits that most often result in depression or are most likely to do so (Pilkonis, 1988).

A measurement issue that applies to both the personality trait research and personality disorder research is the threshold for determining when a personality trait becomes maladaptive. If it is the point at which a trait provides a vulnerability to episodes of depressed mood, then it is likely that most of the cutoff points for diagnosis in DSM-III-R are too high. It is likely that the possession of just three avoidant personality disorder diagnostic criteria (e.g., easily hurt by criticism or disapproval, no close friends or confidants, and unwillingness to get involved with people unless certain of being liked) or just four dependent personality disorder criteria (e.g., easily hurt by criticism or disapproval, feels devastated or helpless when close relationships end, frequently preoccupied with fears of being abandoned, and feels uncomfortable or helpless when alone) are sufficient to provide a predisposition to depression. The DSM-III-R cutoff points for diagnosis do not define the point at which a personality trait becomes a personality disorder. They were determined simply by face validity for the description of each personality disorder (e.g., possessing only four of the dependent criteria did not appear to be sufficiently close to the prototypic dependent personality disorder). If the cutoff points do not provide the threshold for when the disposition to depression occurs (and they may not even be close), then using these cutoff points for assessing the relationship of the maladaptive personality traits to depression is likely to provide an arbitrary and artifactual handicap.

The same concern applied to studies on autonomy, self-criticism, introversion, dependency, and other personality trait constructs that impose arbitrary categorical distinctions. Many studies have simply defined "dependent" or "self-critical" persons on the basis of an arbitrary cutoff in the distribution of scores obtained from their respective sample of normal subjects (e.g., Hammen, Ellicott, Gitlin, & Jamison, 1989; Robins, 1990). These cutoff points have had no apparent relationship to the likely threshold for the vulnerability to depressed mood (nor are they likely to result in a consistent definition of caseness across studies). Persons who are below the 75th percentile or the 50th percentile are less likely to be predisposed to depression than those above the threshold, but many may still be substantially predisposed.

It would be of interest in future personality trait and personality disorder studies to include an independent measure of social and occupational dysfunction and distress, in order to assess whether the diagnostic thresholds do in fact correspond to a meaningful threshold of clinically significant maladaptivity. In the absence of any empirical or conceptual justification for a cutoff point as indicating the threshold for maladaptivity (e.g., disposition to becoming depressed), it would be preferable not to impose an arbitrary cutoff point that would only hinder the identification of a relationship of the personality disposition to the occurrence of depression. Until there is empirical support for a categorical distinction, it is recommended that researchers assess personality trait and personality disorder constructs dimensionally.

## Nomothetic and Idiographic Assessment

Debate concerning the relative advantages and disadvantages of nomothetic and idiographic approaches to personality research has continued since Allport's (1937) early treatise. There is little doubt that scientific personality research must ultimately strive for nomothetic principles, but there can be utility in approaching some issues with idiographic as well as nomothetic procedures (Kenrick & Braver, 1982; Lamiell & Trierweiler, 1986; Pervin, 1985).

The complexity of the relationship of personality to depression may offer one such situation in which idiographic research can be useful. Given the multifactorial etiology of depression, it may be unrealistic to predict that a particular personality disorder or trait will predominate in the premorbid history of a group of depressed patients. If it is the case that avoidant, introverted, autonomous, narcissistic, dependent, self-critical, self-defeating, histrionic, compulsive, borderline, and other personality traits provide a vulnerability or predisposition to depression, then in any single group of depressed patients there is unlikely to be a predominant personality style. Even if most had a personality trait predisposition, the traits that were predisposing would be difficult to verify, since a wide variety of traits would probably be present. Some will have borderline, some will have dependent, some will have narcissistic, and some will have compulsive traits. The hypothesis that avoidant personality traits predispose a person to experience episodes of depression does not imply that a substantial or even a significant proportion of depressed persons will have avoidant traits.

Therefore, rather than assessing the premorbid history of depressed persons, it would be more fruitful to follow the course of persons with the predisposing avoidant, dependent, introverted, or self-critical traits. This is the approach taken by some personality trait and personality disorder researchers. However, it is perhaps unrealistic to expect to find a group of pure cases (without comorbid personality and comorbid depressive symptomatology) who can be followed for a sufficient period of time to verify the presence and specificity of the relationship of the trait to the occurrence of clinically significant episodes of depression.

Intensive studies of prototypic cases might then be of some use. It might be difficult to verify in a 1-year follow-up study that avoidant traits provide a predisposition to depression, but the viability of this hypothesis could be verified in single-case, intensive studies of prototypic persons. Idiographic studies would be useful in illustrating how avoidant (and other) personality traits can result in and interact with depressive episodes. Generalizing from the individual cases would be problematic, but they can be useful in providing vivid and clear examples of the hypothesized interactions and in generating hypotheses.

An illustration of the potential of idiographic research was provided by Zevon and Tellegen (1982). They conducted daily assessments of mood across 90 days. Intraindividual factor analyses of the correlations across days verified the presence of the two broad trait dimensions of positive and negative affectivity that have been repeatedly identified in interindividual studies. "No a priori reasons exist that would prevent idiographic analysis from employing sophisticated measurement and analytic procedures" (Zevon & Tellegen, 1982, p. 121). The potential for intensive studies of prototypic cases has perhaps not been sufficiently appreciated.

## Direct, Subtle, and Probing Assessments

There is a paradox in the assessment of personality disorders that the assessment is based in large part on self-descriptions by persons who are characterized in part by distorted, inaccurate perceptions and presentations of themselves (Widiger, Frances & Trull, 1989). For example, it is perhaps unrealistic to ask psychopathic persons whether they repeatedly con people for personal profit or have no regard for the truth. If a person is disreputable, dishonest, and deceptive, why would he or she admit to being dishonest? It may not be realistic to expect the antisocial person to respond affirmatively to the Personality Diagnostic Questionnaire—Revised (PDQ-R) item "I have lied a lot on this questionnaire" (Hyler & Rieder, 1987).

It may be similarly unrealistic to expect narcissistic persons to acknowledge that they have a grandiose sense of self-importance. Truly narcissistic persons may not consider their sense of self-importance to be grandiose, inappropriate, or exaggerated. Narcissistic persons may also deny that they react to criticism with rage, shame, or humiliation, because they may find the admission itself to be threatening to their self-esteem. It may thus be unrealistic for the PDQ-R assessment of narcissism to ask such a subject to acknowledge that "I often find myself thinking about how great a person I am," "I expect other people to do favors for me even though I do not usually do favors for them," and "I need very much for other people to take notice of me or compliment me" (Hyler & Rieder, 1987). A histrionic person may likewise not have the insight or honesty to acknowledge that "If I don't get my way I get angry and behave childishly." In fact, to the extent that personality disorders involve distorted self-perceptions, persons with personality disorders should provide inaccurate responses to self-report questionnaires.

There is indirect support for the hypothesis that personality disorder patients possess a distorting response style. Hurt et al. (1984) obtained a correlation of .74 between the total number of personality disorder symptoms reported by their predominantly dramatic–emotional (histrionic and borderline) patients and the difference between the *F* and *K* scales of the Minnesota Multiphasic Personality Inventory (MMPI)—an index of "a response style that is characterized by the exaggeration of psychiatric symptoms" (p. 1230). Morey and Smith (1988) suggest interpreting elevations on the *F* scale (a measure of symptom exaggeration) as being diagnostic of BPD, because of the consistent finding of a correlation between the *F* and *BPD* scales. Edell (1984) likewise found a substantial but nonspecific relationship between the Borderline Syndrome Index (BSI) and measures of psychopathology, and concluded that "it would appear that the BSI taps a more general tendency to attribute multiple forms of psychopathology to oneself, which may or may not be particularly characteristic of borderline syndrome patients" (p. 262). Costa and McCrae (1990) and Wiggins and Pincus (1989) reported a negative correlation between narcissism and neuroticism, which could be interpreted as a (defensive) denial of the doubts, insecurities, vulnerabilities, and self-consciousness that characterize neuroticism. Costa and McCrae (1990) further reported that this negative correlation was not replicated by peer and spouse ratings of neuroticism, which may again suggest that the self-report involved a defensive denial.

Most semistructured interviews and self-report inventories do use indirect inquiries, particularly for the most obviously socially undesirable traits. Instead of asking subjects whether they are grandiose, one asks whether they have been successful, have any special talents or abilities, or are destined to accomplish great things (e.g., Loranger, 1988; Pfohl, Blum, Zimmerman, & Stangl, 1989; Widiger et al., 1989). The interviewer then infers the presence of grandiosity on the basis of the lack of a realistic response.

The PDE (Loranger, 1988) uses the tactic of asking, "Have people ever told you that you have too high an opinion of yourself?", "Have people ever told you that you're not affectionate?", "Have you ever been told that you're too much concerned about looking physically attractive?" The PDQ-R uses this approach as well: "People say that I'm self-centered" and "People have complained that though I talk a lot I have trouble getting to the point" (Hyler & Rieder, 1987). Because it is too confrontational and obvious simply to ask people whether they are self-centered, opinionated, or deceptive, one asks whether anyone has ever accused them of or complained about these traits. This approach, however, may be just as transparent and obvious as a direct inquiry. It would be useful in future studies to determine whether persons are in fact able to acknowledge that others have accused them of being grandiose if they are unwilling to acknowledge their own grandiosity.

## Indirect Items

The relative utility and validity of direct versus subtle items have been debated and researched for some time. On the basis of his review of the literature, Graham (1990) concluded that "considerable research evidence indicates that nontest behaviors are most accurately predicted by the obvious rather than by the subtle items" (p. 167). The recent revision of the MMPI retained many of the subtle–obvious scales, but their inclusion was controversial and "does not represent the committee's endorsement of the scales. We urge that they be interpreted with caution" (Butcher, Dahlstrom, Graham, Tellegen, & Kaemmer, 1989, p. 47). The bulk of the research does suggest that subtle (indirect) items are not more successful than obvious (direct) items (Burkhart, Gynther, & Fromuth, 1980; Butcher, 1989; Holden & Jackson, 1985; Snyter & Graham, 1984; Wrobel & Lachar, 1982).

Since most respondents do attempt to provide an honest self-description, and subtle items are only indirectly related to the construct that is being assessed, it is not surprising that direct items have more predictive validity. However, if the population of subjects is characterized in large part by the tendency to provide inaccurate or distorted self-presentations, then subtle items may have some utility. Both the paradox and the potential utility of subtle items are illustrated in the following discussion of their interpretation by Greene (1989):

> These . . . subtle scales are not being used to predict specific clinical phenomena since it is reasonably well established that obvious scales are better predictors of most external criteria than subtle scales . . . Instead, the difference between the obvious and subtle subscales is being used as an index of the accuracy of item endorsement. . . . When a patient's responses have been identified as reflecting overreporting of psychopathology, the standard profile is no longer interpretable since it reflects an invalid response set. The clinician should describe the patient's style of overreporting, determine the potential causes for this response set (see Table 3), and assess the implications . . . The clinician should not attempt to interpret the codetype or any of the individual scales. (Greene, 1989, p. 11)

However, one of the three potential reasons for overreporting that was cited in Greene's Table 3 was the presence of a dependent or a histrionic personality disorder, depression, and anxiety:

> The patient's style is to overreport symptoms because he or she has learned that [this] is the way to receive attention. This style is encountered frequently in patients with dependent or histrionic personality

disorders and depressive mood disorders. Overreporting of psychopathology is particularly common in depressive disorders with anxiety features. (Greene, 1989, p. 11)

Assessment of a personality trait, including dependency, may then be exaggerated or inflated by the presence of a dependent personality disorder (and depression). This exaggeration is indicated in part by the excessive elevation on the obvious items (relative to the subtle items of dependency). One is then advised not to interpret the elevation on dependency as reflecting dependency, but rather as simply inaccurate responding.

Substantive interpretations of validity scales are of course complicated when there are joint reasons for the elevation. Both depression and various personality disorders (e.g., dependent, histrionic, and borderline) are likely to result in the exaggeration of symptomatology. Their comorbidity should further compound the mutual inflation of scales. It will probably not be clear whether the subject is really that depressed or just being histrionic, whether the subject is really that histrionic or just being depressed, or both.

It might thus be useful to explore the utility and validity of subtle and indirect items to diagnose personality disorders that are characterized in part by an exaggeration of symptomatology. It would certainly be useful for self-report inventories and semistructured interviews to include scales that assess for response styles. Only one of the currently published self-report personality disorder inventories contains scales to assess the response styles of symptom exaggeration and denial (i.e., the Millon Clinical Multiaxial Inventory, second edition [MCMI-II]; Millon, 1987), and none of the semistructured interviews includes questions to assess for symptom denial or exaggeration. Such scales might be of considerable use in research on the interaction of personality disorders and depression.

## Unconscious Traits

Subtle or indirect inquiries could be a necessity to the extent that the subject is unaware of the trait. This is perhaps evident in the assessment of defense mechanisms (Vaillant, 1986; Perry & Cooper, 1987). One of the defense mechanisms is in fact essentially equivalent to a response style. Various scales have been developed to assess the tendency to deny or underreport symptomatology. The purpose of these scales has been to assess whether the responses to the other items within the inventory can be considered valid (Greene, 1989), but they may also relate to measures of the defense mechanism of denial developed by Bond (Bond, 1986; Bond & Vaillant, 1986) and Gleser and Ihilevich (1969).

Cramer (1988) recently reviewed the Defense Mechanism Inventory developed by Gleser and Ihilevich (1969) and concluded that "despite some psychometric problems and questions of scale interpretation, the defense scales are found to be meaningfully related to cognitive, personality, pathological, and demographic variables" (p. 142). "The individual scales have proven quite sensitive to rather subtle nuances of clinical behavior" (p. 162). Perry and Cooper (1987), however, are more skeptical of the validity of self-report scales to assess defense mechanisms: "Since a defense mechanism entails a degree of unawareness of its operation on the subject's part, self-report would only measure conscious derivatives of a defense" (p. 13). Perry and Cooper are again suggesting that it may be paradoxical to ask subjects the extent to which they repress, deny, intellectualize, project, or rationalize.

Bond's Defense Style Questionnaire (DSQ) is in fact indistinguishable from a self-report measure of a personality disorder, including such items as "People often call me a sulker," "I act like a child when I'm frustrated," "People tend to mistreat me," and "I often feel superior to people I'm with" (Bond, 1986). Scales from the DSQ would certainly correlate with scales from the PDQ-R, in large part because their respective items are almost identical. The items could be said to be indirect, in that they assess the effects of relying on a particular defense, rather than the defense itself. It is an interesting empirical question whether the approach taken by Bond, Gleser, and Ihilevich is preferable to simply asking subjects whether they tend to deny, rationalize, or intellectualize. The direct approach may be the best approach after all (Graham, 1990; Shrauger & Osberg, 1981). It would also be useful to assess the convergent and discriminant validity of these self-report scales with observational–interview measures of the same defense mechanisms, and the relative validity of each with respect to an external validator.

The approach taken by Perry (1987; Perry & Cooper, 1989) with the Defense Mechanisms Rating Scale (DMRS) is in some respects unique. The DMRS is not a semistructured interview, but rather a system for coding the observation of an interview. The interviewer does not provide any ratings. "Rather, the recent history offered by the subject, relevant life vignettes, and the interaction between the subject and the interviewer serve as the data base from which the observer–raters make their ratings of defense mechanisms" (Perry, 1987, p. 2). The rating is thus rather direct in its assessment, in that the observer rates the subject's actual, *in vivo* behavior with respect to its manner and degree of defensiveness (it is indirect, in that the subjects' self-evaluations are not relevant to the rating). For example, denial is coded as present when

> in several instances the subject denies inquiries or suggestions about certain feelings, affective responses or intentions . . . The subject is hard to interview because he commonly responds with "no" [to questions], at least some of which should yield more elaborate answers . . . The subject responds to the interviewer's questions or statements by denial accompanied by anger [or] vehement attempts to avoid [the] topic. (Perry, 1987, p. 5)

Ratings are also based in part on reports from subjects regarding their past or current behavior; such reports are particularly important for differentiating defenses that are representative of the individuals' usual functioning from those that temporarily arise in a crisis (Perry & Cooper, 1987).

*Probes*

The procedure of Perry (1987) could be extended further through the use of probes. Personality and personality disorders involved the disposition to respond to particular situations in a characteristic manner (Levy, 1983). If the relevant situations do not occur, then the trait may not be evident—and, most importantly here, the trait may be most evident within a particular situation. For example, BPD may be especially evident within unstructured rather than structured situations (Gunderson & Singer, 1975); dependency may be more evident when a relationship is threatened than when it is stable (Trull, Widiger, & Frances, 1987); extraversion (or introversion) is perhaps more evident during a singles party than during a church social (Rorer & Widiger, 1983); and narcissism may be particularly evident in the response to threats to self-esteem. Each personality disorder may have a particular Achilles heel or an environmental press to which it is especially sensitive or vulnerable. Rather than assessing the presence of the personality disorder (or trait) by attempting to identify the person's characteristic style across most situations (or time), it may instead by useful to assess the person's response to provocative or instigating situations.

This approach would be consistent with the interpersonal models of personality disorder and personality assessment (Benjamin, 1986, in press; Kiesler, 1982, 1986; McLemore & Benjamin, 1979; Wiggins, 1982). From this perspective, the personality (or self) is defined primarily with respect to the person's relationships. "What needs to be studied is not conceptually isolated 'human behavior,' but rather the behavior of persons relating to and interacting in a system with other people" (Kiesler, 1982, p. 5). A particular interpersonal (personality) style will be most evident in the context of an interaction. The characteristic manner of relating to others is thus perhaps best observed by providing an interaction in which the extent to which the person is (for example) affiliative or controlling will be revealed.

Interpersonal probes could be interactions that tend to be especially revealing of a person's manner of relating to others, or, for the personality disorders, of a person's maladaptive behavior patterns. For example, narcissists are said to respond to criticism with rage, shame, or humiliation (APA, 1987) or indifference (APA, 1980), whereas the avoidant and dependent are easily hurt by criticism. Providing a subject with criticism and then assessing the response may thus be the most useful method of assessing these criteria. The dependent person volunteers to do things that are unpleasant or demeaning, whereas the passive aggressive protests that others make unreasonable demands (APA, 1987). Both may then be revealed by their response to (reasonable and unreasonable) requests. The dependent tends to agree even when the other person is wrong, whereas the compulsive insists that it be done his or her way. Both may be revealed by a task that requires collaboration with a peer. The histrionic tends to be inappropriately sexually seductive, whereas the schizoid expresses little desire for sexual experiences. Their characteristic manner may thus be revealed best by observing their response to a sexual flirtation or a sexual opportunity. Turner, Beidel, and Townsley (1992), for example, have assessed social anxiety and social skills of avoidant subjects through behavioral challenges (e.g., subjects were asked to make an impromptu 10-minute speech) and interactions with a passive confederate. The use of probes is of course not limited to the interpersonal realm, as in Cloninger's (1987) assessment of learning strategies and abilities administered via computer.

These probes could be presented *in vivo* or through a self-report questionnaire. The former approach offers a more realistic provocation, but may be impractical and poses the risk of ethical problems. Regrettably, the most realistic and informative provocations are likely to be among the most stressful, problematic, and risky. The cost in creating various situations is also prohibitive. An alternative would be to have a subject interact with a significant other (e.g., spouse or friend) while being observed through a one-way mirror. The interaction could be structured with respect to various situations that are likely to be the most revealing (e.g., re-enactment of past significant incidents or role playing of provocative interactions).

A self-report version would consist of a series of brief vignettes to which subjects would indicate their reaction or likely response. The

Thematic Apperception Test has been a traditional projective test of interpersonal (object-relational) issues (Weston, 1991), but the lack of a reliable scoring procedure or a systematic representation of the situations that would be prototypic for each personality disorder would limit its use. In any case, a disadvantage here is that the probes could simply begin to resemble a self-report questionnaire. It may not be any different to read about a sexual situation and note one's reaction or likely response than it would be to respond to the item "Sex doesn't interest me" on a true–false questionnaire. A probe works to the extent that it provokes a person's characteristic manner despite the presence of depression, anxiety, or a distorting response style. Paragraph descriptions or photographs of provocative situations may not themselves be very provocative and could perhaps be readily susceptible to the mood of the subject. What makes a probe distinct from a self-report questionnaire or a semistructured interview is that it involves the assessment of a habitual response to a stimulus, rather than a subject's descriptions of how he or she tends to respond. One wants the subject simply to react to the probe rather than to provide a self-description.

## RECOMMENDATIONS

The issues and complexities in the assessment of the relationship between personality traits and personality disorders to depression are clearly extensive. However, this chapter does suggest a number of approaches that may be worth pursuing. These are outlined below.

Semistructured interviews appear to be more resistant to the artifactual effects of mood states than self-report inventories. However, semistructured interviews are not immune to the effects of depressed mood, and research on the relationship of personality to mood should use a multimethod design, particularly with alternative methods of measurement whose error variances are not correlated. Studies should also contain a measure of mood state to use as a covariate in the analyses, although it is important to recognize that depressive feelings are part of negative affectivity, neuroticism, borderline traits, and other personality trait constructs. It would be useful for future research to further explore the validity and utility of informants (e.g., peers and spouses). Peer report questionnaires (i.e., versions of self-report inventories that are to be completed by an informant) may be particularly fruitful.

Semistructured interviews (and self-report inventories) should be more explicit and stringent with respect to the time duration that is required for a personality trait attribution. If the trait involves a specific behavioral act that is infrequent, then additional acts that are representative of the trait in question should be assessed to ensure that the trait has been present for a specified duration of time (e.g., throughout a 5-year period). LEAD diagnoses offer a potential external validator for cross-sectional personality disorder assessments, but the interrater (or intersite) and test–retest reliability of the LEAD diagnoses should be assessed before they are accepted as "gold standards."

Longitudinal studies are clearly preferable over cross-sectional designs. It is particularly preferable to follow up persons with the personality disorder or trait predisposition, rather than to follow back or to follow up persons with depression. Longitudinal studies, however, also need to recognize the overlap of the constructs of (1) personality traits/ disorders that involve mood with (2) chronic mood disorders with an early onset. Researchers may also consider the use of idiographic longitudinal research with prototypic cases.

Future research should explore the advantages and disadvantages of self-report assessments of specific acts and behaviors with respect to the effects of mood states. The reporting of the frequency of specific acts and incidents may be more resistant to the effects of mood than the self-descriptions that are currently requested in self-report inventories. This research, however, may require the development of prototypic acts for the various personality disorders (and traits) that are more specific than those currently available.

Future research should also explore the relationship among the commonly researched personality traits (e.g., self-criticism, dependency, autonomy, neuroticism, and introversion), defense mechanisms (e.g., denial, intellectualization, and projection), and personality disorders (e.g., obsessive compulsive, dependent, narcissistic, avoidant, schizoid, and borderline). Many of the existing measures might be more parsimoniously subsumed within a single, comprehensive model of personality (e.g., the five-factor model described by McCrae & Costa, 1990, and Digman, 1990, or the seven-factor model described by Tellegen & Waller, in press). This research would also be useful to establish the relationship among adaptive personality traits, maladaptive personality traits, and personality disorders. It is recommended that researchers refrain from imposing arbitrary categorical distinctions that may impair the assessment of the relationship of a personality trait or disorder to depression, or at least that they provide an empirical or a conceptual rationale for whatever categorical distinction is used.

Future research might also explore the use of indirect assessments in the assessment of maladaptive personality traits and personality disorders to determine whether subtle and indirect items are more useful with subjects who have personality disorders. It might be particularly useful for semistructured interviews ans self-report inventories to include items or scales whose purpose it is to assess response styles.

Observational measures of actual interactions of subjects with significant others may also be useful, particularly if such an interaction involves the use of structured situations that provide the optimal context (probe) for the expression of the various personality disorders and maladaptive personality traits. The use of these probes may be more resistant to the effects of mood states, but this hypothesis should itself be explored empirically.

## ACKNOWLEDGMENTS

I wish to express my appreciation to David Kupfer, Auke Tellegen, Lorna Smith Benjamin, Bob Cloninger, Tracie Shea, Marjorie Klein, Chris Perry, and Paul Pilkonis for their very helpful comments on an earlier version of this chapter. Correspondence concerning this chapter should be addressed to Thomas A. Widiger, Ph.D., 115 Kastle Hall, Department of Psychology, University of Kentucky, Lexington, KY 40506-0044.

## REFERENCES

Abramson, L., Metalsky, G., & Alloy, L. (1989). Hopelessness depression: A theory-based subtype of depression. *Psychological Review, 96,* 358–372.

Akiskal, H. (1983). Dysthymic disorder: Psychopathology of proposed chronic depressive subtypes. *American Journal of Psychiatry, 140,* 11–20.

Akiskal, H. (1989). Validating affective personality types. In L. Robins & J. Barrett (Eds.), *The validity of psychiatric diagnosis* (pp. 217–227). New York: Raven Press.

Akiskal, H., Hirschfeld, R., & Yerevanian, B. (1983). The relationship of personality to affective disorders: A critical review. *Archives of General Psychiatry, 40,* 801–810.

Allport, G. (1937). *Personality.* New York: Henry Holt.

American Psychiatric Association (APA). (1980). *Diagnostic and statistical manual of mental disorders* (3rd ed.). Washington, DC: Author.

American Psychiatric Association (APA). (1987). *Diagnostic and statistical manual of mental disorders* (3rd ed., rev.). Washington, DC: Author.

American Psychiatric Association (APA) Task Force on Laboratory Tests in Psychiatry. (1987). The dexamethasone suppression test: An overview of its current status in psychiatry. *American Journal of Psychiatry, 144,* 1253–1262.

Ames-Frankel, J., Walsh, T., Devlin, M., & Oldham, J. (1990, May). Axis II comorbidity and chronicity in bulimia. In J. Oldham (Chair), *Understanding Axis I chronicity: Role of Axis II.* Symposium conducted at the 143rd Annual Meeting of the American Psychiatric Association, New York.

Arana, G., Baldessarini, R., & Ornstein, M. (1985). The dexamethasone suppression test for diagnosis and prognosis in psychiatry. *Archives of General Psychiatry, 42,* 1193–1204.

Barnett, P., & Gotlib, I. (1988). Psychosocial functioning and depression: Distinguishing among antecedents, concomitants, and consequences. *Psychological Bulletin, 104,* 97–126.

Beck, A. (1983). Cognitive therapy of depression: New perspectives. In P. Clayton & J. Barrett (Eds.), *Treatment of depression: Old controversies and new approaches* (pp. 265–290). New York: Raven Press.

Benjamin, L. S. (1986). Adding social and intrapsychic descriptors to Axis I of DSM-III. In T. Millon & G. L. Klerman (Eds.), *Contemporary directions in psychopathology* (pp. 599–638). New York: Guilford Press.

Benjamin, L. S. (in press). *Interpersonal diagnosis and treatment of the DSM personality disorders.* New York: Guilford Press.

Blatt, S., Quinlan, D., Chevron, E., McDonald, C., & Zuroff, D. (1982). Dependency and self-criticism: Psychological dimensions of depression. *Journal of Consulting and Clinical Psychology, 50,* 113–124.

Block, J. (1989). Critique of the act frequency approach to personality. *Journal of Personality and Social Psychology, 56,* 234–245.

Bond, M. (1986). An empirical study of defense styles. In G. Vaillant (Ed.), *Empirical studies of ego mechanisms of defense* (pp. 1–29). Washington, DC: American Psychiatric Press.

Bond, M., & Vaillant, G. (1986). An empirical study of the relationship between diagnostic and defense style. *Archives of General Psychiatry, 43,* 285–288.

Boyce, P., Hadzi-Pavlovic, D., Parker, G., Brodaty, H., Hickle, I., Mitchell, P., & Wilhelm, K. (1989). Depressive type and state effects on personality measures. *Acta Psychiatrica Scandinavica, 81,* 197–200.

Burkhart, B., Gynther, M., & Fromuth, M. (1980). The relative validity of subtle versus obvious items on the MMPI Depression scale. *Journal of Clinical Psychology, 36,* 748–751.

Buss, D., & Craik, K. (1981). The act frequency analysis of interpersonal dispositions: Aloofness, gregariousness, dominance and submissiveness. *Journal of Personality, 49,* 175–192.

Buss, D., & Craik, K. (1987). Act criteria for the diagnosis of personality disorders. *Journal of Personality Disorders, 1,* 73–71.

Butcher, J. (1989). *Minnesota Multiphasic Personality Inventory-2, user's guide, the Minnesota Report: Adult clinical system.* Minneapolis: National Computer Systems.

Butcher, J., Dahlstrom, W., Graham, J., Tellegen, A., & Kaemmer, B. (1989). *Manual for administration and scoring: MMPI-2.* Minneapolis: University of Minnesota Press.

Buysee, D., & Kupfer, D. (in press). Electroencephalographic sleep studies in depression: Sensitivity, specificity, and related conceptual issues. *Journal of Nervous and Mental Disease.*

Campbell, D., & Fiske, D. (1959). Convergent and discriminant validation by the multitrait–multimethod matrix. *Psychological Bulletin, 56,* 81–105.

Chaplin, W., John, O., & Goldberg, L. (1988). Conceptions of states and traits:

Dimensional attributes with ideals as prototypes. *Journal of Personality and Social Psychology, 54,* 541–557.

Chodoff, P. (1972). The depressive personality. *Archives of General Psychiatry, 27,* 666–673.

Cloninger, C. R. (1987). A systematic method for clinical description and classification of personality variants. *Archives of General Psychiatry, 44,* 573–588.

Costa, P., & McCrae, R. (1985). *The NEP Personality Inventory manual.* Odessa, FL: Psychological Assessment Resources.

Costa, P., & McCrae, R. (1990). Personality disorders and the five-factor model of personality. *Journal of Personality Disorders, 4,* 362–371.

Cramer, P. (1988). The Defense Mechanism Inventory: A review of research and discussion of the scales. *Journal of Personality Assessment, 52,* 142–164.

Digman, J. (1990). Personality structure: Emergence of the five-factor model. *Annual Review of Psychology, 41,* 417–440.

Docherty, J., Fiester, S., & Shea, T. (1986). Syndrome diagnosis and personality disorder. In A. Frances & R. Hales (Eds.), *Psychiatry update* (Vol. 5, pp. 315–355). Washington, DC: American Psychiatric Press.

Eaves, G., & Rush, A. (1984). Cognitive patterns in symptomatic and remitted unipolar major depression. *Journal of Abnormal Psychology, 93,* 31–40.

Edell, W. (1984). The Borderline Syndrome Index: Clinical validity and utility. *Journal of Nervous and Mental Disease, 172,* 254–263.

Farmer, R., & Nelson-Gray, R. (1990). Personality disorders and depression: Hypothetical relations, empirical findings, and methodological considerations. *Clinical Psychology Review, 10,* 453–476.

Gleser, G., & Ihilevich, D. (1969). An objective instrument for measuring defense mechanisms. *Journal of Consulting and Clinical Psychology, 33,* 51–60.

Gorton, G., & Akhtar, S. (1990). The literature on personality disorders, 1985–88: Trends, issues, and controversies. *Hospital and Community Psychiatry, 41,* 39–50.

Graham, J. (1990). *MMPI-2: Assessing personality and psychopathology.* New York: Oxford University Press.

Greene, R. (1989). Assessing the validity of MMPI profiles in clinical settings. In M. Maruish, D. Baucom, & K. Moreland (Eds.), *Clinical notes on the MMPI* (No. 11). Minneapolis: National Computer Systems.

Gunderson, J. (1987). Interfaces between psychoanalytic and empirical studies of borderline personality. In J. Grotstein, M. Solomon, & J. Lang (Eds.), *The borderline patient* (Vol. 1, pp. 37–59). Hillsdale, NJ: Analytic Press.

Gunderson, J. (1992). Diagnostic controversies. In A. Tasman & M. B. Riba (Eds.), *Review of psychiatry* (Vol. 11, pp. 9–24). Washington, DC: American Psychiatric Press.

Gunderson, J., & Elliott, G. (1985). The interface between borderline personality disorder and affective disorder. *American Journal of Psychiatry, 142,* 277–288.

Gunderson, J., & Pollack, W. (1985). Conceptual risks of the Axis I–II division. In H. Klar & L. J. Siever (Eds.), *Biologic response styles: Clinical investigations* (pp. 82–95). Washington, DC: American Psychiatric Press.

Gunderson, J., Ronningstam, E., & Bodkin, A. (1990). The Diagnostic Interview for Narcissistic Patients. *Archives of General Psychiatry, 47,* 676–680.

Gunderson, J., & Singer, M. (1975). Defining borderline patients: An overview. *American Journal of Psychiatry, 132,* 1–10.

Hamilton, E., & Abramson, L. (1983). Cognitive patterns and major depressive disorder: A longitudinal study in a hospital setting. *Journal of Abnormal Psychology, 92,* 173–184.

Hammen, C., Ellicott, A., Gitlin, M., & Jamison, K. R. (1989). Sociotropy/autonomy and vulnerability to specific life events in patients with unipolar depression and bipolar disorders. *Journal of Abnormal Psychology, 98,* 154–160.

Hanada, K., & Takahashi, S. (1983). Multi-institutional collaborative studies of diagnostic reliability of DSM-III and ICD-9 in Japan. In R. Spitzer, J. Williams, & A. Skodol (Eds.), *International perspectives on DSM-III* (pp. 273–290). Washington, DC: American Psychiatric Press.

Hirschfeld, R. M. A., Klerman, G. L., Clayton, P., & Keller, M. (1983a). Personality and depression: Empirical findings. *Archives of General Psychiatry, 40,* 993–998.

Hirschfeld, R. M. A., Klerman, G. L., Clayton, P., & Keller, M., McDonald-Scott, P., & Larkin, B. (1983b). Assessing personality: Effects of the depressive state on trait measurement. *American Journal of Psychiatry, 140,* 695–699.

Hirschfeld, R. M. A., Klerman, G. L., Gough, H. G., Barrett, J., Korchin, S. J., & Chodoff, P. (1977). A measure of interpersonal dependency. *Journal of Personality Assessment, 41,* 610–618.

Hirschfeld, R. M. A., Klerman, G. L., Lavori, P., Keller, M., Griffith, P., & Coryell, W. (1989). Premorbid personality assessments of first onset of major depression. *Archives of General Psychiatry, 46,* 345–350.

Hirschfeld, R. M. A., & Shea, M. T. (1990, May). Depressive personality disorder: DSM-IV. In R. M. A. Hirschfeld (Chair), *Depressive personality disorder: Current status.* Symposium conducted at the 143rd Annual Meeting of the American Psychiatric Association, New York.

Holden, R., & Jackson, D. (1985). Disguise and the structured self-report assessment of psychopathology: I. An analogue investigation. *Journal of Consulting and Clinical Psychology, 53,* 211–222.

Hollon, S., Kendall, P., & Lumry, A. (1986). Specificity of depressotypic cognitions in clinical depression. *Journal of Abnormal Psychiatry, 95,* 52–59.

Hurt, S., Hyler, S., Frances, A., Clarkin, J., & Brent, R. (1984). Assessing borderline personality disorder with self-report, clinical interview, or semi-structured interview. *American Journal of Psychiatry, 141,* 1228–1231.

Hyler, S., & Rieder, R. (1987). *PDQ-R: Personality Diagnostic Questionnaire—Revised.* New York: New York State Psychiatric Institute.

Hyler, S., Skodol, A., Kellman, H., Oldham, J., & Rosnick, L. (1990). Validity of the Personality Diagnostic Questionnaire—Revised: Comparison with two structured interviews. *American Journal of Psychiatry, 147,* 1043–1048.

Joffe, R. T., & Regan, J. P. (1988). Personality and depression. *Journal of Psychiatric Research, 22,* 279–286.

Joffe, R. T., & Regan, J. P. (1989). Personality and depression: A further evaluation. *Journal of Psychiatric Research, 23,* 299–301.

Johnson, M., & Magaro, P. (1987). Effects of mood and severity on memory processes in depression and mania. *Psychological Bulletin, 101,* 28–40.

Keller, M. (1989). Current concepts in affective disorders. *Journal of Clinical Psychiatry, 50,* 157–162.

Kenrick, D., & Braver, S. (1982). Personality: Idiographic and nomothetic! *Psychological Bulletin, 89,* 182–186.

Kiesler, D. (1982). Interpersonal theory for personality and psychotherapy. In J. Anchin & D. Kiesler (Eds.), *Handbook of interpersonal psychotherapy* (pp. 3–24). Elmsford, NY: Pergamon Press.

Kiesler, D. (1986). The 1982 Interpersonal Circle: An analysis of DSM-III personality disorders. In T. Millon & G. L. Klerman (Eds.), *Contemporary directions in psychopathology* (pp. 571–597). New York: Guilford Press.

Kiesler, D. (1991). Interpersonal methods of assessment and diagnosis. In C. R. Snyder & D. R. Forsyth (Eds.), *Handbook of social and clinical psychology: The health perspective* (pp. 438–468). Elmsford, NY: Pergamon Press.

Klein, D., Harding, K., Taylor, E., & Dickstein, S. (1988a). Dependency and self-criticism in depression: Evaluation in a clinical population. *Journal of Abnormal Psychology, 97,* 399–404.

Klein, D., Taylor, E., Dickstein, S., & Harding, K. (1988b). Primary early-onset dysthymia: Comparison with primary nonbipolar nonchronic major depression on demographic, clinical, familial, personality, and socioenvironmental characteristics and short-term outcome. *Journal of Abnormal Psychology, 97,* 387–398.

Kroll, J., & Ogata, S. (1987). The relationship of borderline personality disorder to the affective disorders. *Psychiatric Developments, 2,* 105–128.

Kupfer, D., & Ehlers, C. (1989). Two roads to rapid eye movement latency. *Archives of General Psychiatry, 46,* 945–948.

Kupfer, D., Frank, E., Grochocinksi, V., Gregor, M., & McEachran, A. (1988). Electroencephalographic sleep profiles in recurrent depression: A longitudinal investigation. *Archives of General Psychiatry, 45,* 678–681.

Kupfer, D., & Thase, M. (1989). Laboratory studies and validity of psychiatric diagnosis: Has there been progress? In L. Robins & J. Barrett (Eds.), *The validity of psychiatric diagnosis* (pp. 177–200). New York: Raven Press.

Lamiell, J., & Trierweiler, S. (1986). Personality measurement and intuitive personality judgments from an idiothetic point of view. *Clinical Psychology Review, 6,* 471–491.

Levy, L. (1983). Trait approaches. In M. Hersen, A. Kazdin, & A. Bellack (Eds.), *The clinical psychology handbook* (pp. 123–142). New York: Plenum Press.

Lewinsohn, P., Steinmetz, J., Larson, D., & Franklin J. (1981). Depression-related cognitions: Antecedent or consequence? *Journal of Abnormal Psychology, 90,* 213–219.

Libb, J., Stankovic, S., Sokol, R., Freeman, A., Houck, C., & Switzer, P. (1990). Stability of the MCMI among depressed psychiatric outpatients. *Journal of Personality Assessment, 55,* 209–218.

Liebowitz, M., Stallone, F., Dunner, D., & Fieve, R. (1979). Personality features of patients with primary affective disorder. *Acta Psychiatrica Scandinavica, 60,* 214–224.

Livesley, W. (1986). Trait and behavioral prototypes of personality disorder. *American Journal of Psychiatry, 143,* 728–732.

Loranger, A. (1988). *Personality Disorder Examination (PDE) manual.* Yonkers, NY: DV Communications.

McCrae, R. (1983). Extraversion is not a filter, neuroticism is not an outcome: A reply to Lawton. *Experimental Aging Research, 9,* 73–76.

McCrae, R., & Costa, P. (1990). *Personality in adulthood.* New York: Guilford Press.

McGlashan, T. (1987). The borderline syndrome: II. Is it a variant of schizophrenia or affective disorder? *Archives of General Psychiatry, 40,* 1319–1323.

McLemore, C., & Benjamin, L. S. (1979). Whatever happened to interpersonal diagnosis? A psychosocial alternative to DSM-III. *American Psychologist, 34,* 17–34.

Meehl, P. (1986). Diagnostic taxa as open concepts: Metatheoretical and statistical questions about reliability and construct validity in the grand strategy of nosological revision. In T. Millon & G. L. Klerman (Eds.), *Contemporary directions in psychopathology* (pp. 215–231). New York: Guilford Press.

Mellsop, G., Varghese, F., Joshua, S., & Hicks, A. (1982). The reliability of Axis II of DSM-III. *American Journal of Psychiatry, 139,* 1360–1361.

Millon, T. (1987). *Manual for the MCMI-II* (2nd ed.). Minneapolis: National Computer Systems.

Millon, T., & Kotic, D. (1985). The relationship of depression to disorders of personality. In E. Beckham & W. Leber (Eds.), *Handbook of depression* (pp. 700–744). Homewood, IL: Dorsey Press.

Miranda, J., & Persons, J. (1988). Dysfunctional attitudes are mood-state dependent. *Journal of Abnormal Psychology, 97,* 76–79.

Miranda, J., Persons, J., & Byers, C. (1990). Endorsement of dysfunctional beliefs depends on current mood state. *Journal of Abnormal Psychology, 99,* 237–241.

Moore, M. (1975). Some myths about "mental illness." *Archives of General Psychiatry, 32,* 1483–1497.

Morey, L., & Smith, M. (1988). Personality disorders. In R. Greene (Ed.), *The MMPI: Use with specific populations* (pp. 110–158). New York: Grune & Stratton.

O'Boyle, M., & Self, D. (1990). A comparison of two interviews for DSM-III-R personality disorders. *Psychiatry Research, 32,* 85–92.

Nietzel, M., & Harris, M. (1990). Relationship of dependency and achievement/ autonomy to depression. *Clinical Psychology Review, 10,* 279–298.

Perry, J. C. (1987). *Defense Mechanisms Rating Scale.* Unpublished manuscript, Cambridge Hospital, Department of Psychiatry, Cambridge, MA.

Perry, J. C., & Cooper, A. (1987). Empirical studies of psychological defense mechanisms. In R. Michels & J. Cavenar (Eds.), *Psychiatry* (Vol. 1, Ch. 30). Philadelphia: J. B. Lippincott.

Perry, J. C., & Cooper, A. (1989). An empirical study of defense mechanisms: I. Clinical interview and life vignette ratings. *Archives of General Psychiatry, 46,* 444–452.

Persons, J., & Rao, P. (1985). Longitudinal study of cognitions, life events, and depression in psychiatric inpatients. *Journal of Abnormal Psychology, 94,* 51–63.

Pervin, L. A. (1985). Personality: Current controversies, issues, and directions. *Annual Review of Psychology, 36,* 83–114.

Pfohl, B., Blum, N., Zimmerman, M., & Stangl, D. (1989). *Structured Interview for DSM-III-R Personality (SIDP-R).* Iowa City: University of Iowa, Department of Psychiatry.

Phillips, K., Gunderson, J., Hirschfeld, R. M. A., & Smith, L. (1990). A review of the depressive personality. *American Journal of Psychiatry, 147,* 830–837.

Piersma, H. (1986). The stability of the Millon Clinical Multiaxial Inventory for psychiatric inpatients. *Journal of Personality Assessment, 50,* 193–197.

Piersma, H. (1989). The MCMI-II as a treatment outcome measure for psychiatric inpatients. *Journal of Clinical Psychology, 45,* 87–93.

Pilkonis, P. (1988). Personality prototypes among depressives: Themes of dependency and autonomy. *Journal of Personality Disorders, 2,* 144–152.

Reich, J. (1985). Measurement of DSM-III, Axis II. *Comprehensive Psychiatry, 26,* 352–363.

Reich, J., Noyes, R., Hirschfeld, R. M. A., Coryell, W., & O'Gorman, T. (1987). State and personality in depressed and panic patients. *American Journal of Psychiatry, 144,* 181–187.

Rehm, L. (1989). Behavioral models of anxiety and depression. In P. Kendall & D. Watson (Eds.), *Anxiety and depression* (pp. 55–79). New York: Academic Press.

Robins, C. J. (1990). Congruence of personality and life events in depression. *Journal of Abnormal Psychology, 99,* 393–397.

Rorer, L., & Widiger, T. A. (1983). Personality structure and assessment. *Annual Review of Psychology, 34,* 431–463.

Schneider, K. (1958). *Psychopathic personalities.* Springfield, IL: Charles C Thomas.

Schotte, D., Cools, J., & Payvar, S. (1990). Problem-solving deficits in suicidal patients: Trait vulnerability or state phenomenon? *Journal of Consulting and Clinical Psychology, 58,* 562–564.

Segal, Z. (1988). Appraisal of the self-schema construct in cognitive models of depression. *Psychological Bulletin, 103,* 147–162.

Shrauger, J., & Osberg, T. (1981). The relative accuracy of self-predictions and judgments by others in psychological assessment. *Psychological Bulletin, 90,* 322–351.

Silverman, J., Silverman, J., & Eardley, D. (1984). Do maladaptive attitudes cause depression? *Archives of General Psychiatry, 41,* 28–30.

Skodol, A. E., Oldham, J. M., Rosnick, L., Kellman, H. D., & Hyler, S. E. (1991). Diagnosis of DSM-III-R personality disorders: A comparison of two structured interviews. *International Journal of Methods in Psychiatric Research, 1,* 13–26.

Skodol, A., Rosnick, L., Kellman, H. D., Oldham, J. M., & Hyler, S. E. (1988). Validating structured DSM-III-R personality disorder assessments with longitudinal data. *American Journal of Psychiatry, 145,* 1297–1299.

Snyter, C., & Graham, J. (1984). The utility of subtle and obvious MMPI subscales. *Journal of Clinical Psychology, 40,* 981–985.

Spielberger, C. D., Jacobs, G., Russell, S., & Crane, S. R. (1983). Assessment of anger: The State–Trait Anger Scale. In J. Butcher & C. Spielberger (Eds.), *Advances in personality assessment* (Vol. 2, pp. 161–189). Hillsdale, NJ: Erlbaum.

Spitzer, R. (1983). Psychiatric diagnosis: Are clinicians still necessary? *Comprehensive Psychiatry, 24,* 399–411.

Spitzer, R., Williams, J., Gibbons, M., & First, M. (1990). *User's guide for the Structured Clinical Interview for DSM-III-R.* Washington, DC: American Psychiatric Press.

Swartz, M., Blazer, D., George, L., & Winfield, I. (1990). Estimating the prevalence of borderline personality disorder in the community. *Journal of Personality Disorders, 4,* 257–272.

Swartz, M., Blazer, D., George, L., Winfield, D., Zakris, J., & Dye, E. (1989). Identification of borderline personality disorder with the NIMH Diagnostic Interview Schedule. *American Journal of Psychiatry, 146,* 200–205.

Teasdale, J. (1983). Negative thinking in depression: Cause, effect, or reciprocal relationship? *Advances in Behavior Research and Therapy, 5,* 3–25.

Tellegen, A. (1985). Structures of mood and personality and their relevance to assessing anxiety, with an emphasis on self-report. In A. Tuma & J. Maser (Eds.), *Anxiety and the anxiety disorders* (pp. 681–706). Hillsdale, NJ: Erlbaum.

Tellegen, A., Lykken, D., Bouchard, T., Wilcox, K., Segal, N., & Rich, S. (1988). Personality similarity in twins reared apart and together. *Journal of Personality and Social Psychology, 54,* 1031–1039.

Tellegen, A., & Waller, N. (in press). Exploring personality through test construction: Development of the Multidimensional Personality Questionnaire. In S. Briggs & J. Cheeks (Eds.), *Personality measures: Development and evaluation* (Vol. 1). Greenwich, CT: JAI Press.

Trull, T., Widiger, T. A., & Frances, A. (1987). Covariation of avoidant, schizoid, and dependent personality disorder criteria sets. *American Journal of Psychiatry, 144,* 767–771.

Turner, S. M., Beidel, D. C., & Townsley, R. M. (1992). Social phobia: A comparison of specific and generalized subtypes and avoidant personality disorder. *Journal of Abnormal Psychology, 101,* 326–331.

Vaillant, G. (Ed.). (1986). *Empirical studies of ego mechanisms of defense.* Washington, DC: American Psychiatric Press.

Vogel, G., Vogel, F., McAbee, R., & Thurmond, A. (1980). Improvement of depression by REM sleep deprivation. *Archives of General Psychiatry, 37,* 247–253.

Watson, D., & Clark, L. (1984). Negative affectivity: The disposition to experience aversive emotional states. *Psychological Bulletin, 96,* 465–490.

Weston, D. (1991). Clinical assessment of object relations using the TAT. *Journal of Personality Assessment, 56,* 56–74.

Wetzler, S., Kahn, R., Cahn, W., van Praag, H., & Asnis, G. (1990). Psychological test characteristics of depressed and panic patients. *Psychiatry Research, 31,* 179–192.

Widiger, T. A. (1989). The categorical distinction between personality and affective disorders. *Journal of Personality Disorders, 3,* 77–91.

Widiger, T. A., & Frances, A. (1985). The DSM-III personality disorders: Perspectives from psychology. *Archives of General Psychiatry, 42,* 615–623.

Widiger, T. A., & Frances, A. (1987). Interviews and inventories for the measurement of personality disorders. *Clinical Psychology Review, 7,* 49–75.

Widiger, T. A., Frances, A., Spitzer, R., & Williams, J. (1988). The DSM-III-R personality disorders: An overview. *American Journal of Psychiatry, 145,* 786–795.

Widiger, T. A., Frances, A., & Trull, T. (1989). Personality disorders. In R. Craig (Ed.), *Clinical and diagnostic interviewing* (pp. 221–236). Northvale, NJ: Jason Aronson.

Widiger, T. A., Freiman, K., & Bailey, B. (1990). Convergent and discriminant validity of personality disorder prototypic acts. *Psychological Assessment: A Journal of Consulting and Clinical Psychology, 2,* 107–113.

Widiger, T. A., & Hyler, S. E. (1987). Axis I/Axis II interactions. In R. Michels & J. Cavenar (Eds.), *Psychiatry* (Vol. 1, Ch. 29). Philadelphia: J. B. Lippincott.

Widiger, T. A., & Shea, M. T. (1991). The differentiation of Axis I and Axis II disorders. *Journal of Abnormal Psychology, 100,* 399–406.

Widiger, T. A., & Trull, T. (1992). Personality and psychopathology: An application of the five-factor model. *Journal of Personality, 60,* 363–393.

Wiggins, J. (1982). Circumplex models of interpersonal behavior in clinical psychology. In P. Kendall & J. Butcher (Eds.), *Handbook of research methods in clinical psychology* (pp. 183–221). New York: Wiley.

Wiggins, J., & Pincus, A. (1989). Conceptions of personality disorders and dimensions of personality. *Psychological Assessment: A Journal of Consulting and Clinical Psychology, 1,* 305–316.

Wrobel, T., & Lachar, D. (1982). Validity of the Weiner subtle and obvious scales for the MMPI: Another example of the importance of inventory-item content. *Journal of Consulting and Clinical Psychology, 50,* 469–470.

Zarcone, V., Benson, K., & Berger, P. (1987). Abnormal rapid eye movement latencies in schizophrenia. *Archives of General Psychiatry, 44,* 36–45.

Zevon, M. A., & Tellegen, A. (1982). The structure of mood change: An idiographic/nomothetic analysis. *Journal of Personality and Social Psychology, 43,* 111–122.

Zimmerman, M., & Coryell, W. (1989). DSM-III personality disorder diagnoses in a nonpatient sample. *Archives of General Psychiatry, 46,* 682–689.

Zimmerman, M., & Coryell, W. (1990). Diagnosing personality disorders in the community: A comparison of self-report and interview measures. *Archives of General Psychiatry, 47,* 527–531.

Zimmerman, M., Pfohl, B., Coryell, W., Stangl, D., & Corenthal, C. (1988). Diagnosing personality disorder in depressed patients. *Archives of General Psychiatry, 45,* 733–737.

Zonderman, A., Herbst, J., Schmidt, C., Costa, R., & McCrae, R. (1992). *Depressive symptoms as a non-specific, graded risk for psychiatric diagnosis.* Manuscript submitted for publication.

# Commentary

LORNA SMITH BENJAMIN
*University of Utah*

I read Widiger's chapter on assessment issues three times. Each time, I felt like Alice in Wonderland. Numerous impressive ideas came into view, but faded away before I could find the thread that connected them. There was much to occupy my attention: studies and counter-studies, arguments and counterarguments, proposals and counterproposals. Awed by the breadth of the review and fascinated by the surprising perspectives, I was nonetheless frightened by the part that seemed to say, "Off with her head!"

The threat is in the thought about what will happen if this chapter sets the "gold standard." I favor the model that suggests that certain personality traits predispose a person to depression. Widiger favors the overlapping model, which says that personality and depression are functionally inseparable. The models generate different approaches to the assessment of personality and depression. Methods required by one model are not necessarily consistent with those required by the other. Some of the methods that I consider essential to test the predisposing model are dismissed by Widiger as vulnerable to artifact.

Widiger justifiably has enormous influence in determining what is considered the correct way to define and measure psychopathology. He is a strong advocate of empiricism, and has been an important force in the objectification of the descriptions of mental disorders in the *Diagnostic and Statistical Manual of Mental Disorders* (DSM). It is clear that the DSM-III and DSM-III-R have greatly improved the reliability of the definitions of mental disorders. In his present chapter, Widiger carefully applies the standards of empiricism to the question of how to measure (and define) personality and depression. Widiger's analysis of the literature yields a list of attributes for acceptable studies. I paraphrase these as follows:

119

1. Studies should be longitudinal, should assume the trait model for personality and depression, and should be empirical rather than theoretical. Specific behavioral measures are to be preferred. Dimensional rather than categorical definitions of personality are recommended. Good examples of dimensional measurement include the NEO (Neuroticism, Extraversion, Openness) five-factor model or Tellegen's seven-factor model. Self-reports about personality from depressed patients are to be avoided, because they are contaminated by the "distorting lens of depression." Cross-sectional self-ratings made while the subject is in the depressed state are virtually meaningless.

2. "Response styles" are also potential contaminants, and should be assessed. The serious problem of distortion by mood and response set suggests that the most valid information comes from objective observers—namely, informants. The best data are gathered by informants conducting a semistructured interview. Not all informants are equal. In addition to the clinician conducting a semistructured interview, significant others and peers are valid observers. Expert clinical opinion as implemented in the LEAD method is suspect.

3. Probes are recommended. If depression can be elicited by probes, the science of the measurement is improved. Of course there are some fairly problematic ethical considerations here, but the probe model represents good science. Every effort should be made to think of ways of using it.

The underlying value that organizes Widiger's recommendations is objective assessment. It is important to stay close to the data, and the operations for gathering data must be explicit and replicable. Subjective impressions and clinical inference are suspect. This leads to a near-total discounting of the patient's perspective, especially as assessed by self-report in the depressed state.

While one is reading Widiger's intensive and extensive review, it is hard to remember all the studies that are cited and the many alternative views that are considered. Each cross-sectional analysis is sound. The language is tentative, and conclusions are appropriately accompanied by qualifiers and disqualifiers. Unfortunately, the highly empirical perspective yields contradictions in the total picture. The reader who seeks an underlying organizing perspective emerges confused and perplexed. Arduous sequential and contextual analysis yields mutually incompatible arguments. Here is an example.

Widiger proposes that depression and personality are inseparable, overlapping traits (Proposition A). He also says that depression is a state that provides a "distorting lens" that interferes with measurement of personality (Proposition B). Each argument can make sense as it stands alone. The incompatibility is in this thought: If depression and personality are one in the same, how can one be used to adjust the estimate of the other? How can one measure the "distorter" (depression), and use its measurements to correct the estimates of the "real thing" (personality)? If the distorter and the real thing are the same, adjustments for one should effectively eliminate the other!

The impossibility of implementing both perspectives can be illustrated concretely. One example of Proposition A—that personality and mood disorder are the same—is Widiger's proposal that borderline personality disorder (BPD) is a mood disorder. He notes that some people have tried to distinguish between the mood disorder shown by person with BPD and other forms of mood disorder. Widiger comments, "To the extent that the constructs of (borderline) personality and mood disorders do in fact overlap, these proposed distinctions may again be artifactual" (p. 85). He says, in effect, "If I am right that BPD is mood disorder, they are wrong that BPD can be distinguished from mood disorder." Those who are not bothered by tautology might accept Proposition A. They could then go on to Proposition B. Their experiment would define personality (BPD) in terms of mood, as required by Proposition A. They will not readily find methods to implement Proposition B. They would have to find a method that "partials out" the effects of the independent variable that defines the experiment! Existing methods partial out covariates, not the primary independent variable. In other words, Propositions A and B can stand alone, but they cannot work together in the same study. Investigators trying to follow both recommendations would have an impossible design problem.

Widiger recommends that investigators use the semistructured interview as a data source. Since it yields less pathology than self-report inventories in some studies, he concludes that it is less vulnerable to the "distorting lens of depression." Widiger holds that interviewers guided by structure are better data sources than patients because interviewers do not suffer from the "distorting lens" of mood. He holds to this recommendation even though test–retest correlations for self-report inventories are better than the test–retest correlations for semistructured interviews. If a personality trait must be manifested longitudinally, why is the method with the lower test–retest reliability chosen as the best way to assess personality? Does the finding that depressed patients report more pathology than interviewers truly override the better test–retest reliability of self-reports? What about the phenomenon of state-dependent memory? Could it be that depression gives subjects better access to unpleasant perceptions that they otherwise repress or deny? How can we say that the normal condition is categorically more accurate?

The chapter conveys that the literature on personality disorder and depression is rife with artifacts. For example, Swartz et al. (1989) used a semistructured interview (the Diagnostic Interview Schedule) to diagnose the overlap of the BPD diagnosis with various Axis I disorders. Widiger comments, "To the extent that BPD can be diagnosed on the basis of a variety of Axis I symptoms that have been evident within the past year, BPD becomes no more than another name for (nonspecific) Axis I symptomatology" (p. 89). He continues, "This [conclusion that the study affirms findings in the literature that BPD patients suffer from coexisting Axis I disorders] may be all the worse for the literature if the Swartz et al. findings could be attributed in large part to confusing Axis I and Axis II disorders" (p. 89). It should be noted that Swartz et al. used the DSM to diagnose BPD. Widiger's argument about the confusion between Axis I and Axis II for BPD rests on his own reading of the BPD criteria in the DSM. If that perceived logical overlap in the definition is the problem, he might more appropriately criticize the DSM definitions themselves, rather than the researchers who have used them.

As these and other intellectual images in this chapter loomed and receded, I recalled an important paper by Les Morey that assesses the conceptual status of the DSM. Morey (1991) invokes the classical distinction between intervening variables and hypothetical constructs, which was made by MacCorquodale and Meehl in 1951.

> An *intervening variable* was proposed to have three characteristics: (a) the statement of an intervening variable is reducible to the empirical laws that define it; (b) the validity of the empirical laws is necessary and sufficient for statements about the correctness of the concept; and (c) the quantitative expression of the concept can be obtained by grouping empirical terms and functions. . . . In contrast, a *hypothetical construct* was defined as not meeting any of these three conditions. The functional role of intervening variables is convenience, given that they have no factual content beyond those facts that they serve to summarize. On the other hand, hypothetical constructs have a factual referent beyond the data that constitutes their support.
>
> The diagnostic concepts provided by the DSM seem to meet MacCorquodale and Meehl's (1948) rules for an intervening variable. The statement of a DSM diagnosis is reducible to certain explicit rules, such as, at least five of eight diagnostic criteria must be present to assign the diagnosis. . . . However, the DSM label represents an intervening variable for a hypothetical construct whose meaning is not exhausted by a listing of the DSM criteria. Such a construct may include a network of implications about etiology, course, prognosis, treatment, and interrelations with other constructs that comprise meaning surplus to an enumeration of features listed in the DSM.
>
> If one grants this view of the DSM diagnosis as an intervening variable, then it follows that such an operational diagnosis is an in-

dicator of the hypothetical classificatory construct and is not the construct itself. The DSM diagnosis is thus itself a diagnostic instrument that ideally bears a connection to the hypothetical construct in some theoretical space. However, the DSM diagnosis is no more the essence of the construct than a test score is the essence of intelligence; rather, it is an operationalization of the concept, which may or may not be valid. For the purposes of classification research, the use of a DSM diagnosis as the sole criterion against which to validate other instruments (or even its own criteria; cf. Widiger et al., 1986) reifies the diagnosis, inappropriately transforming an intervening variable into a hypothetical construct. (Morey, 1991, pp. 289–290)

This lengthy quotation provides a brief and succinct application of the concepts of intervening variables and hypothetical constructs to the definition of psychopathology. Their relevance to Widiger's chapter may not be apparent at first glance. After all, he is not advocating the DSM definitions of depression or of personality. He speaks of the "depressive state"; he prefers the dimensional to the categorical (i.e., DSM) approach to personality; and he considers as suspect the use of expert clinicians to classify patients in DSM categories. On the other hand, as research coordinator for the forthcoming DSM-IV, he has applied conventional standards of empiricism to the selection, rejection, and revision of items that define the DSM categories. The DSM is empirical, and uses procedures appropriate to the definition of intervening variables. As Morey notes, its resultant categories are treated in clinical and research practice as hypothetical constructs. Widiger himself does not clearly make this error when discussing the DSM. However, in his present analysis of personality and depression, he fails to make an appropriate distinction between intervening variables and hypothetical constructs.

To understand these matters at a subjective level, the reader might ask himself or herself the following question:

Assume I accept the recommendation that personality should be defined as an independent variable in terms of dimensions derived from factor analysis. When I work with a patient's "personality," will I be willing to restrict my thoughts about the nature of the patient's problems to the operations that were used to generate the patient's scores on the seven-factor model? This means that my patients will be described in terms of these dimensions: well-being, social potency, achievement, social closeness, stress reaction, alienation, aggression, control, harm avoidance, traditionalism, absorption, positive affectivity, negative affectivity, and constraint. These descriptions of my patients must not be generalized beyond the items endorsed and the known attributes of the population used to norm the scores.

Such dimensional language is not readily accepted by clinicians, perhaps because it does not relate directly to accepted clinical theory or to typical psychosocial interventions. Even clinicians who are comfortable with this language are likely to want the dimensions to mean a lot more than scores on the test. Clinicians like to think of "things" that have an "existence" over and above the measures themselves. Both the dimensional (e.g., Tellegen's factors or the NEO factors) and categorical (e.g., DSM) definitions of personality must represent hypothetical constructs if they are to be useful clinically. This demand for generality may account for why the DSM categories are typically interpreted as hypothetical constructs even though, as Morey notes, they are actually intervening variables.

Proposition A, mentioned above, treats personality and depression as intervening variables. Their high degree of covariance suggests that BPD and mood disorder are overlapping concepts. On the other hand, if personality and depression are allowed to be hypothetical constructs, then we have the problem introduced by Proposition B. Depression may contaminate measurements of the independent construct, BPD. But if BPD really is a hypothetical construct, it can still be assessed under all conditions, depressed and otherwise. The hypothetical construct, BPD, should generate ideas about how the measures will differ in the depressed and not-depressed conditions. Any observed differences among conditions that are not consistent with the construct are valuable cues. Contradictions would suggest that the constructs BPD or depression need to be refined, and that further data need to be gathered.

If personality and depression are hypothetical constructs, then the patient's point of view is vital to their assessment. I believe that they are valid hypothetical constructs, and I would like to test a predisposing model. I expect that depression follows the patient's *perception* that he or she is helpless, trapped, blocked, overwhelmed, and without recourse. I also believe that depression is likely to be manifested when there is perceived loss of an attachment object, or when there is an event that enhances self-criticism. This view of depressive predispositions has been shaped by the hypotheses of Seligman (helplessness), Blatt (self-criticism), Beck (cognitive style), Bowlby (object loss), and others (e.g., Sullivan, Mischel). Some personalities are predisposed to have these perceptions ("helpless, alone, bad") and are therefore more likely to become depressed. Others are not predisposed in these ways, but they can still become depressed if they find themselves in situations that are harshly critical, that are overwhelming, or that involve the loss of someone or something deeply loved.

Measures of these predispositions toward helplessness, self-criticism, and sensitivity to object loss can be considered indices of aspects of "personality" that are relevant to depression. The affective depressive responses marked by DSM (weight loss, tearfulness, sleep disturbance, etc.) can be considered indicators of "depression." Both "personality" and "depression" are hypothetical constructs or entities that mean more than the measurements used to define them. This position requires that the investigator be able to think of any number of experiments that predict an association between depression and measures of helplessness, self-criticism, or object loss. Here are some examples of such predictions based on the predisposing model just described. A submissive personality will have more depressive episodes than a dominant personality. A submissive personality will become even more submissive when depressed. A self-critical person is more likely to become depressed (self-criticism is the introjective correlate of the position of resentful submission). Depressed people are more likely to be self-critical. A dominant personality subjected to situational stresses that preclude dominance is more likely to have an episode of depression. A dominant personality who is successful in maintaining dominance by social role and circumstance is less likely to have an episode. Persons sensitive to object loss are more likely to perceive rejection and to become depressed about it. If present, social withdrawal is a reaction to the depressive condition rather than a predisposing marker. Persons with BPD and with dependent, histrionic, and passive aggressive personality disorders are more likely to become depressed because they share the trait of dependency. Persons with BPD are also likely to become depressed over perceived object loss. Persons with avoidant personality disorder are vulnerable to depression because of their tendency to feel rejected and to be self-critical. Persons with narcissistic and obsessive compulsive personality disorders are vulnerable to depression because they are easily reduced to self-criticism if they are not in control and "perfect." By contrast, individuals with paranoid, antisocial, and schizoid personality disorders are resistant to depression. The reason is that they are comfortable with autonomy, and so they are neither sensitive to rejection nor dependent. Nor are they self-critical.

A person can feel helpless or self-critical or abandoned because of a predisposition, a reaction to overwhelming external circumstance, or some interaction between the two. The predisposition may be determined by genetics or experience or both. To separate the "broken brain" version of the predisposing model from the "environmentally programmed" version of the predisposing model, one would need to engage in very careful sequential analysis of the development of a person's view of himself or herself and the environment.

Etiology aside, the important point here is that if one accepts any version of the predisposing model (genetic, environmental, or an interaction of the two), one must assess the circumstances as they are seen by the patient. It is also true, as Widiger suggests, that assessments must be made longitudinally.

Because I think of depression and personality as hypothetical constructs, I would favor a logical rather than an empirical analysis of the four models (predisposing, complication, pathoplasty, and spectrum). Such an analysis could organize the contradictions and confusions of empiricism. It could guide investigators and reviewers toward a tolerant and enlightened respect for diversity of approach. If appropriately drawn, the resulting guidelines would leave investigators free to choose any of the four proposed models and still hold to the rules of good science. They would not be tied to the strict empiricism of the overlapping model. Alternative views could receive equal attention, provided that their proposed methods were reliable and valid and were logically consistent with the chosen rationale. Such diversity in approaches would be more likely to yield convincing convergence on truth about the relation between personality and depression.

Despite my objections to Widiger's apparent adherence to strict empiricism, I feel that his chapter is a useful summary of the methodological literature on personality and depression. It points out many important problems, and offers potential solutions from the empiricist's perspective. Investigators and reviewers would do well to carefully consider everything Widiger says. I have suggested ways that readers can go beyond his formulations.

## REFERENCES

MacCorquodale, K., & Meehl, P. (1951). Hypothetical constructs and intervening variables. In H. Feigl & K. Brodbeck (Eds.), *Readings in the philosophy of science*. New York: Basic Books.

Morey, L. (1991). Classification of mental disorder as a collection of hypothetical constructs. *Journal of Abnormal Psychology, 100,* 289–293.

Swartz, M., Blazer, D., George, L., Winfield, D., Zakris, J., & Dye, E. (1989). Identification of borderline personality disorder with the NIMH Diagnostic Interview Schedule. *American Journal of Psychiatry, 146,* 200–205.

Widiger, T. A., Frances, A., Warner, L., & Bluhm, C. (1986). Diagnostic criteria for the borderline and schizotypal personality disorders. *Journal of Abnormal Psychology, 95,* 43–51.

# Commentary

## ROBERT M. A. HIRSCHFELD
*University of Texas Medical Branch*

In his usual scholarly, cogent, and comprehensive fashion, Widiger has provided an overview of current knowledge on personality and depression, focusing on how assessment issues have helped—and have hindered—our understanding of this important relationship.

The study of personality has a long and rich history of theoretical contributions and empirical investigations. This applies also to depression and mood disorders. Personality *disorders* have much more recently become the subject of theory and research. Validational strategies that have been applied to Axis I disorders are being applied to personality disorders. These follow the model proposed by Robins and Guze (1970) for psychiatric disorders; the strategies include consistent and reliable clinical description, follow-up studies, laboratory studies that separate the disorder under investigation from other disorders, and family and genetic studies.

Unfortunately, the application of this model to personality disorders is constrained for several reasons. First, it is less clear what the syndromes are. There has been considerable agreement for a long time on the basic components of schizophrenia and depression. For depression, for example, dysphoria, decreased self-esteem, appetite and sleep disturbances, fatigue, and difficulty in concentrating are widely accepted as fundamental components of the syndrome. There is much less agreement about the components of personality disorders or of an individual personality disorder. Second, it is much less clear how the personality disorders relate to one another. Are they discrete, independent syndromes, or are there an infinite number of continually varying patterns? Third (and perhaps most importantly), should personality disorders be approached from a categorical model, as are other psychiatric disorders, or would a dimensional model be more applicable?

Although these questions are outside Widiger's purview, they are fundamental to assessment issues. Wisely, Widiger does not dodge them, but incorporates them into his thesis.

## WHAT IS IMPORTANT AND WHAT IS NOT IMPORTANT

Widiger identifies three key issues that are important in addressing assessment issues, and one issue that is not. The important issues include personality versus mood, personality disorders versus mood disorders, and temporal concerns. What is not important is the polarity of psychosocial versus biogenetic issues.

### Personality versus Mood

What effect do personality and mood have on each other? All too often people confuse one with the other. For example, irritability can be labeled a personality trait when it may be secondary to a psychiatric illness (such as hypomania), to a medical problem (such as hyperthyroidism), or to a transient life situation. On the other hand, it is sometimes difficult to distinguish between personality traits and mood states when the mood state is more chronic.

Widiger thoroughly discusses the importance of the effect of mood state on assessment of personality traits. This effect has been all but ignored by clinical theorists who have confused chronic depression with personality. They have then incorrectly made judgments about personality features that may have preceded the development of depression, and then compounded their error by implicating these features in the pathogenesis of depression. In fact, personality assessments made of people while they are depressed differ markedly from those made following full recovery from the depression (Hirschfeld et al., 1983). Therefore, it is very important that personality and mood state be carefully separated in research and in clinical practice.

### Personality Disorders versus Mood Disorders

Similarly, it is important to distinguish between personality disorders and mood disorders. The differences between personality traits and mood states parallels the difference between the personality disorders and the mood disorders. One strategy to address this issue is the "spectrum" notion, with personality and personality disorders on one end of the spectrum and mood disorders on the other.

Two spectrums have particular relevance for personality and depression. First, and by far the better known, is the bipolar spectrum. On this spectrum lie bipolar I disorder, bipolar II disorder, cyclothymia, and perhaps depressive temperament. This view was first described by Kraepelin and has been elaborated on by a number of theorists, including Schneider and Akiskal. According to this notion, the depressive temperament and perhaps cyclothymia are subclinical (or slightly clinical) manifestations of bipolar disorder.

A second spectrum encompasses only unipolar depression. One variant of this has been proposed by George Winokur, whose spectrum is defined by family history. "Depressive spectrum disease" is defined by  the presence of alcoholism and/or antisocial personality in first-degree relatives of patients with primary unipolar depression. Winokur characterizes these people as having an earlier age of onset of depression, female gender, personality problems and difficulties, lifelong irritability, and a more variable illness, with less likelihood of long periods of chronicity of depression.

Similar to Winokur's subtype is "character spectrum disorder," identified by Akiskal, King, Rosenthal, Robinson, and Scott-Strauss (1981). These individuals usually have antisocial features and irritable dysphoria. Many are substance abusers and have a family history of alcoholism or sociopathy. However, they have chronic characterological problems rather than a specific family history.

The disorder issue also involves the idea of a line between "normal" and "abnormal." The traditional nosological approach in psychiatry (and most of medicine, for that matter) has been categorical, and is reflected in the notions of "disorder." However, personality disorders may be approached from a dimensional rather than a categorical approach. Widiger discusses the special relevance of the dimensional approach for personality disorders.

Comorbidity among the personality disorders as they are currently defined is extremely high. Pfohl, Coryell, Zimmerman, and Stangl (1986) reported that over half of their patients with at least one personality disorder met criteria for at least one more, and sometimes up to four or five. Pfohl and colleagues reported that a similar high rate of multiple diagnoses has been confirmed by other investigators as well. One reason for this comorbidity may be that personality disorders are not distinct syndromes, but rather an infinite variety of abnormal personality constellations. If this is valid, then the next question is what the requisite personality dimensions are. Here there is little agreement.

Some favor dimensionalizing the existing 11 personality disorders, while others argue for a variety of other schemes. Among them is the so-called five-factor solution, which comes from meta-analysis (Costa & McCrae, 1990).

## Temporal Concerns

There are unique temporal concerns with regard to personality disorders. Most clinicians consider that personality disorders first manifest themselves in adolescence or early adulthood. By definition, personality disorders are long-lasting and presumably must always be there (i.e., they are not "episodic"). The symptomatology should be fairly constant. Such temporal requirements do not exist for other psychiatric disorders.

## Psychosocial versus Biogenetic Issues

Previous clinical theorists have emphasized the importance of early life experience in the development of schizophrenia, depression, and other psychiatric illnesses. Now much more is made of genetically determined proclivities and biogenetic approaches. Some clinicians believe that personality disorders are the only remaining psychiatric illnesses in which abnormal early life experiences contribute to the etiology and pathogenesis of the disorder. Thus, personality disorders are the last major "psychosocial" illnesses, and the last requiring psychotherapy.

Widiger articulately dismisses this line of reasoning. He documents that personality is, in part, clearly biogenetic. He argues that both psychosocial and biogenetic factors are important in the pathogenesis of most psychiatric illnesses, including personality disorders. Both psychotherapeutic and psychopharmacological approaches have utility in the treatment of personality disorders.

## METHODOLOGICAL ISSUES

The very nature of the composite criteria for personality disorders makes them especially difficult to assess. The features of these disorders are often ego-syntonic and often socially undesirable.

Many personality features are ego-syntonic, in that people regard these qualities as being integral parts of themselves, not as something alien and visited upon them. This is not true for most other psychiatric illnesses. For example, the grandiosity and associated behaviors of mania are experienced by an individual as "not the way I usually am" or "not me." Hallucinations are likewise regarded as somehow coming from outside and not part of oneself. These symptoms are usually of limited duration in terms of time. This is not so in personality disorders, in which the qualities may "always" have been there, but are regarded as part of one's personality.

Many of the criteria for personality disorders are socially undesirable. Examples include always wanting to be the center of attention, frequently lying, engaging in criminal behavior, being exploitative of other people, having an excessive and unjustified sense of entitlement, and having an exaggerated sense of self-worth. People possessing these qualities may not regard themselves as having them, and may even be affronted if others suggest that they do. Widiger suggests furthermore that these qualities may be unconscious, and therefore even less accessible for assessment.

Given the unique qualities of the criteria, how is it possible to ascertain them? Widiger discusses the use of direct questions, of informants, and of direct observation. Direct questions have become the standard in the field for assessment of Axis I conditions. Over the past several decades, semistructured and fully structured interviews have been developed for Axis I conditions. However, only recently have they been developed for personality disorders, and their validity is not yet established. Probes have been used to help improve validity; self-report inventories are also utilized.

Use of informants would at first blush seem ideal, because they are the recipients of the behaviors that characterize personality disorders. The problem is that informants themselves may have their own "axes to grind"; in addition, the perspective of many informants may be quite limited. For example, a spouse may be far from objective in his or her viewpoint, and, of course, may only interact with the individual in certain areas.

Direct observation has salient features. Types of direct observation include observation of individual and group experimental situations, naturalistic observations, and performance tests. Though each of these may be useful, none is easy; furthermore, each is limited in its generalizability.

## CONCLUSION

Widiger has overviewed cogently what we have learned about the relationship of personality and depression, with a particular focus on assessment. Many improvements in assessment have occurred, and a great deal of new research has resulted. Presently, the most vexing concern is the continuing lack of clarity about the nature of the conditions themselves. Continuing improvements and contributions in the assessment process will further our knowledge about the relationship between personality and depression.

# REFERENCES

Akiskal, H. S., King, D., Rosenthal, T. L., Robinson, D., & Scott-Strauss, A. (1981). Chronic depression: Part I. Clinical and familial characteristics in 137 probands. *Journal of Affective Disorders, 3,* 297–315.

Costa, P., & McCrae, R. (1990). Personality disorders in the five factor model of personality. *Journal of Personality Disorders, 4,* 362–371.

Hirschfeld, R. M. A., Klerman, G. L., Clayton, P. J., Keller, M. B., McDonald-Scott, P., & Larkin, B. H. (1983). Assessing personality: Effects of the depressive state on trait measure. *American Journal of Psychiatry, 140,*(6), 695–699.

Pfohl, B., Coryell, W., Zimmerman, M., & Stangl, D. (1986). DSM-III personality disorders: Diagnostic overlap and internal consistency of individual DSM-III criteria. *Comprehensive Psychiatry, 27,* 21–34.

Robins, E., & Guze, S. B. (1970). Establishment of diagnostic validity in psychiatric illness: Its application to schizophrenia. *American Journal of Psychiatry, 126,* 983–987.

CHAPTER THREE

# Personality and Depression: Modeling and Measurement Issues

BRIAN W. JUNKER
*Carnegie Mellon University*
PAUL A. PILKONIS
*University of Pittsburgh School of Medicine*
*Western Psychiatric Institute and Clinic*

## INTRODUCTION

In this chapter we offer suggestions about strategies for designing new studies on the relationships between personality and depression, as well as recommendations about the most promising techniques for analyzing the data from such ventures (e.g., potential applications of covariance structure analysis and other model-fitting procedures; the use of exploratory data analysis techniques). A basic issue that we address is the applicability and appropriate use of complex parametric models in this research area (and, by extension, to other areas of clinical research and social science where qualitative, descriptive models predominate).

Our recommendations tend to be conservative. In view of the assumptions and constraints of most multivariate, parametric approaches, it is clear that their use is often premature, given the measurement errors, sampling strategies (relying largely on convenience), and small sample sizes that characterize much clinical research. We see a larger need for first bolstering the foundation upon which such work rests by improving the state of the measurement art (through both exploratory and confirmatory approaches) and encouraging more applications of exploratory data analysis techniques.

The order of authorship is alphabetical.

## THEMES FROM THE EARLIER CHAPTERS

Present understandings of the possible relationships between personality and depression raise more questions than they resolve. In an attempt, however, to identify and integrate the most salient themes from Klein, Wonderlich, and Shea's (Chapter One, this volume) discussion of theory and models, and Widiger's (Chapter Two, this volume) discussion of assessment, we draw four conclusions:

1. A number of descriptive, qualitative accounts of relationships between personality and depression currently exist, and Klein et al. have organized them into a single, superordinate framework at the end of their chapter. This effort is valuable for illustrative purposes, and it provides an example of the use of path diagrams as convenient visual tools, apart from any formal statistical analyses with which they may be associated. The size and complexity of the model, however, quickly become uncomfortable even for heuristic purposes. There is more complexity than we can easily tolerate, either empirically or conceptually.

There appear to be three basic families of models within the larger structure: direct causal models (predisposition or complication hypotheses), in which one domain (personality or depression) accounts for the other; underlying "third-variable" models (spectrum or subclinical hypotheses), in which some predisposition or higher-order variable accounts for both personality disorder and depression; and orthogonal models (pathoplasty or comorbidity hypotheses), in which the two constructs are assumed to be causally independent but do influence each other's manifest characteristics because of their joint probabilities.

Even with this attempt at simplification, there is considerable conceptual overlap among the models and submodels, and it is often difficult to see how they can be distinguished empirically (which perhaps suggests that such distinctions are more apparent than real). The complexity and inclusiveness of the final model also belie the fact that it lacks strong individual components to account for etiology or pathogenesis. We have many good candidates for inclusion as causal factors (on theoretical or common-sense grounds), but few good reasons for exclusion; this suggests that our current models are "weak" ones, or at least that they lack a simple, "deep" structure. Unfortunately, in the domain of model building more is not always better, and we believe that the soundest empirical strategy is to begin with a relatively small piece of the model, to operationalize it satisfactorily (no minor feat itself), and only then to map linkages among separate parts of the model.

2. Widiger makes it clear in his discussion of assessment that there is little current consensus about how to tackle the confounding and

complexities that arise in operationalizing mood (state) and personality (trait) constructs, or even about the best methods (interviews vs. self-reports vs. informant ratings; direct vs. "indirect" measures; observational studies) with which to attempt this. There have been a number of initial explorations of these problems, and our own belief is that the lack of consensus creates a need to focus on fairly broad constructs that are stable and well standardized (through the use of large samples and a common core of assessment tools). Individual, exploratory approaches should yield to broader efforts at cross-validation and confirmatory approaches to measurement problems, with all of this being a necessary first step to more extensive use of structural models (i.e., models that explore relationships between constructs, using either manifest or latent variables).

We follow Hoyle's (1991) conventions in defining different types of models: "Measurement" models examine relationships among within-construct indicators, whereas "structural" models elucidate between-construct relationships, with either manifest variables ("path" models) or latent variables. The general point is that in psychiatric research, we need better measurement before we can rise to the challenge of combined measurement *and* structural models. Better measurement can accommodate both (latent) method variables and (latent) content variables (see the discussion of multitrait–multimethod approaches, below).

3. One theme that runs through both earlier chapters is the need for longitudinal studies, a recommendation that we also endorse. Important prerequisites for the field (before we engage in premature elaboration of structural models) are good studies of "natural history"—that is, closer examinations of the phenomena of personality and depression as they unfold developmentally. Many plausible models of the relationship between the two are available, but as the complexity and inclusiveness of such models increase, there is heightened danger of reifying the models (i.e., of focusing more on the models than on the people or phenomena observed). We emphasize the need to stay close to the clinical phenomena of primary interest, and longitudinal studies provide an excellent vehicle in this regard. They can also serve the purpose of improving measurement. Alternative techniques and instruments can be used, and their reliability, stability, and utility can be examined over time.

4. Klein et al. and Widiger try to be as inclusive as possible in their reviews, consistent with the goals of their chapters. Such surveys illustrate the diversity that exists in this area, but our own review of newer tools available for data analysis (e.g., covariance structure analysis in its various forms) makes it clear that little progress can be made in the

broader application of such techniques (if one insists on this) without the use of larger samples (see our discussion below of recommendations for minimum sample sizes), aggregation of data if single samples are too small, and the use of common assessment measures that make aggregation possible. Diversity of clinical and measurement methodologies at the level of individual investigators may enhance committed, "small-scale" science, but it is not compatible with the use of complex parametric models in most clinical research. This tension between the interests of separate, autonomous researchers and the possible uses of large-sample, parametric techniques within the field as a whole has implications for the feasibility and acceptability of any specific recommendations we can make about implementation of newer data-analytic techniques.

In this chapter, our major focus is on modeling and statistical tools that aid the modeling process. Although we do not treat data collection and clinical research strategies in detail, these issues are obviously important. Kraemer (1981) and Kraemer and Thiemann (1989) provide excellent recommendations for research strategies. Rosnow and Rosenthal (1989) and Cohen (1990) offer additional insights on the application of statistical methodology to questions in clinical research. Such advice is useful to turn to when, for example, limited sample sizes or other constraints preclude the use of some of the less robust approaches we consider below.

## BASIC MODELING AND MEASUREMENT ISSUES

### Science and Models

To give context to our discussion, it is useful to draw some contrasts between the types of models that practicing scientists employ, as well as between the varying usages of the word "model" in statistics and science. In this account, we rely heavily on the excellent discussion of Lehmann (1990).

Many statisticians (Cox, 1990; Lehmann, 1990; Nelder, 1986) distinguish between at least two types of (quantitative) models and modeling activity. On the one hand are "interpolary," "empirical," or "technological" models, which are used to smooth away excessive detail (including noise) in data to reveal important patterns or to provide extrapolations to guide future action and expectations. On the other hand are "explanatory," "theoretical," or "scientific" models, which "embody the search for the basic mechanism underlying the process being studied; they constitute an effort to achieve *understanding*" (Lehmann, 1990, p. 163; emphasis in original).

Of course, most models possess features of both empiricism and explanation. (Lehmann reports a proposal—only partly fanciful—by Kruskal and Neyman [1956] of a scale running from purely empirical models at 0 to purely explanatory models at 10. It may be of interest to the present reader that Kruskal and Neyman assigned to exploratory factor analysis a score of 4 on this scale!) The classification of a model as empirical or explanatory depends as much upon its anticipated use and anticipated criteria of acceptance as on the particular nature of the model itself. Lehmann's comments on the validation of the two extreme model types are especially interesting:

> The difference in the aims and nature of these two types of models implies very different attitudes toward checking their validity. Techniques such as goodness of fit tests or cross validation serve the needs of checking an empirical model by determining whether the model provides an adequate fit for the data. *Many different models could pass such a test, which reflects the fact that there is not a unique correct empirical model.* On the other hand, ideally there is only one model which at the given level of abstraction and generality describes the mechanism or process in question. To check its accuracy requires identification of the details of the model and their functions and interrelations with the corresponding details of the real situation. And the explanation must provide a detailed fit not only for the phenomenon at hand but must also fit appropriately into the existing scientific fabric of related phenomena in which it is to become embedded. (1990, pp. 164–165; emphasis added)

Note that traditional confirmatory statistical issues—specifying a family of parametric models; estimating (selecting) a model from the family; and accounting for the uncertainty of parameter estimates, inferences, and decisions—really are in the domain of validating technological models. It is for this reason that Nelder (1986) is inclined to place statistical methods within the domain of Kuhn's (1970) "normal science" (where scientists act as technicians, refining and improving concepts and measurements), but not at the cusps of scientific revolutions (where new bodies of theory supplant old ones). Good (1983) is more blunt: "Statistics as a whole is more concerned with superficial structure than with deep structure. To discover deep structure in a science usually requires much familiarity with that science" (p. 288).

It is useful to contemplate the two principal aims of statistical modeling in psychiatry in this light. On the one hand are measurement models. These models, all variants of factor-analytic or latent-variable approaches, serve two important technological purposes. First, they smooth away noise, allowing us to quantify a latent construct that is supposed to underlie several indicator or response variables. Second,

used in a careful confirmatory fashion, they can suggest parsimonious
ways to cluster observable variables, based on the first (and higher-
order) factors upon which they depend. On the other hand are structural models, ranging from covariance structure models (which relate
latent and observed variables to one another) to standard regression or
contingency table models (which only relate observable variables to one
another). Again, when used in a careful confirmatory fashion, the
results suggest parsimonious ways to represent associations between
and among variables.

The neither of the techniques is good at constructing "deep" theory for
psychiatric research (or any other kind of research). Technically, the size
of the models that these techniques can handle is quite modest, and the
sample sizes needed to estimate and draw inferences from even small
models are rather larger than the 20 to 100 subjects that might be
expected in a typical clinical setting. Philosophically, these models share
with other statistical approaches the limitation that they can only reveal
goodness of fit with the associational features of data; they cannot
reveal, in principle, anything about causal relationships or the accuracy
of theoretical constructs. The latter must be inferred from assumptions
and reasoning within the scientific domain, not the statistical domain
(see the comments of Hoyle, 1991, or more generally those of Holland,
1986).

## Definition and Measurement of Constructs

In our view, research in personality and mood often suffers from inadequate definition of constructs, inadequate methods for measuring
them, and inadequate validation of measuring instruments. The detail of
many construct taxonomies—such as the summary model proposed by
Klein et al. in Chapter One, or the current revision of the *Diagnostic and
Statistical Manual of Mental Disorders* (DSM-III-R; American Psychiatric
Association, 1987)—is too great to allow for even a clear conceptual
differentiation, let alone careful corroboration or falsification from data.

The current milieu in which quantitative psychiatric research is
done is both too fragmented and too fluid to provide the firm measurement foundation that is needed. Taxonomies of personality and depressive disorders are too finely detailed (i.e., have too many parameters), given the sizes of the data sets with which we work, to offer any
real opportunity to assess their validity with data. Instead, the taxonomies provide names of phenomena that may or may not be distinct and
may or may not be linked to fundamental aspects of mood and personality. The fact that there are probably too many "names" can lead
easily to two kinds of nominalistic fallacies: (1) We may apply names

invalidly (i.e., reify a nonexistent phenomenon by repeatedly referring to a name); or (2) we may label valid phenomena with the "wrong" name, given that there are so many labels in the current research lexicon (see Cliff, 1983).

Moreover, detailed "public" taxonomies such as the DSM have been subject to frequent nontrivial revision, in part because the conception of constructs at this level of detail is not stable over time. One result of this instability is the disincentives it creates to spend time carefully designing operational measures of the constructs in the nomenclature. More generally, this instability is symptomatic of a lack of grounding in reliable and valid observable measures. There is no "gold standard" of constructs, let alone gold standards of measurement for those constructs.

Fundamental measurement issues—from practical "survey-style" issues, such as the impact of item wording and item order on responses to self-report and other rating forms, to basic technical issues, such as the impact of reliability and validity of operational measures of latent constructs on classification error rates—must be addressed before we can arrive at a clear understanding of what is being measured and how well. Careful pursuit of basic measurement issues can help in clearly defining constructs in the theory of personality and depression; without clear definitions and reliable measurement instruments, we really have no way of knowing what we are achieving when we attempt to model the interaction of one construct with another.

Pursuing basic measurement questions is generally more difficult, time-consuming, and data-intensive than performing omnibus tests of model fit, but it will ultimately be more rewarding: These more basic questions must be answered before trustworthy quantitative models of the complex interactions between personality and mood can be constructed. This is not to say that there is no place for structural models in current psychiatric research, but we see a continued need to focus on good measurement (within-construct modeling) before detailed structure (between-construct modeling) can be tackled. We also share with Diaconis (1985) the opinion that good exploratory methods will go further at this stage of theoretical development.

A direction worth pursuing is the development of measures of fairly gross constructs that are stable, well standardized, and comprehensible in unidimensional terms. Learning from work in educational testing may be valuable in this regard. In many forms of educational measurement, there is an effort to keep constructs relatively broad. Thus there are tests of "quantitative reasoning" or "mathematics skills," and although researchers will argue about the relative contributions of trigonometry and algebra items, the general goal is to measure mathematical aptitude and achievement. Also, the questions on such tests tap many "minor dimensions," but they cluster together to produce a gross scale that is essentially unidimensional (see Stout, 1990, for a technical discussion) and sensitive to variation along a general dimension (e.g., "quantitative reasoning").

This approach affects both the analysis and construction of psychological questionnaires and tests. Humphreys (1982, 1986), for example, has encouraged the construction of tests that measure

> one major or dominant dimension, but [in which] numerous small factors representing the nonerror noise intrinsic to behavioral measurement of psychologically important traits also contribute to total variance. Very broad tests can be constructed as long as each item shares some of the common attribute and as long as the systematic noise is widely scattered. (1982, p. 1)

This approach has influenced modern thinking on measurement models that "pay" for the presence of a single dominant dimension by allowing weakly specified conditional dependence among items, given a latent trait (Gibbons, Bock, & Hedeker, 1989; McDonald, 1981; Stout, 1987, 1990). It has also influenced current considerations of test construction and the influence of minor dimensions on model fit and inference when unidimensional item response models are used (Drasgow & Parsons, 1983; Harrison, 1986; Reckase, 1979; Reckase, Ackerman, & Carlson, 1988; Roznowski & Reith, 1991; Yen, 1980, 1984).

Another contrast between educational and psychiatric measurement is that in the former area, the samples studied vary over the the entire spectrum of the construct being measured. For example, math tests are not given only to people who do poorly in mathematics. This approach means (1) that sample sizes are more reasonable and (2) that the investigator is obligated to think about a model for "normals" or for "good" behavior, in addition to "deficient" or "disordered" behavior. Data collection in more varied samples, although difficult, also enables us to gauge the prevalence of disorders in different populations more accurately, and provides access to groups not subject to the biases associated with self-selection for treatment.

## Reliability

After constructs have been defined in a theoretically meaningful way and at a level of generality that suits the phenomena under investigation, the next task is a scrupulous assessment of reliability. A complete discussion of reliability theory (see Cronbach, Gleser, Nanda, & Rajaratnam, 1972) and specific types of reliability (e.g., internal-consistency, split-half, test–retest) is beyond our scope here. In general, however, two kinds of reliability will be most important in the area of personality and depression, depending in part on the method used to collect the data. The first is internal-consistency reliability (most relevant for self-reports from patients and informants), and the second is interrater reliability (of greatest importance when clinical ratings are derived from interviews or as general summary measures; the analogue with self-report measures is test–retest reliability over short intervals, where patients act as their own "control" raters). Paying close attention to reliability is always time well spent because of what it tells us about important "operating characteristics" of our measures. Also, given the constraints placed on sample sizes in clinical research (usually for reasons of feasibility and limited access to patients), the most effective way to increase power and disattenuate effect sizes is to reduce measurement error by improving reliability (see Kraemer, 1981; Kraemer & Thiemann, 1989).

## Internal-Consistency Reliability

The goal in assessing internal-consistency reliability is to arrive at measurement instruments that are unidimensional or nearly so. Although there are models for measuring more than one construct at once, the usual approach is to try to achieve unidimensional measurement and to treat deviations from unidimensionality as interesting manifestations of secondary dimensions (see our discussion of educational measurement, above). Lack of unidimensionality can also lead to hierarchical models combining first- and higher-order factors, but the more general point remains: to try to measure one thing at a time and to measure it well.

## Interrater Reliability

Very useful discussions of methods for assessing interrater reliability are provided by Fleiss for both continuous measures (1986) and categorical measures (1981). He also stresses the general point that we have been making: "The most elegant design of a clinical study will not overcome the damage caused by unreliable or imprecise measurement. . . . Larger sample sizes than otherwise necessary, biased estimates, and even biased samples are some of the untoward consequences of unreliable measurement" (1986, p. 1).

By their very nature, some clinical constructs are elusive and in-ferential, requiring considerable abstraction and complex "pattern recognition" on the part of raters. Such constructs may impose limits on interrater reliability, but may still be valid and important to investigate. For example, in our own work on Axis II assessment and adult attach-ment styles, we find that reliabilities (intraclass correlations) for ratings of adult attachment prototypes tend to be in the .50 to .70 range—adequate but not outstanding. At the same time, these constructs appear to be of some clinical and theoretical importance (Pilkonis, Heape, Proietti, & Smith, 1991).

This situation requires us to improve reliability in order to give additional empirical weight to our work, but not at the cost of sacrificing validity. We have found that the most effective way to do this is to add replicate raters to enhance reliability, although there are costs attached in terms of clinician training and time (Tsujimoto, Hamilton, & Berger, 1990). Fleiss (1986, pp. 24–26) demonstrates mathematically the im-pact of this approach. For example, among a panel of judges whose overall reliability (intraclass correlation) is .50, the average of any three judges from the total pool will boost reliability to .75. To improve reliability from .60 to .75 requires two judges, whereas an improvement from .40 to .75 requires five judges. Regardless of the strategy chosen, such calculations make it possible to assess the pros and cons of different approaches to enhancing reliability (e.g., more intensive training of a small group of judges vs. use of replicate ratings from a larger pool in which moderate but not superb reliability can be established).

## Validity

Validity—the extent to which a model or measurement taps the in-tended substantive construct or research question—is a particularly difficult issue, since it is only partly determined by quantitative or statistical evidence; much of the burden of establishing adequate valid-ity falls on the careful thinking of the investigator. In our discussion, we rely upon the useful general survey of validity in behavioral research provided by Rosenthal and Rosnow (1984, pp. 75–86) and the discus-sion of validity focusing on psychological testing provided by Anastasi (1988, pp. 139–201). The reader may also be interested in the extended technical discussions of validity and reliability given by Messick (1989) and Feldt and Brennan (1989). Three measurement specialists—Angoff, Cronbach, and Messick—offer interesting perspectives on the evolution of validity, from numerical measures of criterion validity in the 1950s to the modern focus on construct and content validity, in the first three chapters of the anthology on test validity edited by Wainer and Braun (1988).

In psychiatric research, as in other behavioral research, the focus must be upon the validity not only of the measurements themselves but also of the research design, inferences, and other uses to which the scientific investigation is put. Thus one must be concerned with such issues as statistical validity (do the observed variables covary?), internal validity (is there a justifiable relationship between the variables?), external validity (does the relationship generalize?), and inferential validity (is the relationship free of confounding?). We are all aware that one must guard against threats to validity throughout a research project, but this need for vigilance deserves special emphasis. Lack of validity leaves one vulnerable to poor reliability (e.g., classical test theory's truism that validity is a lower bound to reliability; Lord & Novick, 1968, p. 72), and poor reliability can undermine statistical significance. Even if reliability is maintained and statistically significant results emerge, however, they are meaningless if they do not reflect differences that are valid and relevant for the constructs and research questions of interest.

In keeping with our theme that a major contribution can be made to quantitative psychiatric research by improving the state of the measurement art itself, we turn now to test validity: the extent to which a test, questionnaire, or inventory measures what it is purported to measure. An important, objective requirement is that the measurement instrument exhibit some sort of predictive, concurrent, or postdictive validity—in other words, that the measurements predict or covary with a future, current, or past external measure of the construct assumed to be measured. In the small, sometimes narrowly defined clinical samples with which psychiatric researchers are likely to work, one can probably only expect good validity with respect to fairly gross external criteria, and this gross level of validity must be kept in mind when evaluating the success or failure of substantive models or when making inferences from them.

In some of our own work, for example, we have been exploring the validity of the Inventory of Interpersonal Problems (IIP; Horowitz, Rosenberg, Baer, Ureño, & Villaseñor, 1988), using consensus clinical diagnoses and Personality Assessment Form (PAF; Shea, Glass, Pilkonis, Watkins, & Docherty, 1987) scores as concurrent criteria, with an eye toward more efficient screening of Axis II disorders. Our initial analyses indicate that IIP scores can be indicative of the general level of personality dysfunction, but our further attempts to refine classifications have not led to clusters or subscales that are very much like those in the psychometric literature on the IIP (Horowitz et al., 1988). For whatever reason—perhaps limited sample size (less than 100 at present), or lack of sufficient variability in our clinical sample (which consists of rather impaired patients in secondary- and tertiary-care settings)—general dysfunction seems to dominate other features of the personality disorder.

The general lesson for research practice is clear: It is necessary but not sufficient to rely upon published validity studies, factor analyses, or other psychometric analyses, even for a well-established instrument. Validity (or lack of it) is a consequence of both the measurement instrument and the context in which it is used. Especially in psychiatric research, this context changes greatly from study to study (and from baseline analysis of an instrument to an "operational study" that uses the instrument); therefore, validity should be assessed anew for each application. To paraphrase Anastasi (1988, p. 165), users must not only consult existing validity data in coming to a tentative judgment about whether a rating scale or other instrument measures constructs that are relevant to a research project; they must also check the validity of the instrument in the context in which it will be used.

A useful quantitative tool in assessing construct validity is the multitrait—multimethod (MTMM) design (Campbell & Fiske, 1959). One or more traits are measured by one or more methods (e.g., self-report, clinical interview), and the covariances of the resulting scores are analyzed. If different tests purporting to measure the same construct covary highly, this result provides evidence of convergent validity; lack of association between tests purporting to measure different traits is evidence of discriminant validity. To supplement the necessary hard thinking about content and other qualitative aspects of construct validity, measures of convergent and discriminant validity are quite helpful.

Cole (1987) makes a cogent argument that when the number of cases with no missing data is sufficiently large (100 subjects at an absolute minimum), confirmatory factor analysis is a logical and useful tool for analyzing MTMM designs (an idea that goes back at least to Jöreskog, 1969). After fitting a model with separate factors for traits and methods (and specified zero loadings to keep them separate), convergent validity is indicated by large loadings on common trait factors and discriminant validity by low correlations between trait factors not shared by different measurement instruments.

## Confirmatory Approaches to Measurement

There are many potential pitfalls to the use of modeling in clinical research (see our discussion below of general problems), but one major advantage is that modeling (both measurement and structural modeling) is confirmatory. Thus, it must be theory-driven, and the hard thinking required to develop even simple models and theories serves important heuristic functions. In the course of such thinking, it quickly becomes obvious that it is not sufficient or practical to throw everything but the kitchen sink into some measurement "soup" and then to try, after the fact, to make good conceptual sense of what emerges. Careful thought must be given both to the conceptual definition of the (latent) constructs being investigated and to the selection of the manifest indicators best reflecting them. Being compelled to make such choices may be the major benefit of structural modeling approaches, although one hopes that this kind of thinking goes on at all stages of investigation and data analysis.

Our general emphasis on the need to focus currently on measurement questions is consistent with Anderson and Gerbing's (1988) recommendations for a "two-step" approach to structural modeling. They propose a progression from exploratory factor analysis to more restrictive, confirmatory analysis (using maximum likelihood or generalized least-squares factoring) to respecification of measurement models, which are then cross-validated with new data in an iterative process. Anderson and Gerbing assert the value of careful estimation and respecification of measurement models before any attempts are made at simultaneous estimation of measurement and structural submodels; they point out that such a two-step approach can help prevent the confounding that occurs when one is unable to distinguish inadequacies of the measurement components from inadequacies of the structural components in one's model.

This seems to us to be good advice, especially since a more informed empirical view of what we are actually measuring and which indicators of our constructs are performing in ways consistent with our expectations is probably the most helpful tool in improving our models. On the one hand, there is the need for a stable theoretical framework on which constructs of personality and depression can be made to depend. On the other hand, it is clear that developing such a stable framework requires valid, reliable measures of these constructs. The theory must already be in place to define the constructs, and the constructs must already be well conceived and well measured to establish the theory. This is the "paradox of conceptualization" identified by Kaplan (1964) and discussed by Jones (1984) in a thoughtful article:

> Every taxonomy is a provisional and implicit theory (or family of theories). As knowledge of a particular subject matter grows, our conception of that subject matter changes; as our concepts become more fitting, we learn more and more. Like all existential dilemmas in science, of which this is an instance, the paradox is resolved by a

process of approximation: the better our concepts, the better the theory
we can formulate with them, and in turn, the better the concepts
available for the next, improved theory. (Kaplan, 1964, p. 24)

The alternation between empiricist exploration and model development on the one hand, and the use of existing models to better understand empirical results on the other, is present whenever science and
statistics meet (Box, 1980). There is an advantage, however, to a frankly
exploratory approach when the fundamental constructs and concepts of
a field are still quite fluid (Diaconis, 1985). Given the relative "weak-
ness" (etiological "shallowness") of psychiatric theories, we think that
the development of better empirical constructs is the appropriate pole of
this dialectical process to emphasize at present.

## METHODOLOGICAL ISSUES

### Covariance Structure Analysis

All of the linear latent-variable models currently in use—factor analysis,
linear structural-equations models, path models—fall under the general
rubric of "covariance structure analysis" (CSA). All have some potential
for expressing complex relationships among latent constructs measured
with multiple overt (observable) indicators. As currently practiced, these
methods are confirmatory; one must develop a model, no matter how
preliminary, against which to test the fit of a data set. The very process of
doing this in an a priori way can be enormously revealing, especially
about parts of one's model that have previously been implicit or poorly
articulated. There is no substitute for good, clear thinking, and when
properly used, these modeling strategies promote such clarity.

We do not underestimate this advantage, but our own view of
detailed modeling based upon CSA is cautionary at best. We are concerned, for example, with the extent to which the technology of linear
structural-equations models overshadows and undermines their suggestive power. Also, much of the rhetoric that has surrounded these models
in the past, including the use of the name "causal modeling," encourages one to think of CSA as a means of generating deep, scientific
models rather than the empirical, technological models it does provide.
Every parametric statistical technique places its users between the un-
welcome extremes of focusing on technical aspects of the model, fitting,
and distributional assumptions (thereby losing sight of the scientific
modeling process), and blindly using of the technique without regard to
distributional assumptions, formal convergence criteria, and so on (un-

dermining inferences made from fitting the model). In our view, a successful modeling technique allows the investigator to "live between" these extremes, presenting some very obvious and important modeling assumptions that must be checked before the technique can be used and possessing some robustness against violations of more subtle assumptions that the investigator may not be able to check.

Despite its name, confirmatory structural-equations modeling should be thought of as a largely exploratory technique. The confirmatory part of the process does mean that one must specify models in advance and that there is a level of confirmation possible. But in principle, the models are not expected to fit well—they are "best regarded as approximations to reality rather than as exact statements of truth" (Cudeck & Browne, 1983, p. 147)—and in practice, the initial specification and fitting of a model is followed by a series of post hoc model modification experiments. In this sense, the practice of fitting structural-equations models is much like an exploratory stepwise regression.

In addition, the full CSA model—with a measurement part and a structural part—is fairly complicated, which places the user far from the data. Given such complications, the question of what constitutes a "comfortable" level of complexity arises. When the CSA model applies, this is a technical issue: overfitting versus underfitting (see Bentler & Chou, 1987). But conceptually, the issue raises questions about how much complexity any of us human information processors can tolerate. When science is "weak" and one takes a "top-down" approach, models tend to be overly inclusive, incorporating many plausible influences because no one or two of them stands out as definitive. Rubin (1988) makes the important point that complex parametric models can be useful in finding out what might be going on with the data, but that these approaches should be accompanied by more down-to-earth analyses that make it obvious what relationships exist among the observed variables.

A related point is that there is always a conflict between the use of CSA and sample size considerations. When the sample size is too small, traditional likelihood-ratio measures of fit tend not to follow the correct chi-squared distributions under the null hypothesis (Bentler & Chou, 1987); when the sample size is larger, the (now correctly distributed) chi-squared statistics tend to consistently reject tractable models that can only approximate reality (Cudeck & Browne, 1983). A large technical literature is now devoted to ad hoc measures of model fit that try to circumvent these problems (Mulaik et al., 1989).

Most difficulty in clincial research, however, is likely to occur because sample sizes are too small for adequate CSA. Measurement models, using standard confirmatory factor-analytic techniques that assume joint normality of variables, require 100–150 subjects for models with up to three factors (Anderson & Gerbing, 1988; Cole, 1987). Cases with missing variables present additional difficulties: Anything but the simplest explanation for the missing cases ("missing completely at random," or MCAR) leads to additional complexities in fitting the CSA model (e.g., Kaplan, 1990), and the MCAR explanation itself requires that the offending cases be deleted completely from the analysis, exacerbating sample size problems.

Small CSA models with both a measurement part and a structural part require even larger samples: 200 subjects at minimum to identify paths correctly (Spirtes, Glymour, & Scheines, 1991, Ch. 11), and perhaps 300 subjects to get reasonably good parameter estimates (Tanaka, 1987). More robust measurement models (using "asymptotically distribution-free" methods) require 400–500 subjects at an absolute minimum (Anderson & Gerbing, 1988). Measurement models relating discrete responses to a small number of continuous latent factors (item response theory models) require at least 1,000 subjects for a probit model with up to four factors (Mislevy, 1986; Muthe'n, 1989) and perhaps as few as 500 subjects for a single-factor logit model (Duncan-Jones, Grayson, & Moran, 1986). After reviewing the literature on sample size considerations for structural-equations models, Bentler and Chou (1987) give the following rule of thumb:

> [For stable parameter estimates,] the ratio of sample size to number of free parameters may be able to go as low as 5 : 1 under normal and elliptical theory, especially when there are many indicators of latent variables and the associated factor loadings are large. Although there is even less experience on which to base a recommendation, a ratio of 10 : 1 may be more appropriate for arbitrary distributions. These ratios need to be larger to obtain trustworthy $z$-tests on the significance of parameters, and still larger to yield correct model evaluation chi-square probabilities. (pp. 90–91)

CSA was developed from classical multivariate-normal linear models and errors-in-variables models. Although CSA has been extended to handle some deviations from normality assumptions, the theory on which CSA is based is still rather restrictive and largely difficult to check; moreover, structural-equations models with latent variables are rather more sensitive to violations of these assumptions, so that the user who does not worry about the assumptions runs a greater risk of incorrect conclusions.

Owing to its "normal theory" heritage—and to problems of calculation complexity—most CSA analyzes only sample means and covariances of observed variables. Although it is possible in principle to examine residuals from the model in the original observed variables, this seems to be an uncommon practice; instead, the residuals that are examined are those between the sample and fitted covariance matrices (e.g., Sörbom, 1991). Although this method may be successful for identifying gross model misfit, it is difficult to interpret covariance matrix residuals more carefully, because they are necessarily dependent. In addition, examining the covariance matrices alone does not aid or encourage identification of outliers; for this purpose, looking at plots of the original variables seems to be the only recourse. Miller (1986, pp. 220–234) provides an enlightening discussion of estimation and diagnostics for simple linear structural-equations models with latent variables (errors-in-variables models). A more complete theoretical discussion is given by Leamer (1978, Ch. 7). Biddle and Marlin (1987) provide some interesting practical comparisons between structural-equations models and common linear regression, and suggestions for when each is appropriate.

Many models, especially when the number of parameters is large, may fit the data to about the same degree. As Cliff (1983) points out in a thoughtful critique, "the very form of the equations underlying LISREL *guarantees* that in virtually every application there are an infinity of models that will fit the data equally well" (p. 118; emphasis in original). Breckler (1990) provides some details on equivalent and nearly equivalent CSA models. Failure to reject a particular model means that none of these equivalent models is disconfirmed either; hence, any of these with substantive merit must be considered (from a theoretical, not a statistical, view) by the researcher (Cliff, 1983). Many authors are already sensitive to this issue, but it does create problems for the unsophisticated use of CSA. The most accurate position may be that of Rogosa (1979): The main benefit of structural-equations modeling is that it helps one to exclude models that the data cannot support.

Direct comparisons can be made of nested models—that is, models ordered so that each one is a special case of the next. It should be incumbent on the investigator to attempt to fit more than a single model, in order to examine the plausibility of the preferred one. Anderson and Gerbing (1988) suggest comparing five nested structures: the null model, where the variables of interest are assumed to be independent; the fully saturated model, where all possible paths among the variables are assumed to be important; the theoretical model of interest; and the next most likely constrained and unconstrained alternatives to the theoretical favorite. Cudeck and Browne (1983) give a more complete discussion of this approach. In many applications, it will be possible (unfortunately) to find that all the theoretically plausible alternatives fit the data to a similar extent, limiting one's ability to make definitive claims.

Comparing non-nested models is also important, especially because they are a common outcome of CSA applications. Indeed, the standard CSA computer packages such as LISREL and EQS offer model modification suggestions as features, and at least one line of research (Glymour, Scheines, Spirtes, & Kelly, 1987) has led to a computer program (TET-RAD II) and other algorithms whose purpose is to generate a menu of statistically plausible path models (without estimating path coefficients) by looking at the raw multivariate data. These aids to model modification are certainly necessary for fitting complex models to data; it is unlikely that a researcher will "get it right" on the first try with linear structural-equations models. However, the respecified models tend not to be nested, invalidating traditional likelihood-ratio measures of fit. Alternatives include the Akaike information criterion and the Schwartz criterion for model fit, as well as cross-validation. Cudeck and Browne (1983) describe all three in the CSA context.

Indeed, cross-validation on a fresh batch of data should be part of every analysis. Cross-validation mean-square error, for example, provides an important check of the predictive power of the (theoretical or statistical) model. In the case of nested models, cross-validation offers an alternative to likelihood ratios and other fit indices whose distributions are not known. In the case of non-nested models, cross-validation criteria are generally easy to interpret. Anderson and Gerbing (1988), Breckler (1990), and Cudeck and Browne (1983) all offer useful advice on cross-validation techniques.

Often it is difficult to find more subjects to "spend" on cross-validation. In this case, "bootstrap" and "jackknife" techniques are helpful. Efron and Gong (1983) provide an interesting example in which the exploratory model-fitting process is replicated many times on rerandomized versions of the original data set ("bootstrapping the exploration," as Diaconis, 1985, calls it). Such a procedure, although time-consuming, encourages careful thought about the formal and informal aspects of model fitting and provides a quantitative cross-check of the validity of the model-fitting process itself (rather than just the "final model" that results).

All of these issues can be addressed—making CSA a useful tool—when enough data can be collected so that the researcher can comfortably divide a sample into a "model-fitting" set and a "cross-validation" set. But with typical clinical psychiatric research, sample sizes tend to be quite small, and the constructs tend to be further from the measurable variables. Moreover, if one wishes to reserve some of the sample for cross-validation, the sample sizes recommended above must be roughly doubled.

The reader is now painfully aware that structural-equations modeling, when done properly, is data-intensive (and therefore expensive in terms of clinician time and effort and patient involvement). The need for large samples and cross-validation (which often exceeds the resources of any individual investigator) leads to two recommendations for the field as a whole: (1) Consider the use of common "core" assessment instruments in any state-of-the-art study (cf. Kupfer & Rush's [1983] recommendations for studies of depression), and (2) pursue the potential advantages of aggregating data across centers. Where possible, we believe that individual researchers should administer a core battery of standardized measurement instruments (in addition to unique measures required for the particular study at hand); should make very clear how their samples were selected (selection bias seems unavoidable in this work); and should make their raw data promptly and easily available. Few mechanisms to promote the use of common instruments or aggregation exist, and it may be important to find ways to achieve this, quite apart from the technical issues involved. Some important general considerations are advanced in the report of the Committee on National Statistics, edited by Fienberg, Martin, and Straf (1985). It is time to examine these ideas in the context of quantitative psychiatric research.

Finally, we make a brief comment on another aspect of mood and personality research that we do not have the space to expand upon. There are a number of largely unacknowledged sampling problems that deserve careful consideration in practice: ascertainment biases in gathering subjects, large proportions of missing data, covarying errors attributable to "family" sampling, and neglect of available collateral information. Gibbons et al. (in press) compare several types of analysis popular in psychiatric research, in view of missing data and covarying errors; Mislevy and Sheehan (1989) and Muthe'n (1988) suggest ways to use collateral information to improve parameter estimation. However, existing computer programs for fitting CSA models (LISREL 7, Jöreskog & Sörbom, 1989; EQS, Bentler, 1989) assume simple random sampling of subjects. More complex sampling strategies (unavoidable in practice) require special adjustments to raw sample statistics, which form the inputs to these programs, to achieve appropriate and consistent estimates of parameters (Bentler & Chou, 1987).

## Measurement Models

Despite our lengthy reservations, there are some valuable examples in the literature of the application of confirmatory approaches to measurement problems in the areas of personality and mood. We mention only a few in the interests of brevity. Also, a special issue of *Sociological Methods and Research*, edited by Eaton and Bohrnstedt (1989), includes excellent introductions to many of the best measurement models in use today in the context of psychiatric epidemiology.

Tanaka and Huba (1984a, 1984b) provided some of the first examples of the use of confirmatory hierarchical factor analysis in the domain of depression. Their work is useful because it relies on standard instruments (the Beck Depression Inventory [BDI], the Psychiatric Epidemiology Research Interview) and emphasizes a broader view of the commonalities these instruments share (i.e., it encourages "lumping" rather than "splitting"). They cross-validate their analyses and demonstrate the similarities of the second-order factor structures that emerge (as well as some of the differences in first-order constructs).

It should be noted, however, that Tanaka and Huba fail to account for the discrete nature of BDI item responses in their analysis. Although this may be acceptable in some situations, it leaves the model-fitting process vulnerable to the creation of extra, artifactual latent variables that are needed to fit discrete, range-restricted observed variables with a linear model based on continuous latent variables. An example where such extra factors were identified and removed with a more careful analysis is provided by Mieczkowski, Sweeney, Haas, Mann, and Brown (1991), using a method of factor analysis designed for discrete response variables (Muthe'n, 1987).

The general problem of "scaling" the discrete response items on a questionnaire with the use of a continuous latent-variable model is well known in educational measurement, and some of these methods have been applied in the psychiatric literature as well. Approaches to this problem include second-order factor analysis of binary data (Muthe'n, 1987, 1989), item response theory (Duncan-Jones et al., 1986; Mislevy & Bock, 1981; Reiser, 1989), and full-information factor analysis (Gibbons et al., 1989; Wilson, Wood, & Gibbons, 1984). Two useful surveys of these methods are provided by Mislevy (1986) and Bartholomew (1987). McDonald (1985) makes some concrete recommendations for practice.

Two model-based methods more suited to taxonomic questions are latent-class models and grade-of-membership models. Latent-class models are usually, but not always, identical with discrete mixture models for contingency table data. Examples are provided by Eaton, McCutcheon, Dryman, and Sorenson (1989) and Stern, Arcus, Kagan, Rubin, and Snidman (1991). A study by Fawcett, Clark, Scheftner, and Gibbons (1983), which also serves as a good example of using a variety of psychometric techniques to develop and interpret an assessment scale "from the ground up," includes a mixture analysis of a depressed patient sample that identifies two subtypes of depression distinguished on the basis of anhedonia. Grade-of-membership models offer a compromise between discrete mixture models and continuous latent-variable models. Although these models are very appealing in principle, not much is known about confirmatory approaches with them. Grade-of-membership models have been used to develop typologies of depression in a large clinical sample by Davidson, Woodbury, Pelton, and Krishnan (1988) and in a very large community sample (the Epidemiologic Catchment Area Program) by Woodbury and Manton (1989).

It is common in the area of personality and depression to administer batteries of instruments over repeated intervals to raters who provide data from somewhat different perspectives: patients, informants who know them well, and clinical evaluators who monitor changes over time. Cole (1987) offers good illustrations of the use of confirmatory factor analysis with MTMM data sets (including multiple informants) that go far beyond the usual "visual inspection of zero-order correlations" (p. 584). Finally, Hoyle (1991) provides an excellent primer on the use of CSA in evaluating measurement models in clinical research. He illustrates the methodology with a first-order measurement model of self-concept and a second-order measurement model of self-esteem.

Our discussion of complex parametric models has been cautionary. Additional useful references on the pros and cons of structural modeling approaches in the social and clinical sciences can be found in a special issue of *Child Development* (Connell & Tanaka, 1987). Especially germane are the articles by Biddle and Marlin (1987), Connell (1987), and Martin (1987). Breckler's (1990) discussion of causes for concern in applications of structural-equations modeling is also quite useful. He surveys 72 applications of CSA in personality and social psychology from 1977 to 1987, and cogently summarizes their strengths and weaknesses.

## Causality and General Statistical Models

Holland (1986) describes a formal statistical approach to questions about assessing causal relationships in data, originally developed by Rubin (1974). This approach provides a philosophical account of causality that is amenable to statistical modeling, as well as an explicit, general statistical model capable of exploring many important causal questions.

Imagine that we wish to determine the effect of using treatment T1 rather than treatment T2 (the discussion easily generalizes to more than two values for the "cause"). We can construct an experiment or observational study in which patients are assigned to, or found to be receiving, one or the other treatment. What we want to know (the object of "causal inference") is usually something like the difference in response to the two treatments *for each individual,* or, at the very least, the difference between the average response of all patients *if only T1 were used* and the average response of all patients if only T2 were used. All we can usually observe is the difference between the average response of *just those patients who received T1* and the average response of *just those patients who received T2.* There is no reason to expect, in general, that the second average difference should equal the first. The fact that these are unequal in general is what Holland (1986, p. 947) calls the "fundamental problem of causal inference."

Under further (usually untestable) assumptions, it will be true that the two average differences are equal, so that the second (observable) average can be used as a proxy for the first (unobservable) average. For example, when patients are assigned at random to treatment groups in a double-blind experiment, it may be reasonable to assume that there are no assignment–response confounds (i.e., assignment to treatment group and response to treatment are statistically independent); under this assumption, the average difference we can see is equal to the one we cannot see. Indeed, much of the theory of experimental design and observational studies is devoted to developing and evaluating assumptions like this one that make causal inference possible.

Holland makes several relevant points. The first is that a statistical model usually takes causes to be "given" and seeks to find effects of the causes. This approach is the inverse of the usual scientific quest, which is to find the causes of phenomena (effects). The reason, perhaps not obvious at first, is that it is difficult to isolate a system for causal study if the goal is to identify *all* the causes. On the other hand, an isolated system can conveniently be defined by listing a few "potential cause" variables and focusing attention on responses that may or may not change when these variables are manipulated (or change).

A second, and related, point is that a theory attempting to identify causes of effects rather than effects of causes is necessarily transient:

> I think that looking for causes of effects is a worthwhile scientific endeavor, but it is not the proper perspective in a theoretical analysis of causation. Moreover, I would hold that the "cause" of a given effect is always subject to revisions as our knowledge about the phenomenon increases. (Holland, 1986, p. 959)

This view certainly dovetails with our earlier discussion of the inevitable refinement that all scientific models undergo.

The third point we wish to stress is that Holland's discussion provides some guidance on what kinds of variables can and cannot be causes. The basic criterion is manipulability: It must be possible in principle to assign to any unit any value of the "causal" variable; otherwise, the individual causal effect and average causal effect are not well defined. For example, the dosage level of a drug in an experimental study can obviously be a cause, as can the number of cigarettes smoked per day in an observational study (under some circumstances). Gender or race, however, can never be a cause. Thus, in an epidemiological study, the strongest statements involving gender or race that one can make under this theory are associational. (Some variables, such as "number of previous depressive episodes," may have a controversial status in this regard.)

The Rubin–Holland formulation is important for several reasons. First, it shows that there is indeed a statistical framework in which some causal questions can be rigorously discussed and decided with data. Second, it makes clear once again that although the scientific endeavor (finding causes of effects) is greatly facilitated by statistical analysis (examining the effects of potential causes), statistics cannot supplant scientific thinking. Third, it illustrates that causal inference necessarily relies upon untested assumptions; assessing the plausibility of a particular set of assumptions in a particular research study is one of the main tasks of the scientific investigator.

Finally, the Rubin–Holland formulation clarifies why most conventional statistical models—from logistic regression to CSA models—do not directly address causal issues. A main feature of Rubin's (1974) model is the explicit provision for responses to treatments *not assigned*, as a means of formalizing what is meant by the effect of a causal manipulation. To the extent that conventional statistical models do not contain this provision, they directly address only associational, not causal, questions. For example, Aneshensel and Yokopenic (1985) use LISREL IV to fit a structural-equations model including a path leading from "sex" (gender) to "depression." If Holland's (1986) arguments are to be taken seriously, such path diagrams must be interpreted rather more carefully than is usually done.

This is not to say that structural-equations models cannot help sort out causal issues. In many situations, under appropriate assumptions, these models may be used to estimate special cases of the average effects in Rubin's theory, for example. Moreover, when a causal interpretation is not supported—even if the model is called a "causal model"—the associations (or lack of associations) suggested by the model fit may be very suggestive in developing further theory or identifying variables on which to stratify to remove confounding. What we emphasize is that despite the rhetoric that surrounds them, even statistically well-behaved confirmatory structural-equations models do not by themselves confer causal status on the arrows in the pictures; that is the role of the clear-thinking scientist. Moreover, the more complex the model becomes, the harder it is to see where to make the necessary assumptions that allow rigorous causal inferences.

## Causality without Covariance Structure Analysis

Reasoning about causality is certainly basic to the construction of scientific theory. As a data-analytic tool, path diagrams are helpful in exactly the same way that other visual summaries of (presumed or discovered) patterns are: Our ability to apprehend a relationship presented visually is usually much better than our ability to apprehend the relationship as presented in a series of numbers or descriptive phrases. There have been several interesting uses of path diagrams that do not involve the full machinery of linear structural-equations models, and we point out some examples here.

Downey and Coyne (1990) present an extensive review of research on the onset of depression in children of depressed parents. Among their main methodological concerns are many of the points we have raised above. In particular, changing definitions of depression, diagnostic practices, and nosological terminology make it difficult to compare studies across time or to replicate past work in the area. Nevertheless, Downey and Coyne are successful in bringing together a variety of evidence on the question of links between and among parental depression, marital discord, childhood adjustment to these problems, and the onset of depression in children. They use several path diagrams to illustrate possible theoretical links between and among these fairly gross constructs, carefully set out conditions for causal links, and consider in detail the evidence for the presence versus absence and the "direction of causality" of these links. Among their recommendations for further progress in this area are the development of theoretical models of greater sophistication, access to patient samples less subject to the biases inherent at a research facility, attention to Axis II factors, and the use of comparison (control) groups that have significantly lower prevalences of depression than the target population.

Duncan (1985) takes a somewhat more model-based approach to the analysis of a single survey question tapping normative views on social conformity. Although the study is not a psychiatric one, it is an example of an investigation that combines exploratory and confirmatory statistical analyses to address theoretical questions. The data are a cross-classification of responses to the item at three points in time with indicators of age, gender, race, education, and income, and they are analyzed with standard contingency table methods. The main analyses address age/cohort × period (time-of-survey) issues. Once again, path diagrams are used to illustrate alternative theoretical formulations in a way that is informative and enlightening, without corresponding exactly to the statistical analyses.

Harris, Brown, and Bifulco (1990) give a detailed analysis of several competing theories for the onset of adult depression among patients suffering the childhood loss of a parent; they combine statistical analysis and substantive experience, and illustrate their theoretical speculations with path diagrams. This thoughtful paper is honest about the exploratory nature of the work, seeking to identify associations in their smallish retrospective study that suggest further directions of inquiry. As well as illustrating the use of logistic regression in analyzing a fairly complex set of dichotomous variables, the paper represents the culmination of several years' examination of an interesting data set. The resulting models obviously cannot be validated on the original data set, but they point to important questions to consider in replication studies.

## EXPLORATORY DATA ANALYSIS

When sophisticated model-based methods cannot be applied (because of insufficient sample size, because distributional assumptions are violated, or because the goal is simply to get a "quick and dirty" idea of what is in the data), we must rely on exploratory methods. These methods are useful, not only in interpreting experimental data and generating hypotheses to be checked on replication data, but also in constructing summary measures that are more amenable to traditional statistical procedures. Their main drawback is that they do not encourage thorough a priori consideration of theoretical and quantitative models. Without such preparation, we tend to fall into post hoc rationalizations for the patterns we find. This "magical thinking" is necessary to make any progress on a modeling problem, but when carried to excess it leads us down the wrong paths; see Diaconis (1985) and Rubin (1988) for useful discussions.

There are currently many accepted "paper-and-pencil" methods for exploratory data analysis (EDA), most of which were developed by or in conjunction with John Tukey. An excellent EDA primer is given by Velleman and Hoaglin (1981). A more advanced treatment is provided by Hoaglin, Mosteller, and Tukey (1985), whereas Fox and Long (1990) provide a middle ground for social and behavioral scientists. Elementary

EDA and contingency table techniques with illustrations from psychiatry are also discussed in Greenhouse and Junker (1992).

We have found stem-and-leaf diagrams useful for inspecting the residuals of a model fit and for quickly comparing distributions of the same variable in two different populations (with back-to-back stem-and-leaf diagrams). Boxplots, lined up against one another, provide a quick visual version of a one-way analysis of variance (ANOVA); in addition, boxplots are legible in any orientation, so that they may easily be incorporated into other displays to indicate variability. One-dimensional scatterplots are nicely illustrated in the article by Clark, Gibbons, Fawcett, and Sheftner (1989). Quantile–quantile (q-q) plots provide a rapid way to see whether two variables have the same distribution or whether a single variable is normally distributed. When variables are not normally distributed, power- or log-transforms are often helpful in "getting back" to normality. Kernel density estimates provide another useful visual aid in examining the distributions of random variables.

When one is considering functional relationships between two variables, smoothing techniques can be helpful. The simplest way to smooth is to fit a model in an exploratory spirit. For example, Duncan (1985) fits quintic polynomials in order to better "eyeball" the age/cohort × period effects in which he is interested. Roberts (1986) incorporates both cluster analysis and polynomial curve fitting to explore nonlinear relationships between child competence and parental warmth. Log-linear models are often fitted for the same reason: The fitted cell probabilities or frequencies are easier to interpret than the raw counts. A variety of more sophisticated smoothing techniques for functional relations between two variables, including moving averages, running medians, locally weighted regression smoothers, and spline interpolation, are discussed in the second chapter of Fox and Long (1990). Further information on selecting a good transformation for data, information on robust regression and regression diagnostics, an introduction to bootstrap methods, and an introduction to statistical analysis with missing data are also contained in this collection.

More complicated exploratory methods have traditionally been associated with psychometrics. Factor analysis, even the exploratory kind, can offer hints about what variables "scale together" in a study. In addition, factor analysis can be a useful dimension-reducing tool as a prelude to other analyses. Cluster analysis seeks to separate variables or cases into groups, based on their distance as defined by some quantitative index (e.g., squared Euclidean distance). Occasionally it is useful to cluster-analyze factor loadings from a factor analysis to give a more detailed picture of which items "hang together" on a test or survey. Plots of factor loadings can also be helpful in this regard. Multidimensional scaling uses similarity comparisons to embed data in the smallest dimensional space that admits the partial ordering of the similarity comparisons. Weisberg (1984) offers a comparative survey of these techniques and other exploratory "scaling" techniques. Since these procedures are now standard parts of common statistical packages (e.g., SAS Institute, 1985; SPSS, 1986), they are as "quick and dirty" to use as paper-and-pencil EDA techniques.

Some exploratory methods are also available for path models. A promising approach to creating path diagrams for a data set has been pursued by Clark Glymour and his associates (many relevant references can be found in Spirtes et al., 1991, or Glymour et al., 1987). A criterion that is sometimes considered to be necessary for *A* to fail to be a direct cause of *B* is that *A* and *B* should be statistically independent when stratified by the direct causes of *A*. In the Glymour et al. approach, a path diagram is correctly specified when this conditional independence relation holds for every single variable *A* and every set of variables *B* that are neither direct causes, nor direct or indirect effects, of *A*. Glymour et al. have developed algorithms that, given a probability distribution on a set of variables, can "work backwards" to find a large set of path diagrams consistent with the distribution in this sense. A similar line of reasoning allows the (partial) identification of latent variables needed to complete a path diagram, according to these criteria for a collection of variables of interest.

## LONGITUDINAL MODELS

Earlier in this chapter, we have emphasized the need for longitudinal work—good studies of "natural history" that allow a closer examination of the phenomena of personality and depression as they unfold developmentally—as an important prerequisite for the field before we engage in elaboration of structural models. If we stay close to the clinical phenomena of primary interest, such studies can provide an excellent vehicle for understanding. They can also serve the purpose of improving measurement: Alternative techniques and instruments can be used, and their reliability, stability, and utility can be examined over time.

Examples from the literature that illustrate some of the elements of this approach (longitudinal investigation of respectably sized cohorts, sensitivity to developmental concerns, careful clinical description) are provided by the work of Akiskal (affective and character spectrum disorders; Akiskal, 1983), Depue (naturalistic, longitudinal investigations of cyclothymia and dysthymia; Depue et al., 1981), Brown (careful examination, with multiple cohorts, of vulnerability to depression that began with a focus on social and environmental factors and has now expanded to encompass internalized personality constructs; Brown, Andrews, Harris, Adler, & Bridge, 1986; Brown & Harris, 1978; Harris et al., 1990), Henderson (a focus on the reciprocal relationships between social support and personality; Henderson with Byrne & Duncan-Jones, 1981), and Tyrer (espousing a "lumping" rather than "splitting" philosophy and providing evidence of the inherent connection between Axis I and Axis II characteristics; Tyrer, Alexander, Remington, & Riley, 1987; Tyrer, Casey, & Gall, 1983).

The work of all these investigators shares certain commonalities that we regard as important: an emphasis on longitudinal observation; a theoretical position that has evolved in an ongoing "discussion" with the collection and analysis of new sets of data; a focus on "larger" issues and constructs; and an appreciation of the reciprocity that exists between internal and external environments. These internal environments can include biological (temperamental) substrates or affective predispositions, endogenous "illness" processes, or internalized personality attributes, whereas external environments can include the types of social networks and supports elicited by different kinds of people and the types of life stresses to which they fall prey (either fortuitously or with some contribution of their own). Again, a longitudinal and developmental approach to such phenomena seems most appropriate as a way of appreciating their emergence over time and the complexity of their interactions. In a similar vein, Barnett and Gotlib (1988) provide an extensive survey of the literature on interactions of psychosocial functioning and depression. In particular, their examination of case–control studies and two-wave panel designs gives some indication of what the most common longitudinal studies look like today.

Kraemer (1981) and Kraemer and Thiemann (1989) consider the problem of using "soft" measures (i.e., measures exhibiting only moderate reliability) on a limited number of subjects to make useful inferences. They advocate the use of an "intensive design": repeated measures on each subject over time, using a weighted average of the subjects' responses—usually the slope of the least-squares regression line fitted to the repeated (longitudinal) assessments—as the outcome measure. This outcome measure pools all the available responses of the subjects, potentially improving reliability over an endpoint outcome measure (which uses only one response) or a change outcome measure (which pools two responses, baseline and endpoint).

Gibbons et al. (in press) and Lavori (1990) survey several competing methods for analyzing longitudinal data, including repeated-measures ANOVA, multivariate analysis of variance (MANOVA), and random regression models. This last technique is a more sophisticated version of Kraemer's intensive design that can accommodate some kinds of missing data, irregularly spaced measurements, correlated errors of measurement, time-varying and time-invariant covariates, and individual (patient) deviations from a group-level, average response trend. The general orientation of these recommendations is to stay close to the data as the longitudinal study unfolds—a position we endorse, especially for the initial longitudinal studies we believe are still needed to stabilize concepts in the field.

More complex approaches to measuring change over time by combining growth-curve models with latent-variable models have been pursued by Rogosa and others; McArdle and Epstein (1987) give a review of latent-growth-curve methods. An interesting variation on these ideas is the study of repeated suicide attempts conducted by Clark et al. (1989). Another interesting latent variable approach is illustrated by Graham, Collins, Wugalter, Chung, and Hansen (1991). They develop a latent Markov-chain model for describing onset of substance abuse among seventh- and eighth-graders. This kind of analysis may be helpful, for example, in modeling state-like constructs (which Graham et al. call "dynamic latent variables").

Plewis (1985) provides a useful primer on a variety of longitudinal designs and analyses, concentrating on two-wave studies. However, it should be noted that the use of linear structural-equations models in this context has become controversial. For example, Rogosa (1987) is emphatic about the failings of path models and structural-equations models to handle basic questions in longitudinal research, especially where multiwave panel studies are concerned. He gives examples where the path coefficients are irrelevant, misleading, or unable to recover the structure of the original model in a variety of longitudinal designs.

## RECOMMENDATIONS

1. *Focus on a limited number of global constructs.* One should begin modestly—that is, start with a small number of relatively broad, theoretically meaningful constructs. It is likely to be more productive to focus on one part of a larger model and to get that part right (or to abandon it because of negative results) than to attempt to do everything and be confident of little (because of limited power, overfitting with an excessive number of parameters, etc.). Since there is considerable noise among our correlational signals, it is probably wiser to use more global rather than narrower constructs, at least as a starting point, and to sort out which parts or indicators of those constructs are accounting for most

of the important variance through careful attention to measurement issues.

In the area of personality and depression, several examples of "global" constructs seem promising. They include the prominent factors that routinely appear in factor analyses of personality traits (i.e., the "big five" factors, especially neuroticism; McCrae & Costa, 1987) and of mood states (i.e., positive and negative affectivity, constraint; Watson, Clark, & Tellegen, 1988). From an interpersonal perspective, the propensity for secure versus insecure attachments (Feeney & Noller, 1990; Richman & Flaherty, 1987) is a leading candidate, and from a cognitive perspective, the global cognitive set associated with helplessness (Abramson, Seligman, & Teasdale, 1978) and with diminished self-efficacy (Bandura, 1977) comes to mind. Closely (but conversely) related to the latter are the attributes associated with active coping, learned resourcefulness, and general "hardiness" (Hull, Van Treuren, & Virnelli, 1987).

2. *Focus on longitudinal and developmental understanding, and remain close to the clinical phenomena of interest.* One should worry less about justifying one's own model or establishing the correctness of abstract, conceptual distinctions (e.g., state vs. trait) than about understanding the phenomena under investigation in longitudinal and developmental terms. As our earlier discussion of science and models is intended to illustrate, genuine advances are more likely to come from better substantive understanding than from more "correct" model-fitting procedures. Statistics is helpful for fleshing out the contours of a robust, valid model or paradigm, but it will not by itself show the way to such a paradigm. This type of understanding is more likely to come from long-term experience with a large number of people (patients and nonpatients) with whom the investigator develops a thorough acquaintanceship, at least in empirical terms.

3. *Exploit the possibilities of sound exploratory data analysis.* Before rushing into the use of modeling approaches that rely on complex, parametric techniques, one should take sufficient time to understand the "manifest" characteristics of one's data. Our discussion of exploratory data analysis is intended to highlight this attitude. There is much to be learned from descriptive analyses of the "operating characteristics" of one's assessment tools. To do this effectively, however, and to promote adequate familiarity with these tools, require that the number of tools or measures be limited. The "kitchen sink" approach to measurement is not the answer; it indicates a reluctance to decide which measures are likely to be most promising.

4. *Consider a "two-step" approach to structural modeling.* When "restricted," confirmatory, or model-fitting procedures involving latent

constructs are implemented, one should consider the use of Anderson and Gerbing's (1988) "two-step" approach—that is, focusing first on developing better measurement models for each of one's constructs before attempting to model the relationships among these constructs. Given the common use of multiple methods and sources of information in clinical research, one potentially important use of covariance structure analysis is more sophisticated analysis of multitrait–multimethod data sets (cf. Cole, 1987).

5. *Use standardized assessment instruments and consider ways to aggregate data.* Given the assumptions of complex, parametric approaches and the constraints typically placed on any individual investigator with regard to sampling strategies and sample sizes, one should consider promoting the use of a standardized, common set of assessment tools and developing systematic ways of sharing and aggregating data. We need data "clearinghouses" and new attitudes and policies about how to develop them, who shall have access to them, and how to credit the role of all those who contribute to them.

## ACKNOWLEDGMENTS

This work was supported in part by the MacArthur Foundation Research Network on the Psychobiology of Depression and Other Affective Disorders; by National Institute of Mental Health (NIMH) Grant No. MH44672 to Paul A. Pilkonis; by the Clinical Research Center for Affective Disorders (Methodology Core) at Western Psychiatric Institute and Clinic, NIMH Grant No. MH30915; by NIMH National Research Service Award, Grant No. MH15758; and by the Office of Naval Research, Cognitive Sciences Division, Grant No. N00014-91-J-1208 to Brian W. Junker.

We are grateful to Robert Gibbons, Joel Greenhouse, Kenneth Howard, David Kaplan, Ratna Nandakumar, and William Stout for their comments on earlier drafts of the chapter.

Correspondence concerning the chapter may sent to either author: Brian W. Junker, Department of Statistics, Carnegie Mellon University, Pittsburgh, PA 15213, or Paul A. Pilkonis, Western Psychiatric Institute and Clinic, 3811 O'Hara Street, Pittsburgh, PA 15213.

## REFERENCES

Abramson, L. Y., Seligman, M. E. P., & Teasdale, J. (1978). Learned helplessness in humans: Critique and reformulation. *Journal of Abnormal Psychology, 87,* 32–48.

Akiskal, H. S. (1983). Dysthymic disorder: Psychopathology of proposed chronic depressive subtypes. *American Journal of Psychiatry, 140,* 11–20.

American Psychiatric Association. (1987). *Diagnostic and statistical manual of mental disorders* (3rd ed., rev.). Washington, DC: Author.

Anastasi, A. (1988). *Psychological testing* (6th ed.). New York: Macmillan.

Anderson, J. C., & Gerbing, D. W. (1988). Structural equation modeling in practice: A review and recommended two-step approach. *Psychological Bulletin, 103*, 411–423.

Aneshensel, C. S., & Yokopenic, P. A. (1985). Tests for the comparability of a causal model of depression under two conditions of interviewing. *Journal of Personality and Social Psychology, 5*, 1337–1348.

Bandura, A. (1977). Self-efficacy: Toward a unifying theory of behavioral change. *Psychological Review, 84*, 191–215.

Barnett, P. A., & Gotlib, I. H. (1988). Psychosocial functioning and depression: Distinguishing among the andecedents, concomitants, and consequences. *Psychological Bulletin, 104*, 97–126.

Bartholomew, D. J. (1987). *Latent variable models and factor analysis.* Oxford: Oxford University Press.

Bentler, P. M. (1989). *EQS structural equations program manual.* Los Angeles: BMDP Statistical Software.

Bentler, P. M., & Chou, C.-P. (1987). Practical issues in structural modeling. *Sociological Methods and Research, 16*, 78–117.

Biddle, B. J., & Marlin, M. M. (1987). Causality, confirmation, credulity, and structural equation modeling. *Child Development, 58*, 4–17.

Box, G. E. P. (1980). Sampling and Bayes' inference in scientific modeling and robustness (with discussion). *Journal of the Royal Statistical Society, 143*(Series A), 383–430.

Breckler, S. J. (1990). Applications of covariance structure modeling in psychology: Cause for concern? *Psychological Bulletin, 107*, 260–273.

Brown, G. W., Andrews, B., Harris, T., Adler, Z., & Bridge, L. (1986). Social support, self-esteem and depression. *Psychological Medicine, 16*, 813–831.

Brown, G. W., & Harris, T. (1978). *Social origins of depression.* New York: Free Press.

Campbell, D. T., & Fiske, D. W. (1959). Convergent and discriminant validation by the multitrait–multimethod matrix. *Psychological Bulletin, 56*, 81–105.

Clark, D. C., Gibbons, R. D., Fawcett, J., & Scheftner, W. A. (1989). What is the mechanism by which suicide attempts predispose to later suicide attempts?: A mathematical model. *Journal of Abnormal Psychology, 98*, 42–49.

Cliff, N. (1983). Some cautions concerning the application of causal modeling methods. *Multivariate Behavioral Research, 18*, 115–126.

Cohen, J. (1990). Things I have learned (so far). *American Psychologist, 45*, 1304–1312.

Cole, D. A. (1987). Utility of confirmatory factor analysis in test validation research. *Journal of Consulting and Clinical Psychology, 55*, 584–594.

Connell, J. P. (1987). Structural equation modeling and the study of child development: A question of goodness of fit. *Child Development, 58*, 167–175.

Connell, J. P., & Tanaka, J. S. (Eds.). (1987). Structural equation modeling [Special section]. *Child Development, 58*, 1–175.

Cox, D. R. (1990). Role of models in statistical analysis. *Statistical Science, 5,* 169–174.

Cronbach, L. J., Gleser, G. C., Nanda, H., & Rajaratnam, N. (1972). *The dependability of behavioral measurements.* New York: Wiley.

Cudeck, R., & Browne, M. W. (1983). Cross-validation of covariance structures. *Multivariate Behavioral Research, 18,* 147–167.

Davidson, J., Woodbury, M. A., Pelton, S., & Krishnan, R. (1988). A study of depressive typologies using grade of membership analysis. *Psychological Medicine, 18,* 179–189.

Depue, R. A., Slater, J. F., Wolfstetter-Kausch, H., Klein, D., Goplerud, E., & Farr, D. (1981). A behavioral paradigm for identifying persons at risk for bipolar depressive disorder: A conceptual framework and five validation studies [Monograph]. *Journal of Abnormal Psychology, 90,* 381–437.

Diaconis, P. (1985). Theories of data analysis: From magical thinking through classical statistics. In D. C. Hoaglin, F. Mosteller, & J. W. Tukey (Eds.), *Exploring data tables, trends, and shapes* (pp. 1–36). New York: Wiley.

Downey, G., & Coyne, J. C. (1990). Children of depressed parents: An integrative review. *Psychological Bulletin, 108,* 50–76.

Drasgow, F., & Parsons, C. K. (1983). Application of unidimensional item response theory models to multidimensional data. *Applied Psychological Measurement, 7,* 189–199.

Duncan, O. D. (1985). Generations, cohorts and conformity. In W. M. Mason & S. E. Fienberg (Eds.), *Cohort analysis in social research: Beyond the identification problem* (pp. 289–321). New York: Springer-Verlag.

Duncan-Jones, P., Grayson, D. A., & Moran, P. A. P. (1986). The utility of latent trait models in psychiatric epidemiology. *Psychological Medicine, 16,* 391–405.

Eaton, W. W., & Bohrnstedt, G. (Eds.). (1989). Latent variable models for dichotomous outcomes: Analysis of the Epidemiological Catchment Area program [Special issue]. *Sociological Methods and Research, 18,* 3–182.

Eaton, W. W., McCutcheon, A., Dryman, A., & Sorenson, A. (1989). Latent class analysis of anxiety and depression. *Sociological Methods and Research, 18,* 104–125.

Efron, B., & Gong, G. (1983). A leisurely look at the bootstrap, the jackknife, and cross-validation. *American Statistician, 37,* 36–48.

Fawcett, J., Clark, D. C., Scheftner, W. A., & Gibbons, R. D. (1983). Assessing anhedonia in psychiatric patients. *Archives of General Psychiatry, 40,* 79–84.

Feeney, J. A., & Noller, P. (1990). Attachment style as a predictor of adult romantic relationships. *Journal of Personality and Social Psychology, 58,* 281–291.

Feldt, L. S., & Brennan, R. L. (1989). Reliability. In R. L. Linn (Ed.), *Educational measurement* (3rd ed., pp. 105–146). New York: Macmillan.

Fienberg, S. E., Martin, M. E., & Straf, M. L. (Eds.). (1985). *Sharing research data.* Washington, DC: National Academy Press.

Fleiss, J. L. (1981). *Statistical methods for rates and proportions* (2nd ed.). New York: Wiley.

Fleiss, J. L. (1986). *The design and analysis of clinical experiments.* New York: Wiley.

Fox, J., & Long, J. S. (Eds.). (1990). *Modern methods of data analysis.* Newbury Park, CA: Sage.

Gibbons, R. D., Bock, R. D., & Hedeker, D. R. (1989). *Conditional dependence* (Final Research Report, Office of Naval Research and Illinois State Psychiatric Institute). Chicago: University of Illinois at Chicago.

Gibbons, R. D., Hedeker, D. R., Elkin, I., Waternaux, C., Kraemer, H. C., Greenhouse, J. B., Shea, M. T., Imber, S. D., Sotsky, S. M., & Watkins, J. T. (in press). Some conceptual and statistical issues in the analysis of longitudinal psychiatric data. *Archives of General Psychiatry.*

Glymour, C., Scheines, R., Spirtes, P., & Kelly, K. (1987). *Discovering causal structure.* San Diego: Academic Press.

Good, I. J. (1983). The philosophy of exploratory data analysis. *Philosophy of Science, 50,* 283–295.

Graham, J. W., Collins, L. M., Wugalter, S. E., Chung, N. K., & Hansen, W. B. (1991). Modeling transitions in latent stage-sequential processes: A substance use prevention example. *Journal of Consulting and Clinical Psychology, 59,* 48–57.

Greenhouse, J. B., & Junker, B. W. (1992). Basic statistical principles. In L. K. G. Hsu & M. Herson (Eds.), *Research in psychiatry: Issues, strategies, and methods* (pp. 149–172). New York: Plenum Press.

Harris, T., Brown, G. W., & Bifulco, A. (1990). Loss of parent in childhood and adult psychiatric disorder: A tentative overall model. *Development and Psychopathology, 2,* 311–328.

Harrison, D. A. (1986). Robustness of IRT parameter estimation to violations of the unidimensionality assumption. *Journal of Educational Statistics, 11,* 91–115.

Henderson, A. S., with Byrne, D. G., & Duncan-Jones, P. (1981). *Neurosis and the social environment.* New York: Academic Press.

Hoaglin, D. C., Mosteller, F., & Tukey, J. W. (Eds.). (1985). *Exploring data tables, trends, and shapes.* New York: Wiley.

Holland, P. W. (1986). Statistics and causal inference (with discussion). *Journal of the American Statistical Association, 81,* 945–968.

Horowitz, L. M., Rosenberg, S. E., Baer, B. A., Ureño, G., & Villaseñor, V. S. (1988). Inventory of Interpersonal Problems: Psychometric properties and clinical applications. *Journal of Consulting and Clinical Psychology, 56,* 885–892.

Hoyle, R. H. (1991). Evaluating measurement models in clinical research: Covariance structure analysis of latent variable models of self-conception. *Journal of Consulting and Clinical Psychology, 59,* 67–76.

Hull, J. G., Van Treuren, R. R., & Virnelli, S. (1987). Hardiness and health: A critique and alternative approach. *Journal of Personality and Social Psychology, 53,* 518–530.

Humphreys, L. G. (1982). *Systematic heterogeneity of items in tests of meaningful psychological attributes: A rejection of unidimensionality.* Unpublished manuscript, University of Illinois, Champaign.

Humphreys, L. G. (1986). An analysis of test and item bias in the prediction context. *Journal of Applied Psychology, 71,* 327–333.

Jones, C. O. (1984). Doing before knowing: Concept development in political research. In H. B. Asher, H. F. Weisberg, J. H. Kessel, & W. P. Shively (Eds.), *Theory building and data analysis in the social sciences* (pp. 51–64). Knoxville: University of Tennessee Press.

Jöreskog, K. G. (1969). A general approach to confirmatory maximum likelihood factor analysis. *Psychometrika, 34,* 363–379.

Jöreskog, K. G., & Sörbom, D. (1989). *LISREL 7 user's guide.* Mooresville, IN: Scientific Software.

Kaplan, A. (1964). *The conduct of inquiry: Methodology for behavioral science.* San Francisco: Chandler.

Kaplan, D. (1990). Evaluating and modifying covariance structure models: A review and recommendation (with discussion). *Multivariate Behavioral Research, 25,* 137–203.

Kraemer, H. C. (1981). Coping strategies in psychiatric clinical research. *Journal of Consulting and Clinical Psychology, 49,* 309–319.

Kraemer, H. C., & Thiemann, S. (1989). A strategy to use soft data effectively in randomized controlled clinical trials. *Journal of Consulting and Clinical Psychology, 57,* 148–154.

Kruskal, W., & Neyman, J. (1956, September). *Stochastic models and their applications to social phenomena.* Paper presented at the joint sessions of the Institute of Mathematical Statistics, the American Statistical Association, and the American Social Society, Detroit.

Kuhn, T. S. (1970). *The structure of scientific revolutions* (2nd ed.). Chicago: University of Chicago Press.

Kupfer, D. J., & Rush, A. J. (1983). Recommendations for depression publications: Information for authors. *Journal of Nervous and Mental Disease, 171,* 459–460.

Lavori, P. (1990). ANOVA, MANOVA, my black hen. *Archives of General Psychiatry, 47,* 775–778.

Leamer, E. E. (1978). *Specification searches.* New York: Wiley.

Lehmann, E. L. (1990). Model specification: The views of Fisher and Neyman, and later developments. *Statistical Science, 5,* 160–168.

Lord, F. M., & Novick, M. R. (1968). *Statistical theories of mental test scores.* Reading, MA: Addison-Wesley.

Martin, J. A. (1987). Structural equation modeling: A guide for the perplexed. *Child Development, 58,* 33–37.

McArdle, J. J., & Epstein, D. (1987). Latent growth curves within developmental structural equations. *Child Development, 58,* 110–133.

McCrae, R. R., & Costa, P. T., Jr. (1987). Validation of the five-factor model of personality across instruments and observers. *Journal of Personality and Social Psychology, 52,* 81–90.

McDonald, R. P. (1981). The dimensionality of tests and items. *British Journal of Mathematical and Statistical Psychology, 34,* 100–117.

McDonald, R. P. (1985). *Factor analysis and related methods.* Hillsdale, NJ: Erlbaum.

Messick, S. (1989). Validity. In R. L. Linn (Ed.), *Educational measurement* (3rd ed., pp. 13–103). New York: Macmillan.

Mieczkowski, T. A., Sweeney, J. M., Haas, G., Mann, J., & Brown, R. P. (1991). *Factor composition of the Suicide Intent Scale.* Unpublished manuscript, Department of Psychiatry, University of Pittsburgh School of Medicine.

Miller, R. G. (1986). *Beyond ANOVA: Basics of applied statistics.* New York: Wiley.

Mislevy, R. J. (1986). Recent developments in the factor analysis of categorical variables. *Journal of Educational Statistics, 11,* 3–31.

Mislevy, R. J., & Bock, R. D. (1981). *BILOG* [Computer program]. Mooresville, IN: Scientific Software.

Mislevy, R. J., & Sheehan, K. M. (1989). The role of collateral information about examinees in item parameter estimation. *Psychometrika, 54,* 661–679.

Mulaik, S. A., James, L. R., Van Alstine, J., Bennett, N., Lind, S., & Stilwell, C. D. (1989). Evaluation of goodness-of-fit indices for structural equation models. *Psychological Bulletin, 105,* 430–445.

Muthe'n, B. (1987). *LISCOMP* [Computer program]. Mooresville, IN: Scientific Software.

Muthe'n, B. (1988). Some uses of structural equation modeling in validity studies: Extending IRT to external variables. In H. Wainer & H. I. Braun (Eds.), *Test validity* (pp. 213–238). Hillsdale, NJ: Erlbaum.

Muthe'n, B. (1989). Dichotomous factor analysis of symptom data. *Sociological Methods and Research, 18,* 19–65.

Nelder, J. A. (1986). Statistics, science and technology. *Journal of the Royal Statistical Society, 149*(Series A), 109–121.

Pilkonis, P. A., Heape, C. L., Proietti, J. M., & Smith, K. (1991, July). *Prototypes of adult attachment styles: Reliability of clinical judgments and validity in predicting treatment outcomes in depression.* Paper presented at the meeting of the Society for Psychotherapy Research, Lyon, France.

Plewis, I. (1985). *Analysing change: Measurement and explanation using longitudinal data.* New York: Wiley.

Reckase, M. D. (1979). Unifactor latent trait models applied to multifactor tests: Results and implications. *Journal of Educational Statistics, 4,* 207–230.

Reckase, M. D., Ackerman, T. A., & Carlson, J. E. (1988). Building a unidimensional test using multidimensional items. *Journal of Educational Measurement, 25,* 193–203.

Reiser, M. (1989). An application of the item-response model to psychiatric epidemiology. *Sociological Methods and Research, 18,* 66–103.

Richman, J. A., & Flaherty, J. A. (1987). Adult psychosocial assets and depressive mood over time: Effects of internalized childhood attachments. *Journal of Nervous and Mental Disease, 175,* 703–712.

Roberts, W. L. (1986). Nonlinear models of development: An example from the socialization of competence. *Child Development, 57,* 1166–1178.

Rogosa, D. (1979). Causal models in longitudinal research: Rationale, formulation, and interpretation. In J. R. Nesselroade & P. B. Baltes (Eds.), *Longitudinal research in the development of behavior* (pp. 263–302). New York: Academic Press.

Rogosa, D. (1987). Causal models do not support scientific conclusions. *Journal of Educational Measurement, 12,* 185–195.

Rosenthal, R., & Rosnow, R. L. (1984). *Essentials of behavioral research: Methods and data analysis.* New York: McGraw-Hill.

Rosnow, R. L., & Rosenthal, R. (1989). Statistical procedures and the justification of knowledge in psychological science. *American Psychologist, 44,* 1276–1284.

Roznowski, M., & Reith, J. (1991). *Measurement quality of tests containing differentially functioning items: Do biased items result in poor tests?* Technical Report TR92-1, Department of Psychology, Ohio State University. Manuscript submitted for publication.

Rubin, D. B. (1974). Estimating causal effects of treatments in randomized and nonrandomized studies. *Journal of Educational Psychology, 66,* 688–701.

Rubin, D. B. (1988). Discussion. In H. Wainer & H. I. Braun (Eds.), *Test validity* (pp. 241–256). Hillsdale, NJ: Erlbaum.

SAS Institute, Inc. (1985). *SAS user's guide: Statistics* (Version 5 ed.). Cary, NC: Author.

Shea, M. T., Glass, D. R., Pilkonis, P. A., Watkins, J., & Docherty, J. P. (1987). Frequency and implications of personality disorders in a sample of depressed outpatients. *Journal of Personality Disorders, 1,* 27–42.

Sörbom, D. (1991). *An illustration of analysis with the LISREL computer program.* Paper presented at the North American meeting of the Psychometric Society, New Brunswick, NJ.

Spirtes, P., Glymour, C., & Scheines, R. (1991). *Causality, statistics and search.* Unpublished manuscript, Department of Philosophy, Carnegie-Mellon University.

SPSS, Inc. (1986). *SPSS^x user's guide* (2nd ed.). New York: McGraw-Hill.

Stern, H., Arcus, D., Kagan, J., Rubin, D. B., & Snidman, N. (1991). *Statistical choices in temperament research.* Technical Report, Department of Statistics, Harvard University. Manuscript submitted for publication.

Stout, W. F. (1987). A nonparametric approach for assessing latent trait unidimensionality. *Psychometrika, 52,* 589–617.

Stout, W. F. (1990). A new item response theory modeling approach with applications to unidimensionality assessment and ability estimation. *Psychometrika, 55,* 293–325.

Tanaka, J. S. (1987). "How big is big enough?": Sample size and goodness of fit in structural equation models with latent variables. *Child Development, 58,* 134–146.

Tanaka, J. S., & Huba, G. J. (1984a). Confirmatory hierarchical factor analyses of psychological distress measures. *Journal of Personality and Social Psychology, 46,* 621–635.

Tanaka, J. S., & Huba, G. J. (1984b). Structures of psychological distress: Testing confirmatory hierarchical models. *Journal of Consulting and Clinical Psychology, 52,* 719–721.

Tsujimoto, R. N., Hamilton, M., & Berger, D. E. (1990). Averaging multiple judges to improve validity: Aid to planning cost-effective clinical research. *Psychological Assessment: A Journal of Consulting and Clinical Psychology, 2,* 432–437.

Tyrer, P., Alexander, J., Remington, M., & Riley, P. (1987). Relationship between neurotic symptoms and neurotic diagnosis: A longitudinal study. *Journal of Affective Disorders, 13,* 13–21.

Tyrer, P., Casey, P., & Gall, J. (1983). Relationship between neurosis and personality disorder. *British Journal of Psychiatry, 142,* 404–408.

Velleman, P. F., & Hoaglin, D. C. (1981). *Applications, basics and computing of exploratory data analysis.* Boston: Duxbury Press.

Wainer, H., & Braun, H. I. (Eds.). (1988). *Test validity.* Hillsdale, NJ: Erlbaum.

Watson, D., Clark, L. A., & Tellegen, A. (1988). Development and validation of brief measures of positive and negative affect: The PANAS scales. *Journal of Personality and Social Psychology, 54,* 1063–1070.

Weisberg, H. F. (1984). Scaling objectives and procedures. In H. B. Asher, H. F. Weisberg, J. H. Kessel, & W. P. Shively (Eds.), *Theory-building and data analysis in the social sciences* (pp. 329–355). Knoxville: University of Tennessee Press.

Wilson, D., Wood, R., & Gibbons, R. D. (1984). *TESTFACT* [Computer program]. Mooresville, IN: Scientific Software.

Woodbury, M. A., & Manton, K. G. (1989). Grade of membership analysis of depression-related psychiatric disorders. *Sociological Methods and Research, 18,* 126–163.

Yen, W. M. (1980). The extent, causes and importance of context effects on item parameters for two latent trait models. *Journal of Educational Measurement, 17,* 297–311.

Yen, W. M. (1984). Effects of local item dependence on the fit and equating performance of the three-parameter logistic model. *Applied Psychological Measurement, 8,* 125–145.

# Commentary

HELENA CHMURA KRAEMER
*Stanford University School of Medicine*

## INTRODUCTION

I remember reading about the pain and anger expressed by those theoretical physicists whose breakthrough concepts led to the development of the atomic bomb and ultimately to its use. Many of this group (and, since then, their intellectual heirs) have led efforts to restrict the use of atomic power to peaceful purposes. Certainly that was not the first time—nor, in all likelihood, will it be the last—that ethical and concerned scientists lost control of their own intellectual product and witnessed its use to do harm.

What is at stake here is obviously not as profound as the annihilation of humanity. Nevertheless, generating false and misleading results is of concern in any context where those results may affect clinical decision making, public health policy, educational policy, social policy, economic policy—in other words, any context in which the health and well-being of people are at stake (i.e., "people sciences"). Somewhere there is a line dividing trivial research topics in which false and misleading results are of no concern, and important research topics in which such results are of strong concern. As a biostatistician, I do not always know where that line is, and consequently follow a simple rule: If the researchers indicate by word or action their lack of concern about false-positive or false-negative findings in their research, I take that as indication that their research is trivial. I excuse myself from consulting on such research; as a reviewer, I recommend against funding or publishing it; as a reader, I do not take the results seriously. But when those most knowledgeable about an intellectual product to be used to generate research results (i.e., those most closely akin to its developers), warn about the consequences of its promiscuous use and abuse, its shortcomings, limitations, and dangers—when they urge control, restraint, moderation, and scrupulous care in its use—I pay close attention to their concerns and would expect researchers dealing with *important* research areas to do so as well.

In their chapter, Junker and Pilkonis have expressed their reservations about the use of complex parametric models in the "people sciences," and have done so in a comprehensive, balanced, and clear discussion of the issues. Although the stimulus for their comments is the use of various forms of covariance structure analysis in the study of personality and depression, the authors note that these issues extend to the use of these models in other areas of "people sciences"—and, I would add, to other complex parametric models, such as genetic linkage analyses. Such models are mathematically elegant and enticing, for they seem to afford a window to the study of complex systems not otherwise available. However, that window is highly opaque unless a great deal already known about the complex system is built into the model. In the absence of such knowledge, one ends up studying the window, and not the complex scene still obscured outside.

The authors make one comment that well summarizes their thesis: "although the scientific endeavor . . . is greatly facilitated by statistical analysis . . . , statistics cannot supplant scientific thinking" (p. 155). This comment parallels that of Paulos (1990) in his treatise on innumeracy and its effects:

> Innumeracy and pseudoscience are often associated, in part because of the ease with which mathematical certainty can be invoked to bludgeon the innumerate into a dumb acquiescence. Pure mathematics does indeed deal with certainties, but its applications are only as good as the underlying empirical assumptions, simplifications, and estimations that go into them. (p. 67)

I would add two other parallel admonitions:

1. *Although our knowledge and understanding of humanity are greatly illuminated by scientific endeavor, scientific methods cannot supplant seeing, hearing, and interacting with human beings.* This is a stance that is clearly implied in the Junker and Pilkonis advice to "remain close to the clinical phenomena of interest" (p. 162; cf. Jaffee & Spirer, 1987, Ch. 2).

2. *Although statistical analysis is greatly facilitated by computer processing, computer analysis cannot supplant statistical reasoning.* The wide dissemination of computer software to apply complex mathematical and statistical models, especially when these are made available to those with little or no understanding of the mathematical or statistical bases of

the models, is a serious problem. Naive users have no motivation or means to check crucial assumptions of a model against the realities of the situation in which they use it. When results generated under these circumstances are submitted to review for publication, reviewers, editors, and readers can only assume that the methods were properly used. The risk of false-positive results is very high, as is that of producing results that cannot be independently replicated or confirmed (and are only sometimes later refuted).

Both these admonitions are implied in the Junker and Pilkonis discussion. Indeed, there is little that I can add to or expand on what they have said. I can only agree and endorse their stance, and second their recommendations. Instead, let me take the opposite stance, and both state and try to counter the likely objections to what they say.

## POSSIBLE OBJECTIONS TO JUNKER AND PILKONIS

*Objection 1: "If you statisticians did not mean these models to be used, then why did you make them?"*
There are many different answers to this question. The most trivial is simply that model building is fun and challenging to a statistician. Any hobbyist who builds models of any kind would understand this.

More seriously, theoretical statisticians build models to advance their own knowledge and understanding of statistical concepts. Basic scientists in any field would understand this. An applied statistician or a researcher might develop a model as a means of organizing what is already known about a complex system, and of presenting and communicating this information (as Junker and Pilkonis suggest). This process is quite distinct from using a mathematical model in analyses designed to advance and develop new knowledge about a complex system.

Finally, a mathematical model is very useful in detecting the limits of a complex system. Not rejecting a model with a goodness-of-fit test is tantamount to a "hung jury." It may merely reflect a lack of sensitivity or power, not a good model. However, rejecting a model is an indication that something is wrong in the model. If the model is carefully structured so that rejection localizes what is wrong in the model, this provides valuable guidance.

As can be seen, the reasons why a model may be valued may be different for theoretical statisticians, for applied statisticians, and for other researchers in "people sciences." Whether or not a particular mathematical or statistical model is appropriate for use in some research context is a determination the researchers are responsible for, not the model builders—a judgment based on the researchers' knowledge of the field of application (see Feinstein, 1987, Chs. 8–9).

*Objection 2: "If we don't use mathematical models, then what do we use?"*

The question here is not whether to use mathematical models or not. All statistical approaches (i.e., methods used to draw inferences about populations from samples) are based on models. There is no alternative. The issue here is only the complexity of the model. What is suggested is that the complexity of a model that can be used as a basis of inference is limited by the state of knowledge in the field of application. In a field in which there are empirical studies that support the assumptions of a complex mathematical model, the use of such a model is both appropriate and warranted. However, in a field in which little is known of structure and content, only the simplest mathematical models should be used (see Jaffee & Spirer, 1987, Ch. 11).

*Objection 3: "Sticking to simple models takes all the joy, innovation, and excitement out of science!"*

The third objection is a point well taken. Most of the excitement in science lies in exploration, in generating hypotheses, in reading and critiquing previous work, in mulling over the issues and discussing them with colleagues, and most of all in the "Aha!" experience. This excitement is the reason why we all go into science. It is certainly not often found in the step-by-step, slow, careful, controlled, monitored, check-and-recheck discipline of the application of the scientific method. Thomas Edison's comment that "Genius is 1% inspiration and 99% perspiration" applies in particular to scientific genius. Scientists must accept the perspiration along with the inspiration (see Kohn, 1986, Ch. 1).

Yet it should be noted that Junker and Pilkonis are advocating well-done exploratory research, not opposing it. By and large, I believe, applied statisticians, epidemiologists, and psychometricians tend to be much more liberal in their view of the value of well-done exploratory studies than other researchers in the "people sciences." Their objections focus on misrepresenting exploratory studies as something other than what they are—for example, reporting invalid $p$ values or statistical tests, and drawing premature and unwarranted conclusions.

*Objection 4: "The issues with which we are dealing are important and urgent. What Junker and Pilkonis propose is simply too slow. They would have us move step by plodding step, rather than take the giant strides and great leaps that the use of complex models would enable us to do."*

Which giant strides, which great leaps, are here being referred to? How many of the results from the use of these complex models in the biobehavioral sciences have been replicated and confirmed in the hands of other researchers, at other sites, using independent approaches? How many such results have gone on to become the basis of valuable and productive new "knowledge"? Without doubt, the results have produced many published papers. However, I would argue that far more time, effort, and resources are wasted trying to confirm false-positive results reported in such papers, and trying to "fit" those results into the contradictory indications of other studies.

*Objection 5: "What does it matter whether the statistical approaches used are valid and justified or not? Everyone knows that until a result is confirmed, it is not a 'finding.' It is naive to believe any published result until it is suitably replicated and confirmed. Thus whether or not the initial result is wrong or not does not matter; the proof is in the pudding."*

This comment, first of all, labels the research being done as "trivial," for the researchers themselves are not concerned about false-positive or false-negative results. However, beyond that, there are problems with counting on replication to expose false results.

First of all, there is limited enthusiasm among funding agencies for funding simple replication studies, as well as among editors for publishing the results of such studies. If the original study does not find significant results, the authors will find the results hard to publish because of the premium placed on statistical significance levels. If a later study cannot confirm the original significant result, there are always many explanations for "Why not?" other than that the original was a false-positive result or the later a false-negative one. The result is that there are typically many studies addressing different forms of the same issue, none exactly confirming and none exactly disproving any other. The waters merely get muddier and muddier as more studies are done. This can be clearly seen in the background and rationale sections of proposals and papers.

I would argue that ethical and concerned scientists are responsible for making every possible effort to avoid either false positives or false negatives in their own results. Under the best of circumstances, some of those results will be wrong, but there will be fewer wrong answers than if scientists take such a casual stance about errors as is demonstrated in this objection.

*Objection 6: "My statistician doesn't agree."*

This is quite possible, for statisticians are as argumentative as a group as every other group of scientists. However, when there are disagreements in the "people sciences" among professionals in different fields, these disagreements are frequently attributable to differing bases of knowledge and experience. Often these differences can be argued out, and a consensus satisfactory to all fields can be reached. When, however, such a disagreement arises between professionals in the same field, one or the other must be wrong, and the disagreement must be taken more seriously.

Thus let us first clarify whom we are discussing. The word "statistician," like the word "engineer," is often so broadly applied as to have little meaning. Those who track strikes, balls, hits, and errors at the baseball game are "statisticians." Those who tabulate data, enter them into computers, and tally the numbers are "statisticians." Many who have had a course or two in statistics, or who have only read the computer manuals for running statistical programs, are "statisticians." Those who have spent a lifetime of study, teaching, and research in the field, and are professors of statistics, are also "statisticians."

The "statisticians" of concern here are those who can and routinely do critically read and evaluate papers from the journals in the reference list in the Junker and Pilkonis chapter, most particularly those in the *Journal of the American Statistical Association*, the *Journal of the Royal Statistical Society*, and *Psychometrika*. This will exclude both extremes in the spectrum of "statisticians." Those who are fundamentally "blue-collar" statisticians will find the theoretical statistical papers beyond their ken; those who are "white-collar" theoreticians will find the papers in the psychiatry/psychology literature beyond their ken. This leaves those with sufficient training to fully understand the mathematical and statistical issues, *and* with interest and experience in the application of statistical methods in psychiatry and psychology.

Now does the sixth objection still hold? Frequently, I find that "my statistician" refers to one or the other extremes of the definition of "statisticians" referred to above, and a broader information and experience base will resolve the disagreement. If the objection still holds, and the statistician, having explored with the whole research team all the issues (both mathematical and clinical) involved in making the judgments about the applicability of the models, feels that the models are appropriate in your research context, I would defer to his or her judgment. If the result of reading the Junker and Pilkonis chapter is the fostering of such interactions, in which both the mathematical and the clinical issues are thoroughly discussed and considered, and the decision to use mathematical models is predicated on such a basis, I believe that Junker and Pilkonis would be well pleased. Furthermore, we should all be well pleased, for their chapter would have served to improve the quality of science in these areas.

## ACKNOWLEDGMENT

This work was supported by the MacArthur Foundation Research Network on the Psychobiology of Depression and Other Affective Disorders.

## REFERENCES

Feinstein, A. R. (1987). *Clinimetrics*. New Haven, CT: Yale University Press.
Jaffee, A. J., & Spirer, H. F. (1987). *Misused statistics: Straight talk for twisted numbers*. New York: Marcel Dekker.
Kohn, A. (1986). *False prophets: Fraud and error in science and medicine*. Oxford: Basil Blackwell.
Paulos, J. A. (1990). *Innumeracy: Mathematical illiteracy and its consequences*. New York: Vintage Books.

# Commentary

ROBERT D. GIBBONS
*University of Illinois at Chicago*

## OVERVIEW

It gives me great pleasure to provide commentary on the excellent chapter by Junker and Pilkonis. These authors have thoroughly reviewed good quantitative thinking in behavioral science and applied it to psychiatric research, particularly personality research. Their review spans an enormous range of methods, and the authors have cited most psychiatric research applications. Principal areas covered include measurement, structural-equation models with manifest and latent variables, exploratory data analysis, and analysis of longitudinal data. In my opinion, the most valuable discussion concerns the importance of measurement issues, and the most comprehensive discussion considers structural-equation models. However, I find limited discussion of the important topic of longitudinal data. Having made this sweeping generalization, I must add that this is the first time I have ever seen these topics discussed in one review, let alone discussed in the thoughtful and rigorous manner evident here.

I also greatly enjoyed the commentary by Helena Kraemer. She clearly illustrates the never-ending battle that statisticians interested in psychiatric research applications must endure. As if it were not difficult enough to know how to choose the correct statistical model and provide precise justification for our choice, we must also convince our psychiatric colleagues that the process is warranted, often in language quite foreign to our own. In fairness, it is all too common that we as statisticians present our ideas in a language that is *completely* foreign to psychiatric researchers. For example, I recently worked on a survival analysis problem in consultation with a psychiatric colleague. The manuscript reviewer criticized the use of advanced statistical methods as "suboptimal," and suggested that we should have analyzed these time-to-event data using an "old-fashioned multiple-regression analysis" because readers of this major psychiatric journal would be more "comfortable" with this presentation. In a world where simplicity and comfort replace concern for validity of assumptions, there is indeed great cause for concern.

What makes psychiatric data so special? Why do we need "advanced" statistical models? If psychiatric phenomena were "hard" like phenomena of interest in chemistry and physics, could we rely on simpler statistical methods to test our hypotheses? Are statistical methods simply ways of extracting something out of nothing? I have been told many times by biologists, "If you can't see it in the data, it is not worth looking for." Interestingly, these same biologists plot standard error bars (which tell us about sample size) rather than standard deviation bars (which tell us about effect size) on graphical displays of their data. When questioned, they reply, "You would never see anything if we used standard deviation bars."

I suppose that the "hardness" of a science has some impact on choice of statistical method, but I also like to think that there are no soft sciences, only soft scientists. Conversely, I think that variability in human behavior can be decomposed into numerous significant components, whereas variance decomposition of the behavior of inorganic materials is of less concern. This is the reason why psychiatric data are special: They involve measurements and manipulations of complex human behaviors. Furthermore, psychiatric data often represent measurements of chaotic human behavior; hence the complexity of variance decomposition further increases. The statistical/psychological theory I present here is influenced largely by the work of R. Darrell Bock, and I tailor it to the realm of psychiatric research. This theory helps explicate the relationship between the complexities of psychiatric data and the need for statistical models that incorporate rather than ignore these complexities. Since I am most conversant with issues of measurement and change (i.e., longitudinal data), I focus on these topics.

## A THEORY OF PSYCHIATRIC MEASUREMENT

In traditional psychiatric measurement, symptoms, characteristics, traits, and the like are selected on the basis of clinical judgment to form a scale or measuring instrument. In theory, items or symptoms are selected to measure a single underlying construct (e.g., depression or anxiety), although it can be argued that these constructs are inherently multidimensional. To locate an individual on this continuum, a total score is obtained by summing individual item scores—either a binary score (presence or absence of a symptom) or a graded classification (e.g., mild, moderate, or major severity).

This classic form of measurement suffers from serious limitations. Bock (1986) illustrates the problem with this approach by using a sports analogy:

> Imagine a track and field event in which ten athletes participate in [the] 110 meter hurdles race and also in [the] high jump. Suppose that the hurdles race is not quite conventional in that the hurdles are not all the same height and the score is determined, not only by the runner's time, but also by the number of hurdles successfully cleared, i.e., not tipped over. The high jump on the other hand is conducted in the conventional way: the cross bar is raised by, say, 2 cm increments on the uprights, and the athletes try to turn to jump over the bar without dislodging it.

Bock points out that the first event is like a traditionally scored test. Hurdles of varying heights correspond to items of varying difficulty that the examinee tries to answer correctly in the time allowed (in the present context, symptoms of varying severity). In these cases, only a counting operation is used in measurement of ability (severity of the underlying disorder). In contrast, measurement of ability on the high jump is distinctly different. A scale in millimeters on the uprights provides a direct measurement for the athletes' jumping ability. Item response theory (IRT) measurement has the same logic as the high jump: Test items are considered to be arranged on a continuum at fixed points corresponding to increasing difficulty (severity). In the testing situation, the examinee attempts to answer successive items until after some point he or she can no longer do so correctly. His or her ability is measured by the location on the continuum of the last item answered correctly. In psychiatric measurement, a patient's illness or personality impairment is measured by location on the continuum of the most severe symptom or characteristic observed. In this theory of measurement, ability is a scale point, not a count.

These measurement theories are fundamentally different. If hurdles are arbitrarily added or removed, the count of number of hurdles cleared cannot be compared to other scores. An analogy from psychiatric research is that of the 17-item, 21-item, and 24-item versions of the Hamilton Depression Rating Scale; the total scores on the different versions are not comparable. This is not true of high-jump or IRT scoring. If the high-jump bar is changed or a position is omitted, the interpretation of heights remains unchanged; only the precision of measurement is affected. With IRT, new symptom items can be added as more is learned about personality constructs. This does not arbitrarily change the scale of measurement; it increases measurement precision.

I hope that this discussion sparks interest in a more modern view of psychiatric measurement, and that this introduction helps to orient the reader to the fine discussion of methodologies by Junker and Pilkonis. The reader is referred to Lord and Novick (1968) and Lord (1980) for a complete discussion of this theory and related methodologies.

## LONGITUDINAL DATA

In the last decade, the search for etiology and causation has led to a demand for prospective longitudinal studies in psychiatric research. Many studies have been conducted; however, sophistication of methods for statistical analysis is not always commensurate with the cost and effort required to collect these data. Most often, "endpoint" analyses are conducted, in which all but the first and last measurements are discarded. Alternately, simplistic models with unrealistic assumptions are applied (e.g., mixed-model analysis of variance [ANOVA] or "repeated-measures" ANOVA), often producing biased and even misleading results. Elsewhere, my colleagues and I (Gibbons et al., in press) discuss the issue and propose alternatives. Here, I present a basis for questioning traditional methods as applied to longitudinal psychiatric data. Again, I borrow an analogy from Bock (1983b):

> Suppose that a panel study has been carried out to assess, among other things, the TV viewing habits of children from their 10th to 14th birthdays. Perhaps once a year near his or her birthday, each child responds to an interviewer's questions concerning TV viewing during the previous week. At the end of the five-year study, the data comprise a file of number of hours of TV viewing by each child at each age level. (p. 103)

I can easily imagine some data analyst computing means for each age group and perhaps fitting a linear or curvilinear trend line to those means depicting the average number of viewing hours over the age range. A somewhat more sophisticated analyst might fit the line more efficiently using a growth curve model (see Bock, 1979), but this would require complete data for all subjects and identical measurement occasions. As Bock (1983b) points out, "apart from the obvious confounding of developmental and secular trends in these types of analyses, what we should object to most is the use of a mean trend in the population to represent a behavioral relationship taken to be acting within individual subjects" (p. 104).

Reporting only mean trend lines suggests that as a child matures, he or she will watch more TV. This ignores everything we know about individual differences in behavioral characteristics. The truth is that some children watch more TV, some watch less, and others' habits are unchanged. We should not be interested only in mean trend lines, but in the distribution of trends in the population of children. Then we can speak of the number or proportion of children whose TV viewing increases, decreases, or remains unchanged. As Bock (1983b) points out, behavioral relationships are not fixed laws; they are a family of laws whose parameters describe individual behavioral tendencies of subjects in the population.

These ideas are *essential* for the measurement of psychiatric change. Response to treatment, life events, social support, hospitalization, and homelessness, for example, have unique "person-specific" components of variation and deviate systematically from mean trends. To imagine that deviations from average responses are random across time is to ignore our knowledge of human behavior. We do not accept unrealistic behavioral theories, and we should not accept statistical methods with unrealistic assumptions.

This view of psychiatric and/or personality research leads to Bayesian methods of statistical analysis, most broadly described as two-stage models (i.e., sampling responses within subjects and subjects within populations). Relevant distributions can be investigated empirically; hence these approaches are termed "empirical Bayesian" methods. These ideas are the basis of a class of statistical problems called variously "mixed-model" (Elston & Grizzle, 1962), "exchangeability between multiple regression" (Lindley & Smith, 1972), "regression with randomly dispersed parameters" (Rosenberg, 1973), "two-stage stochastic regression" (Fearn, 1975), "James–Stein estimation" (James & Stein, 1961), "variance component models" (Harville, 1977), "random-effect regression models" (Laird & Ware, 1982), "hierarchical regression models" (Bryk & Raudenbush, 1987), and "random regression models" (Bock, 1983a, 1983b, 1989; Jennrich & Schluchter, 1986; Gibbons, Hedeker, Waternaux, & Davis, 1988; Hedeker, Gibbons, Waternaux, & Davis, 1989). Although these ideas generally lead to "sophisticated" statistical models, they dramatically reduce the gap between the reality of data and the assumed reality of the statistical model.

I hope these two illustrations have shown that it is possible for statisticians and psychiatric researchers to live in the same world, speak to each other, and share the same objectives. Certainly, the same careful thought involved in developing theories of personality and psychopathology must also be present in constructing corresponding statistical models. On the other hand, we could just use a good "old-fashioned multiple-regression analysis" and spend the rest of our time at the beach.

## REFERENCES

Bock, R. D. (1979). Univariate and multivariate analysis of time-structured data. In J. R. Nesselroade & P. B. Baltes (Eds.), *Longitudinal research in the study of behavior and development*. New York: Academic Press.

Bock, R. D. (1983a). The discrete Bayesian. In H. Wainer & S. Messick (Eds.), *Principles of modern psychological measurement*. Hillsdale, NJ: Erlbaum.

Bock, R. D. (1983b). Within-subject experimentation in psychiatric research. In R. D. Gibbons & M. W. Dysken (Eds.), *Statistical and methodological advances in psychiatric research*. New York: Spectrum.

Bock, R. D. (1986). *The logic of item response theory*. Unpublished manuscript, Department of Behavioral Sciences, University of Chicago.

Bock, R. D. (1989). Measurement of human variation: A two-stage model. In R. D. Bock (Ed.), *Multilevel analysis of educational data*. New York: Academic Press.

Bryk, A. S., & Raudenbush, S. W. (1987). Application of hierarchical linear models to assessing change. *Psychological Bulletin, 101*, 147–158.

Elston, R. C., & Grizzle, J. E. (1962). Estimation of time-response curves and their confidence bands. *Biometrics, 18*, 148–159.

Fearn, T. A. (1975). Bayesian approach to growth curves. *Biometrika, 62*, 89–100.

Gibbons, R. D., Hedeker, D., Waternaux, C. M., & Davis, J. M. (1988). Random regression models: A comprehensive approach to the analysis of longitudinal psychiatric data. *Psychopharmacology Bulletin, 24*, 438–443.

Gibbons, R. D., Hedeker, D., Elkin, I., Waternaux, C., Kraemer, H. C., Greenhouse, J. B., Shea, M. T., Imber, S. D., Sotsky, S. M., & Watkins, J. T. (in press). Some conceptual and statistical issues in the analysis of longitudinal psychiatric data. *Archives of General Psychiatry*.

Harville, D. A. (1977). Maximum likelihood approaches to variance component estimation and to related problems. *Journal of the American Statistical Association, 72*, 320–340.

Hedeker, D., Gibbons, R. D., Waternaux, C. M., & Davis, J. M. (1989). Investigating drug plasma levels and clinical response using random regression models. *Psychopharmacology Bulletin, 25*, 227–231.

James, W., & Stein, C. (1961). Estimation with quadratic loss. In *Proceedings of the Berkeley Symposium on Mathematical Statistics and Probability*, pp. 361–379.

Jennrich, R. I., & Schluchter, M. D. (1986). Unbalanced repeated-measures models with structured covariance matrices. *Biometrics, 42*, 805–820.

Laird, N. M., & Ware, J. H. (1982). Random effects models for longitudinal data. *Biometrics, 38,* 963–974.

Lindley, D. V., & Smith, A. F. M. (1972). Bayes estimation for linear models (with discussion). *Journal of the Royal Statistical Society, 34*(Series B), 1–41.

Lord, F. M. (1980). *Applications of item response theory to practical testing problems.* Hillsdale, NJ: Erlbaum.

Lord, F. M., & Novick, M. R. (1968). *Statistical theories of mental test scores.* Reading, MA: Addison-Wesley.

Rosenberg, B. (1973). Linear regression with randomly dispersed parameters. *Biometrika, 60,* 65–72.

# Epilogue

ALLEN FRANCES
*Duke University Medical Center*

With its provision of a separate Axis II especially for the diagnosis of personality disorders, the third edition of the *Diagnostic and Statistical Manual of Mental Disorders* (DSM-III) succeeded in directing research and clinical attention toward what had previously been a neglected feature of psychopathology. It was no accident that the research efforts on personality disorders had lagged so far behind investigations of the other psychiatric disorders. Researchers are attracted most to questions that can be answered with incisive and well-established methodologies. Unfortunately, the personality disorders are inherently difficult to define, to diagnose reliably, and to study systematically and longitudinally. With the realization that the diagnosis of personality disorders is too important to ignore, a group of intrepid investigators have begun to develop the research tools and designs necessary to begin the enterprise. The present volume is a culmination of such efforts and provides a fascinating overview of a number of theoretical, practical, and statistical issues in the study of personality disorders. This epilogue briefly indicates why this endeavor is worth pursuing and why it is difficult to pursue; it also suggests some of the future lines of research that are likely to be informed by the methodological clarifications offered in the book.

There are a number of compelling reasons for expanding research on personality disorders. Personality disorders are important both in themselves and also in the ways in which they interact with other psychiatric and medical problems. Two of the personality disorders (i.e., the antisocial and borderline) are associated with high rates of suicidal behavior (and completed suicide), and cause enormous public health and societal problems. A number of the personality disorders (e.g., schizotypal, paranoid, borderline, avoidant, obsessive compulsive) may represent spectrum variants related to Axis I psychiatric disorders. These Axis II and related Axis I disorders may share genetic, central nervous system, and environmental mediators that could lead to a fundamental understanding of pathogenesis and treatment response. The presence or absence of personality disorders may also be important in explaining the heterogeneity often encountered in studies of the course, family loading, biology, or treatment outcome of Axis I conditions. Finally, from a clinical viewpoint, it is often the presence of personality disorders that is responsible for treatment noncompliance and for treatment nonresponse. The more we learn about personality disorders, the more we will understand about the development of psychopathology and about how best to help our patients.

Unfortunately, the study of personality disorders confronts a number of thorny theoretical and practical conundrums that have been comprehensively described in this book. As outlined by Klein, Wonderlich, and Shea in Chapter One, the possible relationships between personality disorders and the other psychiatric disorders are complex and heterogeneous. It seems clear that each of the possible models of relationship (i.e., common cause, spectrum, vulnerability, pathoplasty, scar, or artifact) has face validity and is likely to explain some but not all of the situations encountered. As outlined by Widiger in Chapter Two, personality disorder assessment is inherently difficult because (1) there are so many personality disorders; (2) they merge dimensionally with one another and with normality; (3) measures (especially cross-sectional ones) meant to tap traits are inherently confounded with current state and role expectations; (4) long-lasting states may be impossible to distinguish from traits; and (5) descriptive results obtained from self-report, clinical interview, and informants tend to disagree and provide different views of the patient. It has also been very difficult to get agreement on which personality disorders are most crucial to assess, which items best tap them, and how to deal with multiple diagnoses. Efforts at developing a dimensional system of personality assessment might solve many of these problems, but they are still in a relatively formative stage, without consensus on which dimensions and which instruments would be most germane. Perhaps most problematic of all, we still lack a "gold standard" with which to judge the validity of personality assessments.

Despite all of these difficulties, it is fair to say that enormous progress has been made in personality disorder research. The foundation now exists for what will undoubtedly be a fascinating research enterprise—one that will be rich in both clinical and theoretical implications. We now have available a variety of instruments that can reliably assess personality disorders and personality dimensions. These have been applied in studies of course, familial aggregation, biological test functioning, and treatment outcome. The available literature has provided a great deal of data on the descriptive validity of the various personality disorders and dimensions. It suggests that temperamental factors (e.g., aggression, avoidance) measured quite early in life are stable over time and predictive of later personality development and psychopathology. Available studies also provide suggestive evidence that personality disorders and temperaments tend to improve over time. The familial aggregation of personality features, and their relationship to Axis I disorders, has been demonstrated in a number of studies. There is an accumulating body of literature on the biological and physiological correlates of personality, with perhaps the most intriguing finding being the relationship between the serotonin system and impulse control and aggressivity. Finally, a number of studies have documented that personality disorder is a predictor of poor or delayed treatment response, highlighting this as a crucial arena for clinical innovation and as an explanation of the heterogeneity in the results of treatment outcome studies.

What approaches are most likely to further personality disorder research? Junker and Pilkonis suggest in Chapter Three that we develop broader and simpler constructs and test these with widely accepted assessment tools, using sufficiently large populations studied over sufficiently long periods of time. The current literature represents a good start, but progress has been hindered by the variety of competing instruments meant to tap virtually identical constructs in slightly different ways. This makes it difficult or impossible to aggregate, or even generalize, results across studies. The potential gain of comparing the advantages and disadvantages of diverse instruments must be balanced against the current loss of comparability across investigations, which is a major impediment to progress in this field. Virtually all personality studies have been limited by the size and specificity of sampling. It is very difficult to generalize from the results of any given study, because the specific conditions of sampling may highlight certain relationships and obscure others (e.g., impulsivity is a powerful discriminator of borderline personality disorder in an outpatient psychiatric sample, but is nonspecific in a prison sample that has different comparison groups). As suggested by Junker and Pilkonis, it is crucial that we develop methods to allow for the aggregation of results across data sets. This is necessary to determine generalizability of results, to provide an adequate range to study the measures tested, and to generate sufficient sample sizes for statistical modeling. Such aggregation requires a consensus (thus far sought but not achieved) among the leading investigators in the field to use a core battery of measures that can be applied across studies.

Research endeavors will soon exhaust the descriptive approaches that are now so prominent in the literature and will instead search for a deeper understanding of personality functioning. Perhaps the most promising arena of research will be the study of temperament. Fortunately, temperament is a construct that cuts broadly and deeply across a number of the most crucial issues in personality research and allows the integration of diverse methodologies and spheres of observation. Temperament can be studied in various mammalian species, as well as in human infants and adults; its impact can be studied naturalistically or manipulated experimentally; and temperament studies can apply the broadest range of methods (including methods from molecular and population genetics, neuropharmacology, physiology, and attachment and social systems research). It is entirely possible that we will, within the foreseeable future, have a much greater understanding of the genetic differences that influence temperament and of how these are mediated by psychobiological mechanisms and environmental releasers.

It seems likely that personality measures will become increasingly important in genetic studies of Axis I disorders. This method has already been demonstrated by the importance of measuring schizotypal personality disorder in the study of the familial distribution of schizophrenia. Similar approaches should enlighten our understanding of the relationship of avoidant personality to anxiety disorders and borderline personality to the mood disorders.

As I conclude this book, I am gratified with how far we have come and how interesting are the questions that we can now be asked. In the near future, we seem certain to make discoveries that will help us understand the fundamental nature of personality disorder and its relation to depression. Such discoveries cannot fail at the same time to answer much broader questions about human nature that have confronted us from the dawn of our self-awareness. It should be noted that the ancient Greeks had a perfectly respectable descriptive model of personality (i.e., the melancholic, choleric, sanguine, and phlegmatic types), which they related to a biological model of humours (black bile, yellow bile, blood, and phlegm) and to a biophysical model of ultimate causation (the balance of the four elements—earth, fire, water, and air). Our own descriptive models are not clearly superior to those developed by our predecessors. The major advantage we have now is the remarkable recent growth of our power to design sophisticated research investigations, to measure biological processes, and to study the results generated with powerful statistical methods. Undoubtedly, this will be an exciting time for personality research.

# Index